The Bandit King

Lampião of Brazil

By BILLY JAYNES CHANDLER

TEXAS A&M UNIVERSITY PRESS
College Station and London

Library of Congress Cataloging in Publication Data

Chandler, Billy Jaynes.
   The bandit king.

   Bibliography: p.
   Includes index.
   1. Ferreira da Silva, Virgolino, known as Lampeão,
1900-1938. 2. Brigands and robbers—Brazil, Northeast—
Biography. 3. Brazil, Northeast—History.
I. Title.
F2583.F472C48   364.1'5'0924 [B]   77-99275
ISBN 0-89096-050-X (cloth)
ISBN 0-89096-194-8 (pbk.)

Manufactured in the United States of America
First Paperback Edition

For Rosemary Cunningham

Contents

List of Illustrations

Preface

THE story to be told in these pages belongs to Lampião, the Brazilian who quite likely will stand as the twentieth century's most successful traditional rural bandit. He may also have been one of the last major figures of his kind, for, as the world changes, that type of banditry is rapidly disappearing. Those acquainted with Brazil's history will know that this is not the first time Lampião's story has been told. But much of what has been written before consists of unverified stories either borrowed from earlier writers or indiscriminately gathered from much-diffused and frequently embellished oral tradition. Even the best of the accounts are fragmentary and undocumented, and many of the events described in them are unconnected to both time and place. This study seeks to present a reasonably complete version of the bandit's story, adequately researched, documented, chronologically ordered, and factually accurate. The need for such a record at this time is imperative, since many of the sources of information about Lampião will not long survive. This is true not only of that now rapidly dwindling body of folk who knew him, but also of a considerable quantity of aged and crumbling documents about him. My major aim then in commencing my research and writing this book was to set the historical record straight while there was still time. Lampião's importance to the recent history of his region, as well as to the general history of banditry, merits thorough and careful study. At the same time, I hope that those who have broad interests in the study of banditry or the social history of underdeveloped rural societies will find my approach useful. The story, I believe, has considerable significance for such interests, for I have sought to bring to light the intimate links between the bandit and his society.

There are no doubt unfortunate instances in which I too have unwittingly fallen into error. Bandits' lives, in their telling, are universally subject to exaggeration and outright falsification, and some of the stories I have accepted as true may be at least partially untrue. Yet, I believe that the episodes related here are in character with what I know the famed desperado to have been. This is a reasoned judgment arrived at only after I had read many a yellowing newspaper and dusty document, had been in places where Lampião's life unfolded, and had talked with many people who knew him or who knew some of those who knew him. I am thus convinced that the story possesses the quality of reliability.

Research for the study was done in Brazil during portions of 1973, 1974, and 1975 and was partially supported by a grant from the Penrose Fund of the American Philosophical Society, to which I am grateful. So many Brazilians aided me in my research that they are too numerous to mention here one by one. Yet, a few of them merit special recognition: an old friend of more than a decade, Dr. Lourenço Alves Feitosa of Campos Sales, Ceará; Miguel Feitosa of Araripina, Pernambuco; Aldemar de Mendonça of Pão de Açúcar, Alagoas; João Ferreira dos Santos of Propriá, Sergipe (the brother of the subject of this work); José Melquiades de Oliveira of Pinhão, Sergipe; Manuel Leitão of Mata Grande, Alagoas. Other valuable contributors are found in references to personal interviews. I owe a great personal debt to my friend Major Alberto Salles Paraiso Borges of the Bahia Military Police. He and his charming family of Salvador took me in and cared for me when in 1974 I was one of the victims of a disastrous bus accident in Bahia.

Professors Alfred Hower, Neill Macaulay, and Charles Wagley, all of the University of Florida, read the manuscript and offered worthy counsel for its improvement and publication. Errors and other infelicities that remain are, of course, mine and not theirs.

Kingsville, Texas   B. J. C.

The Bandit King

1. Banditry in the Backlands

BANDITS in backward rural societies have long captured people's interests and imaginations. Indeed, fascination with individual bandits and the creation of legends about them—not to mention the phenomenon of banditry itself—have been so widespread as to suggest an element of universality. The man and the occasional woman who live in that land outside the law as roving bandits, seemingly free of the restrictions of repressive society, touch a responsive chord in the minds of many. Especially appealing are those figures from long ago or far away. Thus, Englishmen have long thrilled to stories of the feats of Robin Hood and his merry men, Americans recount the exploits of Jesse James, Mexicans tell of the raids of Pancho Villa, and Brazilians narrate the deeds of Lampião.

The lives of such men have long been left to the telling of balladeers and other popular storytellers whose tendency was to idealize their subjects, exaggerating whatever good deeds they may have done but neglecting to tell of their many evil ones. So legend has too often preempted historical reality. In recent years, fortunately, historians and social scientists, some of whom are motivated by the suggestive writings of Eric Hobsbawm, have found an interest in banditry.[1] The discussion stimulated by Hobsbawm, whose own interest lies as much in the legends of the bandits as in the bandits' deeds, has led some scholars to conclude that before much more of significance can be said about bandits it is necessary to look at the reality of their lives and the societies in which they lived and died.[2] While it is not the intention of

[1] Eric Hobsbawm, *Primitive Rebels: Studies in Archaic Forms of Social Movement in the 19th and 20th Centuries*, pp. 13–29; idem, *Bandits*.

[2] For instance, see Anton Blok, "The Peasant and the Brigand: Social Banditry Reconsidered," *Comparative Studies in Society and History* 14 (September,

this study to disparage the significance of legend, the principal aim is the historical recreation of one bandit, who, among the world's practitioners of that profession, stands second to none.

Lampião,[3] whose setting was the impoverished and decadent backlands (*sertão*) of northeastern Brazil, began his slide toward outlawry in 1916, when he was nineteen years old, because of a dispute with a neighboring family. When, five years later, the police killed his father, he declared that he would live as a bandit and die as one. As a bandit, he operated in classic fashion. Roaming with his band of malefactors on foot or horseback over several states, he lived by extortion, seizing persons for ransom, and robbery. He could be trustworthy, generous, and gentlemanly to those who earned his loyalty or struck his fancy; those who aroused his enmity were met with sackings, burnings, torture, and death. A wily fellow who was a consummate guerrilla warrior, he outwitted and vanquished the state military forces so often and so skillfully that his fellow backlanders came to believe he possessed extraordinary powers. Whatever the source of his strength—many believed that it emanated from his religious fervor—he earned the fear and respect of a vast region. He purchased the police, met landed barons and political chiefs as equals, and developed amicable relations with a state governor. Commissioned a captain in a bizarre move by one of the region's most prestigious leaders, he might have bridged the chasm to respectability had circumstances been more propitious. He talked on occasion, perhaps only half in jest, of declaring himself governor of a new backlands state. Long before he met his death in 1938 as the result of betrayal by one of his trusted protectors, Captain Lampião had become a legend.[4]

1972): 495; also T. H. Aston, "Robin Hood: Communication," *Past and Present* 20 (November, 1961): 9.

[3] Lampião's real name was Virgulino Ferreira da Silva. He acquired the nickname of Lampião, meaning lantern or lamp, early in his career. It formerly was spelled "Lampeão," but the newer spelling is now common.

[4] There has been a steady flow of purportedly factual books published in Brazil about Lampião. Among the most notable are the following: Ranulfo Prata, *Lampeão*; Optato Gueiros *"Lampeão": Memórias de um oficial ex-commandante de forças volantes*; Cícero Rodrigues de Carvalho, *Serrote Preto (Lampião e seus sequazes)*; Nertan Macedo, *Capitão Virgulino Ferreira: Lampião*; Luiz Luna, *Lampião e seus cabras*; Joaquim Góis, *Lampião: O último cangaceiro*; Manoel Bezerra e Silva, *Lampião e suas façanhas*; Christina Matta Machado, *As táticas de guerra dos cangaceiros*; Aglae Lima de Oliveira, *Lampião, cangaço e nordeste*.

Lampião's career was not an isolated phenomenon; rather, it was part of a regional epidemic of banditry that commenced around 1900 and lasted some forty years. The bands of outlaws were known as the *cangaço*, and the bandits themselves were called *cangaceiros*. The words *cangaceiro* and *cangaço* apparently came into use as early as the 1830s and were related to *canga* or *cangalho*, meaning a yoke for oxen. Presumably, the cangaceiro carried his rifle over his shoulders as the steer wore his yoke. At first signifying a group of armed men who acted in behalf of a landlord, *cangaceiros* by the early 1900s had come to denote bands that operated independently. The word apparently began to be used widely only at this time.[5]

Tales of the cangaço are a distinctive part of backlands history and folklore. In reality, the banditry differed little, except in its intensity, from the brigandage that had long existed intermittently in the region. Its chief feature was simple bands of roving outlaws who operated on their own account. The cangaço achieved distinction, however, in the minds of the public and of the bandits themselves, for both generally recognized it as an identifiable social phenomenon. The cangaceiros of the various bands tacitly declared themselves to be a group or subculture by adopting a peculiar form of dress. Most of them could be identified by a colorful kerchief and a leather hat (a backlands cowboy hat) whose brim, usually decorated, was turned upward at the front; numerous cartridge belts, worn over the shoulders (crossing each other over the chest) and around the waist, added to the striking appearance. Cangaceiros also asserted their distinctiveness in their avowed reasons for becoming bandits. They fell outside the law, many of them said, only because of the necessity of avenging wrongs done to them or their families. In a society in which injustice was rife, such explanations often met considerable sympathy. Understandably, they achieved greater acceptance among intellectuals who surveyed the happenings from afar than among the inhabitants of the zones in which the bandits spread their murder and destruction. Nonetheless, the view that the cangaço was an understandable—though deplorable—reaction to the poverty and lack of justice in the northeastern backlands served to set the bandits apart from ordinary outlaws in the popular mind.

[5] See Maria Isaura Pereira de Queiroz, "Notas sociológicas sobre o cangaço," *Ciência e Cultura* 77 (May, 1975): 495–516; and Esmaregado de Freitas in *Diário de Pernambuco* (Recife), March 12, 1926.

The cangaço was exclusively a backlands phenomenon. Lampião operated in his home state of Pernambuco, as well as in Alagoas, Ceará, Paraíba, northern Bahia, Sergipe, and, on one ill-fated occasion, Rio Grande do Norte. Confining his operations entirely to the interior, he never set foot in any of the state capitals, which in that region all lie on the coast. Geographically, the area is not especially favorable to human habitation, although many of its natives, as well as an occasional outsider, are captivated by its forbidding charm. Often erroneously thought of as a flat, monotonous, and barren land, it is in fact surprisingly varied in appearance and physical characteristics. Some of its parts, to be sure, are relatively flat and give the appearance of unbroken monotony, but, in the main, it is highly accidented by hills, plateaus, and low mountain ranges (*serras*) rising as high as 3,000 feet. Rivers generally are shallow and often dry; the only exception of note is the São Francisco, the chief "highway" of the lower backlands, which empties its precious waters into the sea between Alagoas and Sergipe but whose value for transportation is limited by the falls of Paulo Afonso.

While the climate is tropical and semiarid, it has peculiar characteristics, especially in the amounts and patterns of rainfall. The quantity of rain varies greatly within the region. In the better-watered mountains of far backlands Alagoas, for example—one of Lampião's favorite haunts—annual precipitation averages forty-seven inches. In contrast, many of the drier portions, such as the Juàzeiro area of Bahia, are lucky to receive half that amount. In all backlands areas, substantial rain is likely to fall only in one season, known by natives as the winter. The winter normally stretches over five or six months and begins, depending on the particular place, in the period from December to March. Within that normal pattern, considerable variation exists. Not only may the onset and the termination of the winter vary greatly, but the distribution of rain through the season often is dangerously erratic. Most of the rain for a year may fall within a few days or a few weeks, or it may come only at the beginning or the end of the season. Thus not only the relative scarcity of rainfall but also its distribution creates severe problems for backlands agriculturists and ranchers.

The drought (*sêca*) is a harsh reality that backlanders have come to accept stoically. Severe droughts, affecting virtually the entire region, occur about every ten years. While they normally last only one season, droughts having a duration of two or three years have been recorded, the disaster of 1877–1879 being one of the best known. Localized droughts occur even more frequently. Average temperatures in the backlands are high; extremes may vary from an early morning low of near 55° Fahrenheit in an area of high elevation to a maximum of about 95° on a hot day in the dry season, which natives call the summer.

The vegetation of the backlands is understandably as distinctive as the climate, and here too considerable variation exists. On the plateaus (*chapadas*) of the higher elevations, one finds a cross between savanna and true forest. There, the ground is covered by grasses and a thick combination of small trees and bushes of permanent foliage, and the cactuses of the lower elevations also occasionally appear. The natural vegetation of the lower regions is the *caatinga*, a kind of gnarled, spiny growth of short stature suitable to a hot, dry land. Small trees and bushes predominate, along with an often luxuriant growth of various species of cactus—some of which, like the *facheiro* or *mandacarú*, rise majestically to a height of twenty feet or more. Most of the trees and bushes lose their leaves during the summer. A few, like the *joazeiro* tree, retain theirs the year around, and their verdant beauty stands out uniquely in the midst of the brownness and desolation of the dry season. The density of the *caatinga* varies greatly, in some areas relatively sparse and in others impenetrable. Overall, the backlands, with their long dry seasons, frequent droughts, thorny and grotesque vegetation, and often difficult terrain, do not extend man a cordial welcome. Like the bandits, who often came from their far recesses, they are forbidding.[6]

If the physical characteristics of the land inhabited by Lampião appear to be unduly emphasized, let it be said that the society of which

[6] The classic description of the backlands is found in Euclides da Cunha, *Os sertões*, first published in 1902 in Brazil and available in many subsequent Brazilian editions. It is available to English readers in Samuel Putnam's translation entitled *Rebellion in the Backlands (Os sertões)*, but the reader should be warned that Putnam's rendering of da Cunha is not always accurate. Nor, for that matter, does da Cunha himself always portray the backlands and its people realistically. He saw them through the eyes of an urban intellectual who was in the area for only a short time during one summer and his picture is overdrawn. I have relied on my observations, as well as on the portion dedicated to the geography of the Northeast in Instituto Brasileiro de Geografia e Estatística, *Grande região nordeste*, vol. 5 of *Enciclopédia dos municípios brasileiros*, especially pp. 64–278.

he was a not atypical member was molded in part by these physical factors. Yet, the society that produced Lampião was molded by other things as well, and, while its confines had always sheltered various kinds of criminality, conditions during Lampião's lifetime became even more favorable to such behavior. That this was the case is revealed in an examination of selected aspects of backlands social, political, and economic history.[7]

The original Portuguese settlements in northeastern Brazil were not in the backlands but in the humid zone, seldom more than fifty miles in width, which stretches along the coast as far northward as the city of Natal. There, in the course of the sixteenth century, a flourishing plantation society, based on the cultivation of sugar cane, was established. Brazil became in this period Europe's first major supplier of sugar. The native Indians, who were of a relatively low cultural level, were either assimilated or eliminated. Black hands, imported as slaves from sub-Saharan Africa, came to constitute the major portion of the work force and, for that matter, of the society in general. A proud, aristocratic white elite, emerging most notably in such fertile and intensively cultivated areas as Salvador and Olinda (an old city near Recife), dominated the colony. The coastal regions were so valuable for the cultivation of sugar cane, however, that the production of food there to sustain the increasing population began to be looked upon with disfavor. It was then that interest was manifested in the interior as potentially valuable lands for ranching and general agriculture. Thus the backlands began to be conquered and settled—though often sparse-

---

[7] Practically all of the works on Lampião and the cangaço attempt to point to those aspects of the backlands that favored banditry. Among the earlier attempts are two books by Gustavo Barroso, *Heróes e bandidos (Os cangaceiros do nordeste)*, and *Almas de lama e de aço (Lampeão e outros cangaceiros)*. Also see: Pedro Baptista, *Cangaceiros do nordeste*; Ademar Vidal, *Terra de homens*; Rui Facó, *Cangaceiros e fanáticos*, pp. 15–71; Amaury de Souza, "The Cangaço and the Politics of Violence in Northeast Brazil," in *Protest and Resistance in Angola and Brazil*, ed. Ronald L. Chilcote, pp. 109–131; Maria Isaura Pereira de Queiroz, *Os cangaceiros: Les bandits d'honneur brésiliens*, pp. 19–47, and the same author's "Notas sociológicas"; Maria Christina da Matta Machado, "Aspectos do fenômeno do cangaço no nordeste brasileiro," a book-length study published in five installments in *Revista de História*, in 1973 and 1974 in vols. 46, 47, and 49 (nos. 93, pp. 139–175; 95, pp. 177–212; 96, pp. 473–489; 97, pp. 161–200; 99, pp. 145–180). Each of these studies, although often giving special emphasis to one matter or another, points to similar problems. While the analysis that follows here refers to those same general problems, it is essentially my own.

ly so. By the early decades of the eighteenth century, even the more remote reaches of that vast land had been claimed and the framework of backlands society had been built.

The general lines of the society constructed there were pale and poor imitations of the aristocratic and class-ridden forms that existed on the coast.[8] Lands were handed out in large tracts by high colonial officials to those who had influence and, it was hoped, the means to subdue and utilize the land. In this manner, the base was laid for a system of *latifundia* (large estates) that was eroded by the passing of time but never eliminated. The cattle baron, who owned the land, was a backlands potentate equal in his own world to the sugar plantation lord (*senhor do engenho*) of the coast. He ruled his world almost at will, often giving short shrift to the few officials sent to impose larger law and discipline. In reality, Portugal, small and increasingly impoverished, seldom rose to exercise any considerable authority in the region, whose potential for the collection of royal income was, after all, meager. Hence, from its origins, backlands society was left to the wisdom, caprice, or neglect, as the case might be, of those few of its members who were fortunate enough to own large amounts of land. The termination of Portuguese rule and the subsequent passing of independent Brazil through the Empire (1822–1889) and Old Republic (1889–1930) periods did not radically alter that circumstance for the vast majority of backlanders.

The cattle barons aside, the overwhelming majority of the people lived in abject poverty, and it was from this class that many of the bandits of Lampião's time were to come. Initially, the lower classes comprised the peoples brought in by the potentates in their penetration of the region. Some of them were cowboys, while others mainly served as troops for the conquest of the Indians. That some of those who were brought in were Negro and mulatto slaves might seem strange, in view of the fact that there were few highly lucrative, intensively worked enterprises to which such expensive labor could be directed. Nonetheless,

8 The history of the backlands has not been well investigated. A brief survey may be found in Ernani Silva Bruno, *História do Brasil: Geral e regional*, vols. 2 and 3. Manoel Correia de Andrade, *A terra e o homen no nordeste*, is valuable, especially for its discussion of aspects of the history of the economy. Billy Jaynes Chandler, *The Feitosas and the Sertão dos Inhamuns: The History of a Family and a Community in Northeast Brazil, 1700-1930*, although confined to one part of the backlands, describes a society that has much in common with the region in general.

evidence suggests that such persons made up a small but significant portion of the backlands population. They represented, to say the least, a good investment and they became skilled at the work—from cattle herding to blacksmithing—that the backlands life demanded.

Over the years, their status as slaves gradually came to an end, in part through voluntary manumission but in large measure as a result of the abolitionist efforts that dealt a final blow to the institution in 1888. Because they intermixed with both whites and Indians from the time of their introduction to the area, blacks and mulattoes became an integral portion of the submerged class.[9] The sparse Indian population also helped to form that class. Being a warlike people, Indians were killed in great numbers in the initial conquests; the remainder were assimilated, some almost immediately, others first passing through the mission system.

Thus the backlands lower class was composed of a mixture of the native Indians, the Negro and mulatto slaves and their descendants, and the free persons, usually also of mixed heritage, who accompanied the cattle barons from the coast. In time, the lower class also came to contain many who traced their ancestry back to those cattle barons, for backlands customs and conditions almost relentlessly imposed a leveling process. Landed estates eventually fragmented, since they were divided on the death of the owner among the various heirs. Because successful ranching required extensive acreage, increasingly smaller properties led to the impoverishment of the owners. Misfortune of any kind, but especially the periodic droughts, decimated the herds and other resources of small ranchers. Consequently, they were forced to sell or abandon their properties, sinking thereupon into the dispossessed class.

From the foregoing, it would seem that in time backlands latifundia would have disappeared. In fact, it did not survive extensively in its original form, but there was a countervailing tendency that prevented its disappearance. Through varying sets of circumstances, but especially through personal drive and well-made marriages, individual ranchers were frequently able not only to halt the process of disintegration but even to rebuild the fortunes in herds and land that their forefathers had

[9] See Billy Jaynes Chandler, "The Role of Negroes in the Ethnic Formation of Ceará: The Need for a Reappraisal," *Revista de Ciências Sociais* 4, no. 1 (1973): 31–43.

lost. Hence, while land ownership ceased to be as monolithic as it was in the epoch of the conquest, latifundia nonetheless persisted as a main determining factor in the patterns of backlands society. Crucially, in terms of those patterns, the society continued to be dominated by the relatively few who possessed large amounts of land. The distinguishing feature of the colonial backlands potentate and his successor, the *coronel* ("colonel" or, better, "political boss") of later times, was the prestige and power that his land holdings conferred.

The significant economic activity in the backlands was cattle ranching; that is, it was the significant economic activity in terms of the production of a surplus for export. As we have noted, it was for this reason that the area was conquered, and, in conformance with this aim, the main highways of the region became the long cattle trails that stretched from its far corners to coastal capitals like Recife and Salvador. But, while ranching provided the base for the few to accumulate a modest measure of wealth, it was not the labor from which the larger population subsisted. As physical conditions mandated, cattle raising was extensively practiced and, as such, required few hands. Apart from the never numerous and relatively privileged cowboys, hands might be required only on special occasions, such as roundup time. As generation followed generation, the increasing population of the backlands was largely superfluous. They constituted the tenant (*morador*) class, which by leave of the landlord was permitted to eke out a meager living through subsistence agriculture. Other than furnishing something now and then for the table of their patron (*patrão*) and, perhaps, hiring out as laborers a few days each year, their contribution to society was keeping themselves alive.

There was an economic function that this surplus class could potentially serve—the production of agricultural products for export to the coastal population. Such production had long occurred in the region called the *agreste*, immediately adjacent to the sugar zone. However, the difficulties of transportation over the long distances, together with lethargy and tradition, long hindered agricultural development in the far backlands, even though portions of the region were capable of producing exportable quantities of foodstuffs and other plant products in normal years. Notable change in the situation began to occur only in the nineteenth century, initially as the result of the planting of cotton in some areas. Transportation facilities remained poor, however, and, income from such a crop being subject to the fluctuations of the world market, benefits to backlands society were meager.[10]

Changes of greater consequence awaited the penetration of railroads into the region, a development that began to take place only in the late nineteenth and early twentieth centuries. While railroads reached only a few areas of the backlands, they nonetheless formed by far the best transportation system in the region until the coming of passable roads for motor trucks nearly a half century later. In those areas that they served, and for many miles distant, the railroads stimulated the first significant cultivation of food crops for export.[11]

The beneficial effects that might have accrued to the tenant class as a consequence of this development seemed never to materialize. In the first place, the owners of the land began to require a portion of the tenant's production as rent. This was a natural result, in part, of the valorization of agricultural products. Second, the backlands population, which appears to have been on the increase—quite possibly, some scholars believe, because of the vaccination campaigns that lessened the incidence of epidemic diseases such as smallpox[12]—tended to congregate in those regions most suitable for agriculture. Such a trend had begun with the cotton boom of the mid-nineteenth century, but it was of relatively short duration and its effects were not pronounced. In contrast, the turning toward the production of foodstuffs for market proved to be a trend of seemingly permanent duration. It not only renewed the earlier tendency but also greatly accelerated its rate of increase.

Unfortunately, areas suitable for agriculture soon became overcrowded and over utilized. A result of this was the extreme fragmentation of properties in these areas—again through inheritance. The countervailing tendency toward regrouping that occurred in the ranching country was not as pronounced in this area, quite probably because agriculture lends itself to minifundia far more than does extensive cattle production. The economic group that profited most from the commercialization of agricultural products seems to have been those middlemen who purchased the products for export to population centers.

---

[10] On cotton production and its declining importance by the late 1860s, see Roger Lee Cunniff, "The Great Drought: Northeast Brazil, 1877–1880" (Ph.D. diss., University of Texas, Austin, 1971), pp. 78–97.

[11] For one example of this, see Chandler, *Feitosas*, pp. 135, 141–142.

[12] Queiroz, "Notas sociológicas," pp. 506–507.

Characteristically, the middlemen often were enterprising ranchers who not only had an economic base from which to go into the business but who also used their new profits to acquire more land. The result was economic decline in the backlands for most of the population.

The failure of agricultural production to better living standards was only one of a series of unfavorable economic circumstances that may have increased the discontent of the region's most dispossessed classes. One view of the rise of the cangaço emphasizes world market crises that affected the economic well-being of the northeastern region, both coastal and interior. The collapse of the demand for Brazilian cotton following the end of the North American Civil War and a depressed sugar market produced a period of economic setbacks that reached its lowest point with the end of the Amazon rubber boom in the second and third decades of the twentieth century. These economic factors, it is suggested, combined with the increase in backlands population, produced the cangaço. While it seems generally preferable to seek explanations more directly related to the backlands communities in which the cangaço thrived, this larger view should not go unmentioned.[13]

It was not economic conditions alone, however, that brought about the outbreak of banditry in the period. The fragility of the institutions of law, order, and justice also constituted a major contributing factor. Of course, such a condition was not new. It was implanted in the period of colonization when the authorities consigned the region to the landowning potentates. In those early years, the potentates maintained some order within their respective dominions but, at the same time, seriously disrupted general order by engaging in wars with each other.

Attempts subsequently were made during the Empire to impose greater order and institute impartial justice, mainly through entrusting law enforcement powers to imperially controlled county police chiefs. The promise of the innovation was never fully realized because the police chief, who usually was shifted with the rotation of the two national political parties, generally favored the local faction identified with the party of the ministry that had appointed him. The introduction by the Empire of the jury system in criminal cases, moreover, further weakened the attempt. Jurors functioned in reality in accord-

---

[13] Ibid., pp. 505–508.

ance with the wishes of the local colonel or boss; living under his domination, they seldom dared to oppose him. The organization of opposing
political parties in the communities served as an additional inducement
to conflict. Formerly, the backlands were wracked by family wars; to
this continuing violence were now added political antagonisms.[14]

The Old Republic, which succeeded the Empire in 1889, retreated
in the main from any centralized attempt to bring justice and order to
the region. Its extreme federalism, delivering effective governance to
the states, fostered the development of political machines. Most of these
state machines interested themselves in the backlands only to ensure
that the local colonels delivered the vote in proper fashion. In return
for the service, the colonels were assured of noninterference in their
dominions. The local police force, now under state control, normally
could be expected to work with the colonels.[15]

Nonetheless, the local colonels were seldom able to achieve effective domination of their communities. They were still the heads of important family groupings, or *parentelas,* but they were not the potentates of the earlier era. Neither did they and their immediate family
monopolize land to the same extent as had their predecessors. The own-
ing of land in significant amounts still was confined to a small propor-
tion of the population, but in any county there were likely to be not
one but several families that fell into that privileged category. Hence,
power and prestige in most backlands communities had become considerably fractionalized in comparison with the colonial period.

Under such conditions, disorder increased and hope for protection
and justice decreased. In the earlier time, people had achieved a measure of protection by attaching themselves to, or simply living within
the domain of, a potentate. To the degree that the potentate fulfilled
the role of differentiated authority, the people also may have secured a
measure of justice. In contrast, the chaos that followed the fragmentation of the potentates' authority brought a worsened condition. People
still were linked, generally, to one or another of the colonels or influ-

---

[14] Chandler, *Feitosas,* provides ample evidence of this (see especially pp.
46–78). The standard work on family wars is L. A. Costa Pinto, *Lutas de famílias
no Brasil.* It is based, however, on inadequate research and contains many factual
errors.

[15] The now classic study of politics in the period is Victor Nunes Leal, *Coronelismo, enxada e voto.*

ential family groupings, but little security was to be found in such ties, since few of the colonels were sufficiently powerful to dominate their communities. Nor was security to be found in the institutions of the state, which in backlands communities were notoriously weak. Moreover, the power of the institutions was used in behalf of whichever local faction enjoyed the favors of the state machine at the moment. With reliable guarantees of protection to be found neither in one's patron nor in the state, many backlands communities became virtual jungles in which it was every man for himself. It appears certain that the rise of the cangaço was linked intimately to this state of social disorganization.[16]

Lawlessness and disorder—probably more widespread in the backlands during portions of the Old Republic than at any other time—were, however, only parts of a mounting and interlocking complex of conditions that may account for the rise of the cangaço. The droughts, which came in those years in unusual frequency and severity, caused serious disruptions in the society. The disastrous drought of 1877–1879 was followed in quick order by others in 1888–1889, 1891, 1898, 1900, 1902–1903, 1907, 1915, and 1919. The worst of these caused practical evacuations of the ranching country as refugees fled from hunger and starvation, and many of these people never returned. Some migrated to the Amazon region, where they were employed in the rubber industry, while others settled in the cities of the coastal region. Still others congregated in the better-watered agricultural regions in such numbers that they created severe social tensions and put a strain on available resources. Such migrations, whether temporary or permanent, contributed to the breakdown of social control exercised by the landlords over the peasants. The economic dislocations occasioned by the rise and fall of the cotton boom in the mid-nineteenth century may also have had similar effects. Thus, the severe droughts of 1877 and after may have accelerated a process already begun.[17]

Banditry generally flourished during severe droughts and was especially bad during the late 1870s. Although banditry also existed on a minimal level in ordinary times, it is probable that the unusually fre-

[16] Souza in "The Cangaço" takes a similar view, arguing that the cangaço in part came out of a conjunction of political factors that included the inability of either the state or the colonels to dominate the community (see especially pp. 111, 123).

[17] Cunniff, "The Great Drought," pp. 78–96.

quent droughts of the late nineteenth and early twentieth centuries contributed to the uncommonly high level of sustained banditry that characterized the cangaço. Indeed, the drought of 1919 seems to have inaugurated the worst of it.[18]

Evidence of a crisis in backlands society in the period is found also in the manifestations of messianism or religious fanaticism. Here, too, not only were the already weakening bonds of social control severed and loyalties transferred, but significant population shifts also occurred. Such messianism, based on the superstition, ignorance, and poverty of backlanders, had long existed. Two of the most prominent outbreaks of messianism, however, virtually paralleled the rise of the cangaço. Both banditry and messianism, apparently, fed on the same complex of conditions.[19] Antônio Conselheiro's community at Canudos in Bahia, founded in 1893, was the first of these two religious movements; Padre Cícero Romão Batista's "Holy City" of Juàzeiro, which emerged in the decades after 1889, was the second.[20] Conselheiro brought together some several thousand followers in his short-lived settlement, which was destroyed by the federal army in 1897. Juàzeiro, located in the Cariri of southeastern Ceará—a region suitable for agriculture—survived and prospered, going on to become the focus of the backlands' largest concentration of people. The Cariri, attracting a wide assortment of the region's displaced and dispossessed population—criminals and adventurers among them—served as an especially fertile field for the recruitment of men to whom violence was commonplace. Indeed, the concentration of people in the Cariri, and its violent political life

18 Frederico Pernambucano de Mello in "Aspectos do banditismo rural nordestino" (MS furnished by the author) contends that this was the case and names twenty-five bands that operated between 1919 and 1927. On one of the groups that operated during the 1877–1879 drought, see Raimundo Nonato, *Jesuíno Brilhante: O cangaceiro romântico*. However, Brilhante and his band were not produced by the drought, having been in existence when it began.

19 This is a commonly held view, propounded especially by Facó in *Cangaceiros*.

20 Da Cunha's *Rebellion in the Backlands*, the story of Canudos, is one of Brazil's most famous literary works, but it should be balanced with other views, especially that set forth in Ataliba Nogueira, *Antônio Conselheiro e Canudos: Revisão histórica*. Padre Cícero and Juàzeiro are treated in greater detail in chapter 4 of the present study. In addition to the works cited there, Facó's *Cangaceiros* should be consulted on Juàzeiro's rise and its influence on the region.

during the first decades of the twentieth century, may be counted as another development that influenced the rise of the cangaço.[21]

Antônio Silvino, the first of the prominent cangaceiros, ought also to be mentioned in any discussion of the conditions that favored an increase in banditry in the period.[22] The stories and legends of his exploits, and the wonder and respect that he called forth among many backlanders, helped to mold popular conceptions of the cangaço and give it a selfsustaining force. Born in 1875 to a respected ranching family of backlands Pernambuco, Silvino became a bandit in 1897 when he angrily killed two men whom he associated with the murderers of his father. His criminal career came to an end only in 1914 when he was wounded and captured by the Pernambuco police. During the seventeen intervening years, he roamed with his small group of followers over four states, operating in bandit fashion but also creating a legend of a gentlemanly bandit who respected those who merited such treatment and rendered justice to those who deserved it. There were few backlands boys who did not know of Silvino's feats. When, and if, the course of their lives suggested a similar path, the celebrated outlaw chieftain served as a laudable example.

Lampião was born and grew up within an area often frequented by Silvino. He was born in the year in which Silvino became an outlaw; he was seventeen when the famed bandit was captured. Silvino no doubt served as an example for Lampião, but he was not the only one. Nor, for that matter, was he the most important one. After Silvino, the best-known cangaceiro chieftain came from São Francisco, the district of Vila Bela County in which Lampião was born and reared. Sebastião Pereira (also known as Sinhô Pereira), like Silvino, was a unique bandit, a gentleman who came from one of the area's most prestigious families. Also like Silvino, he fell outside the law in an attempt to avenge his family's honor. That he should follow that course was not surprising, for his family had long been engaged in one of the

21 See Facó, *Cangaceiros*, especially part 3.

22 No adequate historical treatment of Silvino has yet been published, but Mário Souto Maior, *Antônio Silvino: Capitão de trabuco*, and Carvalho, *Serrote Preto*, pp. 428–470, provide brief sketches. An interesting interpretation of aspects of his story is found in Linda Lewin, "The Oligarchical Limitations of Social Banditry in Brazil: The Case of the 'Good' Thief Antônio Silvino," *Past and Present*, forthcoming.

backlands' most rancorous interfamily conflicts. The troubles of the Pereira family form an intimate part of the social environment in which Lampião became a cangaceiro.[23]

Trouble between the Pereiras and the Carvalhos originated apparently in political rivalries in the late 1840s, but it was in the decade and a half after 1905 that the trouble entered its most violent phase. The violence appears to have helped generate an explosion of lawlessness that, reaching well beyond the original combatants, came to encompass not only the Pajeú River region of central Pernambuco but neighboring areas as well.

The reopening of the conflict in 1905 involved a matter common to the backlands, the attempted disarming on a highway of two of the Carvalho clan by two Pereiras. Life in the backlands being dangerous, the wearing of arms was viewed as a right and any attempt to interfere with it a serious breach of honor. Thus, when word of the incident reached the Carvalhos, various altercations between members of the two families ensued. In one of them, Né Pereira, a former county police chief, was killed on market day at Vila Bela. When the accused killers were absolved by the jury, the Pereiras were left in an angry mood. Additional violence followed, culminating in the 1907 ambush slaying of Manuel Pereira (also known as Padre Pereira, for he once studied in a seminary), the seventy-two-year-old chief of the Pereira clan. Three days later, Né Dadú, one of the murdered chief's nephews, killed two Carvalhos—an action taken, it was said, on the request of the widow. Attacks and killings, of course, continued. In the absence of a strong arm of institutionalized law and justice, the Mosaic law, privately executed, reigned. In one well-remembered episode, the Carvalhos, at the head of three hundred armed men, attacked the Pereira stronghold of São Francisco in 1908. Only after twenty-four hours, when they learned that a Pereira force was on its way to aid the besieged village, did the Carvalhos retreat.

The ability of the Carvalhos to marshal such a large number of gunmen was indicative of what was happening to the Pajeú River area. In the absence of strong and impartial governmental authority—what

[23] On Sebastião Pereira and his family, see: Abelardo Parreira, *Sertanejos e cangaceiros*; Luís Wilson, *Vila Bela, os Pereiras e outras históricas*; Ulisses Lins de Albuquerque, *Um sertanejo e o sertão*, pp. 321–345. Also see the notes of chapter 2 of the present study.

did exist was used by one faction or the other—the general population was being drawn into the conflict; that is, when they were not attending to smaller, lesser-known feuds of their own. One such feud pitted Casimiro Honório, a rancher and head of a large family, against Zé de Sousa, a valiant mulatto who had run off with Casimiro's daughter. After a bitter and prolonged conflict, Zé was killed by Casimiro, who was allied with the Carvalhos.[24] Casimiro was the uncle of the man with whom Lampião and his brothers had their first major conflict. Another conflict involved Casimiro and an uncle (by marriage) of Lampião. These examples could be multiplied almost endlessly, for there were few families unaffected by the violence of those years.

Well-to-do ranchers were virtually forced by circumstances to arm their cowboys and tenants for the protection of family and property or, as some did, to recruit a special squad from among the area's more fearless young men. In view of the social disorganization indicated by these conditions, the increasing number of armed bands—cangaceiros—operating at times for hire but mostly on their own, was not an unexpected development.

One of those bands was formed by Sebastião Pereira in 1916 when Né Dadú, one of his older brothers, was killed. Né, who had avenged the killing of the Pereira chieftain in 1907, had managed to survive until 1916 in spite of the numerous acts of violence that had marked the continuation of the Carvalho-Pereira conflict. He was killed while he slept by one of his own trusted gunmen. Other members of his family, however, had suspected that the man was secretly in the hire of the Carvalhos and had warned Né against him. Years later Sebastião said that he entered the cangaço because of the cowardly and brutal murder of his brother and the total absence of any hope for justice from the hands of government officials. His family, he continued, asked State Governor Dantas Barreto for help; the governor, in reply, reenforced the police, which, at the moment, were with the Carvalhos.[25] With this turn of events, twenty-year-old Sebastião resolved to dedicate himself full time to avenging his brother's death. Traveling to Ceará to visit a relative, he returned with a band of eighteen men. Also accompanying him and sharing leadership of the band was his cousin, Luís Padre, a son of the chieftain who had been assassinated in 1907. It was the chief-

---

[24] David Jurubeba, interview, Serra Talhada, Pernambuco, July 29, 1975.
[25] Wilson, *Vila Bela*, p. 308.

tain's widow who counseled her son to accompany his cousin on the mission of vengeance.

Lampião joined the band of Sebastião Pereira and Luís Padre some five years later. Not many months thereafter, he found himself, by the turn of events, at the head of it. Yet, neither the existence of that band nor, for that matter, any of the other probable causes of the rise of the cangaço fully explains why Lampião became an outlaw. His story, with its peculiarities, is his own. Nor does it fully explain why so many of his contemporaries became cangaceiros. The story of each would possess its own unique qualities. An understanding of broader social conditions makes the emergence of Lampião and the other cangaceiros more comprehensible, but it may be that the greater understanding is to be found in the stories of the bandits themselves. Without those stories, the historical record is merely skeletal, containing nothing of the drama and the ambiguities of the bandits' lives or of the societies in which those unfortunate lives unfolded.

2. Virgulino

THAT Lampião was not just another ordinary backlands bandit was recognized at an early date. Until 1922 he was known only locally, but before that year had run its course his fame was spreading throughout northeastern Brazil. In June of that year, he and his band made a spectacular raid on Agua Branca, a county seat nestled in the green hills of back-country Alagoas State. Soon the region's most influential newspaper, commenting on the extent to which his exploits were attracting popular attention, called him the "renowned Lampião."[1] The newspaper was perceptive in its notice and somewhat prophetic, for from 1922 until 1938 he was out of regional and national news for scarcely more than a few weeks at a time. Seldom had a bandit captured for so long a time a nation's interest.

Yet, Lampião's boyhood was a usual one for the time and place, and probably none of those who knew him as a child could have predicted the fame he was to achieve. He was born in Vila Bela County in the state of Pernambuco on July 7, 1897, and was given the name Virgulino Ferreira da Silva.[2] The place of his birth was his father's ranch, Passagem das Pedras ("Rocky Pass"), lying at the foot of Serra

[1] *Diário de Pernambuco* (Recife), July 22, 1922.
[2] Authenticated copy of registry of birth furnished by Irací Alves dos Santos, official of the Civil Registry of Tauapiranga, Serra Talhada (formerly Vila Bela) County, Pernambuco. The date of Lampião's birth often has been given erroneously as 1900, and he apparently believed it to be that year. The following account of his early years is based mainly on my interviews with his brother, João Ferreira, Propriá, Sergipe, December 14–15, 1973, and July 1–3, 1974. Additional data were obtained from interviews with Olympo Campos, São José de Belmonte, Pernambuco, July 30–31, 1975; Maria Correia, Agua, Branca, Alagoas, June 27, 1974; Genésio Ferreira, Serra Talhada, Pernambuco, July 21 and 28, 1975; Venáncio Nogueira, Floresta, Pernambuco, August 5, 1975. All of these persons knew Lampião as a youth.

Vermelha ("Red Mountain"), which rises abruptly from its lightly hilled surroundings. Like most of the backlands, the ranch was covered with cactus and other forms of scrub vegetation and was dedicated to subsistence agriculture and the raising of cattle, sheep, and goats. Virgulino's father, José Ferreira dos Santos, also transported merchandise throughout the immediate region, using mules and burros, since roads were often impassable to any kind of wheeled vehicle. He was not wealthy, but neither was he poor. He was a member of the land-owning class that stood between the elite which dominated the society and the vast majority of landless peasantry. The Ferreira family had the reputation of being intelligent, honest, and hardworking folk.[3]

Virgulino, the third of José Ferreira's nine children, spent his childhood in the house of his grandparents, Manoel and Jaçosa Lopez, the parents of his mother, Maria. This did not mean any real separation from his parents, for the two houses were only a few hundred yards from each other on opposite sides of a creek. Virgulino never attended a regular school, although he did manage to learn rudimentary reading, writing, and counting from a private instructor. His father was illiterate, not unusual for those of their class; until mid–twentieth century, few schools were found outside cities and towns in northeastern Brazil. Education, then, for the young Virgulino consisted mostly of learning through experience those things necessary to equip him for the same kind of life lived by his father and grandfathers, other opportunities not being anticipated.

On a Brazilian ranch there usually is a division of labor among the inhabitants, and so it was with the family of José Ferreira. Antônio, the eldest son, cared for the plantings, while Levino, the next in line, helped his father with the mule pack. The task of caring for the cattle, sheep, and goats fell to the third son, Virgulino. For the young boy, this entailed daily tracking through the vast pasture lands to round up the sheep and goats in order to pen them at night for protection from predatory animals. He gradually took on the work of caring for cattle, in

---

[3] Racially, Lampião was a mixture of Portuguese, Negro, and Indian, the Portuguese predominating. It has been argued in several works that he was a descendant, through his father, of the Feitosa family of the Inhamuns area of Ceará, but this has not been proved. Surviving members of the Ferreira family know nothing of this, nor do the Feitosas. A typical argument for the relationship is in Macedo, *Capitão Virgulino*, pp. 143–146. On the Feitosas, see Chandler, *Feitosas*.

the course of which he became a skilled cowboy. Many boys of the backlands are expert horsemen by the age of ten or twelve, and so it seems to have been with Virgulino.

He also assumed another important task on the ranch: the making and caring for articles of leather. Halters, bridles, and saddles had to be made and repaired, and the clothing of the cowboys was made of leather as protection from the spiny vegetation. Within the home, much of the furniture, especially chairs, was made at least partially of leather. While leather working had a utilitarian end, it was also a work of art in which the creator took pride, not only in his ability to manufacture a good article but also in making it beautiful. Bridles and saddles, in particular, were often elaborate examples of the leather worker's art. That Virgulino's skills were more than adequate is attested to by several persons who remember him as a young man.

Fortunately, not all was work for Virgulino. The land of northeastern Brazil was neither ranched nor cultivated intensively, and there was plenty of free time. As a young boy, he played the games that backlands boys have long played, and, as is usual, many of them were imitations of adult activities. One of the most popular was the rodeo (*vaquejada*) game, in which two boys, who pretended to be mounted on horses, ranged themselves on either side of a third, who pretended to be the cow; as the three raced down a path, one of the mounted ones sought to throw the cow to the ground. As can be imagined, the cow often took a hard spill. The bodies of the boys, especially their legs, soon possessed numerous scars from the roughness of the games and from contact with the thorny vegetation. Probably, though, the favorite game was cangaceiros and police, the backlands version of cops and robbers. It too involved rough play. While the boys sometimes used corn cobs, arranged under their "cartridge" belts, to throw at each other, they also at times used slingshots and rocks. It is not surprising that cangaceiros and police was a popular game. Not only did the boys frequently see the many cangaceiros who infested the backlands in that era, but they also heard their exploits celebrated in verse and song.

The games just described were, of course, those of boys, and as Virgulino became a youth he began to cultivate adult pastimes. He participated in rodeos and soon became one of the area's most popular young rodeo riders. He also taught himself to play the accordion, the basic instrument in the folk music of the Northeast. A slim, moderately tall, darkly good-looking fellow who danced well, he was popular at the dances that were held frequently on the ranches of the area. All in all, Virgulino was a well-rounded young man who excelled in a number of things.

This view of Lampião's early years may well seem exaggerated, in effect the invention of a romantic boyhood to suit an image of him as a celebrated bandit. Yet, if there is error in this account it is probably on the side of caution, since friend and foe alike remember him as a remarkable young man. Given his abilities, it is a special pity for himself and his society that Virgulino Ferreira was to devote his twenty or so years of adult life to crime and to be eventually gunned down in a rocky mountain creek of a neighboring state.

Historical materials with which to recreate the entry of Virgulino into the cangaço are fragmentary, confusing, and usually contradictory.[4] Nonetheless, at the heart of the matter, it is universally agreed, was a neighbor of the Ferreiras, José Saturnino. Saturnino, only two years older than Virgulino, owned a ranch adjoining the Ferreira property. In local society he was a cut above the Ferreiras, for he had close links with prestigious families. His wife was of the Nogueiras, who counted themselves among the local elite, while his father was a prestigious landowner who himself maintained a band of armed men. His uncle, Casimiro Honório, was a well-known leader of cangaceiros who served the powerful Carvalho family in their rancorous and bloody

---

[4] Again, the João Ferreira interviews are a major source. In addition, João told his story to Luciano Carneiro in "Porque Lampeão entrou no cangaço," *O Cruzeiro*, October 3, 1953, and years earlier to Alvaró Barbosa Gomes, *Diário de Notícias* (Salvador), June 4, 1930. José Saturnino, Lampião's first major enemy, told me his version in an interview in Serra Talhada, Pernambuco, July 26 and 28, 1975; for Saturnino's story, also see Oliveira, *Lampião*, pp. 28–35. Also helpful were interviews with the following men who knew Lampião: Olympo Campos; João Jurubeba (Serra Talhada, Pernambuco, July 29, 1975); Genésio Ferreira; and Miguel Feitosa (Araripina, Pernambuco, July 15–16, 1975). See also the following published interviews with people who knew him: J. Martins Cavalcante, *Correio de Aracajú*, October 9, 1930; José Abílio, *Jornal de Alagoas* (Maceió), August 10, 1938; Sebastião Pereira, in Oswaldo Amorim, "O homem que chefiou Lampião," *Jornal do Brasil* (Rio de Janeiro), December 26, 1969. The several books on Lampião are unreliable for this period. Few give any indication of sources, and events and dates are often hopelessly jumbled and inaccurate. I have chosen thus to reconstruct the story of his life from interviews, documents, and contemporary news accounts.

wars with the Pereiras. He was, in addition, the head of his own clan. The Ferreiras, in comparison, were relatively humble people.

Enmity between the Ferreiras and Saturnino began in 1916, when Virgulino was nineteen. Trespass and alleged thefts of animals and halters were the cause. Such complaints were endemic in the backlands. Range land was unfenced, and ranchers commonly exhibited an exaggerated sense of honor in protection of their flocks and herds. According to the Ferreiras, a tenant of Saturnino was stealing their goats. On their complaint, the local constable, who was Virgulino's uncle, investigated. Accompanied by Virgulino and Levino, he went to the tenant's house and charged that hides found there bore the mark of the Ferreiras. Saturnino, as was usual, took the incursion of the Ferreiras and their constable relative on his land, as well as the accusations, as an insult. He stated that his tenant need have no fear, that he would be protected. He also accused the Ferreira boys of mistreating his animals and stealing their halters and warned them to stay off his land. Judging the validity of the charges today is difficult. If the Ferreiras were guilty of the accusations, their actions may well have been in retaliation for having their goats stolen. The thievery of small animals was a common crime for tenants. They were a miserably poor, subjugated, and sometimes depraved class.

The cult of honor and the avenging of insult were integral parts of the code of the backlands, and José Ferreira's sons were known already as valiant young men. Quite clearly, they were not disposed toward backing down, and they could be insulting on their own. In a nearby village, for example, Antônio had said that he had a horse which he wanted to breed to Saturnino's wife. That was one of the worst forms of insult to Brazilians, who often are overly protective of the females in their families.

Whatever its origins, the ill will between the two families soon erupted into violence. On a day in early December, 1916, Virgulino and Levino, returning from rounding up cattle, passed by a field where some of Saturnino's men were working. As the story is told by one of Saturnino's men, the Ferreira boys, when counseled not to trespass on that land, answered that they would go where they pleased and warned Saturnino not to interfere. Virgulino claimed that two shots were fired on him and his brother by one of Saturnino's gang. The next day, the two boys, now in the company of Antônio and one of their tenants, went again to round up the cattle, but this time they were armed with rifles. As they passed near Saturnino's house, a battle erupted. Who fired first is disputed, but, at any rate, the Ferreira boys and their companion fought against a superior force of Saturnino and his men, and Antônio received a wound in the hip.[5]

All of this was disturbing to José Ferreira, who, it seems, had little of the flamboyant bravery and wildness of his sons and wanted only to live a peaceful life. He, in concert with influential community leaders, sought to work out an accord with Saturnino and his relatives, hoping to avert further violence. Such private solutions to problems of justice were not rare in a land where public institutions were weak and often corrupt. Virgulino's father, being less influential than Saturnino, bore the brunt of the accommodation. The Ferreiras were to sell their ranch and move to a place near the village of Nazaré in the adjoining county of Floresta. They were, in addition, forbidden to set foot in the area of their former home. José Saturnino and his close relatives were not to go near Nazaré.

The move completed, the Ferreiras settled down in their new ranch, known as Poço do Negro ("Black Well"). There they looked forward to a period of peace. Unfortunately, José Ferreira did not find the peace he sought, and this move was to be only one of a series before he met his untimely death. Things did not work out as Ferreira had hoped; Saturnino and his brother-in-law, José Nogueira, broke the accord. One day, probably several months after their family's move, Virgulino and Manoel Lopez (an uncle who lived with the Ferreiras) decided to go to the weekly market day in Nazaré. In the village, Virgulino and his uncle saw Saturnino and Nogueira. Saturnino was there, he has said, only to collect an over-due debt from a person to whom he had sold a horse. Be that as it may, the two men's presence in Nazaré was disturbing to young Virgulino. He wanted to confront them right away in the middle of the street, but Manoel Lopez, the older and apparently the cooler of the two, succeeded in convincing his aroused

[5] Valuable information on this dispute and its violence is found in the criminal proceedings against José Alves de Barros et al., December 7, 1916, First Cartório, Serra Talhada, Pernambuco. This is the process initiated against Saturnino, whose real name was Barros, for the wounding of Antônio. Testimony was offered by Virgulino, among others.

nephew that it would be more prudent to ambush the men on their way home. Saturnino and Nogueira, rightly supposing that something might be in store for them, tried to outlast their adversaries, but, with nightfall near, they set out for home. As they had anticipated, Virgulino and Manoel were waiting for them, and a few shots were exchanged. Whether Virgulino and his uncle really wanted to kill their enemies or wished merely to scare them is unclear. Whichever it was, no one was injured.

Now, it was Saturnino and his clan who were aroused. Early on the next day, some fifteen men launched an attack on Poço do Negro. Virgulino and Manoel were there alone; the elder Ferreira was traveling with his mule team and other members of the family had gone to visit relatives many miles to the north. The attack was not unexpected. Well stocked with ammunition, Virgulino and his uncle put up fierce resistance and succeeded in wounding one of Saturnino's band. After a half hour of firing, the attackers withdrew.

The assault on Poço do Negro alarmed the Ferreiras because it endangered the safety of the entire family. It vividly underscored the insecurity of their lives. The Ferreira boys now went about constantly armed and were beginning to acquire the reputations of cangaceiros. They also began to affect the dress that symbolized the professional bandit: hats with the brims turned up in front, colorful kerchiefs around their necks, and cartridge belts.

Serving as an inspiration for them, as we have already noted, was Sebastião Pereira, a cangaceiro whom they knew well. The most famous of the bandits after Silvino, he came from the village of São Francisco, located near the Ferreira's former ranch, Passagem das Pedras, and he was, moreover, approximately the same age as the Ferreira boys. Accompanied by a numerous band, Pereira since 1916 had been operating in the area of the backlands in which the Ferreiras lived, and an uncle by marriage of the Ferreira boys, Antônio Matildes, was one of those who protected the Pereira band. Interestingly, too, the Nogueiras and Saturnino formed a part of the Carvalho clan, Pereira's chief antagonists. It was thus quite to be expected that Pereira would serve as an example for the Ferreiras and that, when their situation later worsened, they would seek him out for help, for they had common enemies.[6]

[6] Pereira's story as told in Amorim, "O homem que chefiou Lampião." Also see Wilson, *Vila Bela*, pp. 307–326.

The stance of the three Ferreira boys as budding cangaceiros, belligerent in defense of themselves and their family, was disturbing to the Nazaré community, which was dominated by families linked by blood and marriage to the Saturninos and Nogueiras. The Ferreiras had not moved far enough away to escape the influence of their enemies. If their new neighbors were not initially hostile, they were at least predisposed toward the other side.

The first difficulties of the Ferreira boys with the dominant clan of Nazaré (bearing the names variously of Flor, Ferraz, Gomes, Jurubeba, and Nogueira) were occasioned by the insistence of the boys that they wear their arms within the village. Prudence had long dictated—and this was true throughout the backlands—that firearms not be carried in town. It was the custom on entering town to deposit one's weapons in a store or the house of an acquaintance, and to pick them up only when ready to leave. Antônio, Levino, and Virgulino refused to follow this custom, alleging that their lives were in danger, and their refusal led to exchanges of threats between them and Nazaré's leading citizens. Claiming that the Ferreiras were upsetting the peace of the community and harming its commerce, influential residents of the village succeeded in getting a soldier of the state police stationed there. It was expected that he would do their bidding, for impartial police authority was rare in the rural Brazil of that era.

In time, the Ferreira boys did get into serious trouble in Nazaré. The exact cause again is disputed, but the most plausible account leaves them free of guilt. It was market day in Nazaré and, because of a robbery nearby by Pereira and his bandits, the usual prohibition on arms had been lifted. Many persons feared a raid on the village itself. Some people alleged that the Ferreiras had accompanied Pereira in his recent robbery, and Antônio and Virgulino were fired upon as they approached the village. Levino, who had arrived there shortly before without incident, at first participated in the attack on his brothers, apparently thinking that they were men from Pereira's band. This action would seem to cast doubt on the allegations that the Ferreira boys had been riding with Pereira, since Levino was not likely to attack his brothers or their friends.[7] However, he did not long participate in the attack; recognizing them, he went over to their side and assisted in the

[7] Olympo Campos, an acquaintance of the Ferreiras who later fought against them as a soldier, says that the charge against them is untrue (interview).

defense, whereupon he took a bullet in the arm. Found hiding in the house of an acquaintance on the edge of town, he was threatened with being shot on the spot. Fortunately, cooler heads prevailed, and he was taken in custody by the soldier and sent to the county seat of Floresta. Virgulino and Antônio escaped without injury.

The Ferreiras were now in deeper trouble, having had an armed confrontation with the dominant families in their new home. Levino had been wounded and taken away. The continued residence of the Ferreira family in the Nazaré area seemed impossible, and José Ferreira again pondered the fate of his family. His three oldest sons were virtual outlaws, and two of them had now been wounded in gun battles. What might happen further if they remained in Poço do Negro was frightening to contemplate. A new move seemed to be almost a necessity. But first there was the problem of securing the freedom of Levino. This did not turn out to be as difficult as expected, probably because the authorities in the county seat were more interested in securing peace in the outlying district than in securing convictions. It was agreed that Levino could return to his family if the Ferreiras would leave the county. The Ferreiras accepted the conditions and Levino was released. In the meantime, he had been living in the county seat in relative freedom while the local priest, a German immigrant who was a former veterinarian, treated his wound.[8]

The family now moved to the county of Agua Branca in the neighboring state of Alagoas, a choice suggested by the Ferreira boys. They pointed out that Antônio Matildes, their uncle by marriage, had moved there recently and was living under the protection of one of the local colonels, Dr. Ulysses Luna. The move to Alagoas was probably completed in 1920, something over three years after the troubles with Saturnino began. The new home of the family was a rented property in a place called Olho da'Agua ("Eye of Water," meaning a natural spring), a few miles from the county seat. The Ferreiras were no longer as well off as they had been, for their troubles and moves had taken their toll. They had lost most of their cattle and were reduced to making their living from subsistence agriculture and the mule team.

The peace that José Ferreira was seeking for his family was also to elude him in Alagoas. The reasons for this are several, but the Fe-

_____

[8] Interview with the priest, Fr. José Kehrle, in Ricardo Noblat, "Lampião morreu envenenado," *Manchete*, April 29, 1972, pp. 154–157.

rreiras blamed their continuing problems on their enemies in Pernambuco and alleged that Saturnino and Nogueira sent word to authorities in Agua Branca branding them as bandits. That may not have been necessary, for, as João Ferreira—the only one of the brothers who never became a cangaceiro—has said, the boys had their blood up and were not willing to give up their desire to exact revenge from Saturnino. In addition, they had ties with Matildes, a veteran figure in the violence of central Pernambuco, who also had left because of difficulties with the police and the dominant families. While he was still living in Pernambuco in late 1919, his home had been surrounded by police and he had been beaten and arrested, the police alleging that he had been hiding cangaceiros. He had then been taken to the county seat but was soon released for lack of proof. He blamed his difficulties on Saturnino and the Nogueiras, whom he believed had told police that he regularly protected Pereira and his band. Dr. Luna, Matildes' protector in Agua Branca, could do little to help him now in his new home, since he was at the time in the political opposition. Nor could he help the Ferreiras.

At any rate, neither Matildes nor the Ferreira boys wanted to forget Saturnino, and at least twice in the next few months they returned to Pernambuco to raid him and his relatives. The first of the two attacks occurred September 15, 1920. A band of fifteen, including Matildes and the three Ferreira brothers, attacked Saturnino's ranches and also one owned by the Nogueiras, setting fire to houses and wooden fences, killing cattle, and firing at anyone in sight. The raid was led, a witness reported, by Matildes and Virgulino Ferreira. Virgulino already was assuming a position of leadership in the group, even though he was the youngest of the three brothers. Early in December, the same band again raided ranches owned by the Nogueiras.[9]

Given these occurrences, the police in Agua Branca quite naturally were suspicious of Matildes and the Ferreiras. Agua Branca was, after all, only some seventy-five miles from Serra Vermelha, where the raids occurred, and news of them soon reached there. Thereupon, the police searched the homes of Matildes and the Ferreiras, looking for arms and possible stolen goods. Police in those days were little more than bandits themselves, and such a search usually meant the near destruction of the house and its contents and mistreatment of its occupants as well.

[9] Criminal proceedings against Antônio Matildes et al., October 15 and December 3, 1920, First Cartório, Serra Talhada, Pernambuco.

So it was in these cases, except that the families were not in their homes at the time of the searches and thus escaped injury.

The Ferreiras in their new home were now clearly under suspicion of being criminals, and it was not long before a clash with the police occurred. Again, the Ferreiras' luck was bad, for the origins of the incident were not really of their making. One of the Ferreira girls had married Matildes' nephew, and a child of theirs was ill. Someone needed to go to the county seat to purchase medicine, and it was decided that João, one of the two youngest sons of José Ferreira, would make the trip. None of the other male members of the clan could go. With the exception of José Ferreira, they were all unwelcome in the city. Upon arriving in Agua Branca, João was arrested and accused by the police of having come to buy ammunition for Matildes. When news of his arrest reached his home, Virgulino, Antônio, and Levino, accompanied by a friend, took their weapons and set out to free him. This was the reaction that the police chief in Agua Branca had expected, and he was waiting in ambush not far from the Ferreira residence. As the Ferreira party passed, they were fired upon, but, offering stiff resistance, they succeeded in putting the ambuscaders to flight. The Ferreiras then returned home. The next day, they sent word to the police chief that if João were not home by five o'clock in the afternoon they would burn the town. The police chief, counseled by citizens who feared a confrontation, permitted João to return home.

Remaining in Agua Branca now being out of the question, José Ferreira again faced the unhappy necessity of moving. The prospect of moving was clouded by the serious illness of his wife, who, because of her condition, could not travel far. For José, however, the problem of what to do with the three oldest sons was the most pressing, for they were in danger. He thus sent them away, along with the younger children, instructing them to seek out the family later in its new location, wherever that might be. Only José and his wife and João remained. In the next few days, they packed the few belongings they had, made hasty arrangements with the owner of the property, and set out in the direction of nearby Mata Grande. Their destination was not definitely fixed, but they had friends in that county and, moreover, believed its police chief to be sympathetic to their plight. On the road between the towns of Agua Branca and Mata Grande, they stopped to rest at the house of a friend, Senhô Fragoso, at the place known as Engenho ("the

Mill"). There, having worsened rapidly as a result of the journey, José Ferreira's wife died. Now, sad and disheartened, Ferreira decided that he and João would remain with Fragoso until his other sons returned. He accepted his host's offer of a house on the property as a place to live, although, fearing a surprise attack by police at night, he and his son slept in the *caatinga*.

Well they might have feared an attack. In the meantime, Virgulino and his brothers had returned to the area and, with Matildes and seven others, raided Pariconhas, a village in Agua Branca. The attack was motivated by the close ties between the police deputy there and the county police chief, Amarilo Batista. Batista, of course, had been responsible for the arrest of João and, along with the deputy from Pariconhas, had searched and depredated the Matildes and Ferreira homes. This was revenge, and Matildes and his band took full advantage of the opportunity. On arriving in the village at about four-thirty in the afternoon, they seized Manoel Pereira, the deputy, and, after sacking his place of business, tied him to a stake. Matildes told him that this was payment for the earlier plunder of Matildes' own house. Next, the band went to the general store of the county's intendant and invaded it, removing what they could carry away and destroying the rest. Taking money, gold, jewels, and watches, and ordering bottled beverages poured over the dry goods, Matildes charged that the intendant too was responsible for his sufferings. One of the band also went to the home of the county attorney and robbed him. All told, the victims claimed that they had suffered losses and damage of 18:000$000 (about five thousand U.S. dollars), a major fortune in the backlands of that day.[10] Leaving town, the bandits forced the police deputy to accompany them for a few miles, apparently so that he could not organize any immediate pursuit.

Interestingly, some of the witnesses referred to Virgulino Ferreira as "Lampião." He had by this time acquired the nickname with which he was to achieve fame. The origin of the nickname has been variously described, but the most popular version states that it resulted from

[10] Until 1942, Brazilian currency was divided into *contos* written (1:000$000) and *milréis* (1$000). A *conto* in 1922 was the equivalent of $129.00 U.S., and its value remained fairly stable through the remainder of the decade. Between 1930 and 1938, its value fell, in U.S. equivalent, from $107.00 to $58.00, but, during most of those years, ranged from $70.00 to $85.00. See the chart in Robert M. Levine, *The Vargas Regime*, p. 193.

Virgulino's ability to fire a lever-action rifle so rapidly as to create almost continuous light in the darkness. However, nicknames were common in the society and were bestowed often for no particular reason.

Lampião's achievement of fame was not without cost. This particular step toward fame at Pariconhas seems to have led directly to his father's death. The attack on the village took place on May 9, 1921. Nine days later, on the eighteenth, José Ferreira died at the hands of the police. Ferreira, at the time of his death, was preparing to leave Fragoso's property. He had planned to go into Mata Grande on that morning to purchase supplies for the journey and was shelling corn on the front porch of Fragoso's house when the police arrived. His son João was in the pasture in search of the mules. The force, led by Chief of Police Amarilo Batista of Agua Branca and Sergeant José Lucena of the state police, asked no questions. They simply surrounded the house and opened fire on its occupants, believing, they said, that it was a nest of the cangaceiros who had raided Pariconhas. José Ferreira and his host, Fragoso, were killed. The police claimed that they found in the house some of the objects stolen in Pariconhas. If this be so—and there seems little reason to doubt it—the boys had been back to see their father since the raid.[11]

The death of José Ferreira is one of the major tragedies of Lampião's story. He seems to have been a good, hard-working father who earnestly sought to steer his family safely through the difficulties into which they fell. He was at the time of his death not yet an aged man, less than fifty years old.

At the time of their father's death, the older Ferreira sons were on

[11] An inventory of the stolen goods apprehended, dated May 21, 1921, is in the Arquivo Público, Maceió, Alagoas, package M-10 = E = 2. The best source on the Pariconhas raid is the criminal proceedings against Antônio Matildes et al., May 9, 1921, Cartório, Agua Branca, Alagoas. A document appended to the proceedings gives the date of José Ferreira's death. Newspapers made only brief mention of the Pariconhas attack, for example, *Estado das Alagoas* (Maceió), May 29, 1921. Most works on Lampião give 1920 as the date of these events and most of them place José Ferreira's death before the Pariconhas raid. This is a crucial point, if one is arguing, as the popular version of the story does, that the attack on Fragoso's house was unjustified by any past events and consequently that Lampião became a bandit because of the killing of his father by the police. João Ferreira, understandably, has taken that point of view; however, he admitted that he has a clear memory neither of whether it was 1920 or 1921 nor of the exact sequence of events (interview).

their way back to Mata Grande with the younger children to rejoin the family. João, in the meantime, was hiding out near the Fragoso home, fearing for his life. Learning of their father's death before their arrival, the boys hurried to Fragoso's property. There they found João and told him to take the four younger children (three girls and a boy) to Pernambuco in the hope that someone would take them in. João departed, and, unlike the rest of José Ferreira's sons, never joined his brothers in banditry.

For Virgulino, Antônio, and Levino, the die was cast. Virgulino said that having lost a father to the police—and he blamed the death of his mother on them as well—he would fight until death and added that, if he could, he would burn Alagoas. Whatever chance there had been that the lives of the Ferreira boys could be directed into peaceful avenues was shut off. Already, by their attacks on their private enemies and their several skirmishes with police, they were branded as criminals. Now, resolving to live from crime and to avenge the death of their father by fighting the police, they relinquished any reasonable hope of ever being able to return to normality. For better or worse, they had chosen the life of bandits. If they had been "tame cangaceiros" to this point—that is to say, living normal lives but employing violence occasionally in defense of family and honor—it was soon to be no longer true. Shortly, they were to fall so far outside the law that making a normal living became impossible; they could live only from banditry.

Although placing the story of Virgulino's fall into banditry in the context of the conditions of his society and examining the details of his own actions explain in part why it happened, there are still unanswered questions. The event may always evade full comprehension. It is difficult to know why some men become criminals while others, living within the same general set of social conditions and beset by similar tribulations, do not. In the main, the differences would seem to lie in the interaction of events and conditions with individual temperaments. It is to be assumed that the weight of the knowledge that one's family has been dealt with unfairly and brought to disaster—even when one's own actions may have partially contributed to that disaster—lies more heavily on the mind of a strong man than a weak one. The weight is doubly burdensome when there is little hope for relief or retribution through legally sanctioned or socially approved channels. Maybe, then, it was Virgulino's strength, courage, daring, and, quite possibly, a dash of perversity, combined with ever-increasing frustration, that propelled him, that led him to take the paths that worsened his family's condition, and that in the end, when others might have held back still, led him across the line into outlawry. Perhaps it was that combination of character and circumstance that turned the brave and brash Virgulino into the terrible Lampião.[12]

It is ironic that Lampião and his brothers never satisfactorily avenged the death of their father. Both the men whom they blamed most for his death, José Saturnino and Sergeant José Lucena, outlived the Ferreira boys by several decades. Saturnino entered the Pernambuco state police for protection, and he now lives on a ranch where he can look out toward the Serra Vermelha and see the spot where he and Lampião first exchanged shots. Lucena continued to rise in the Alagoas police and eventually became mayor of the state capital. It may well be that Lampião and his brothers relinquished their dedicated efforts to kill the pair. They soon became more preoccupied with preserving their own lives. Nonetheless, the stated aim of Lampião to avenge his father's death gave his career outside the law a *raison d'être* that helped to create the legend of the avenging bandit.

[12] For long, much of the literature on criminality and social disorder emphasized social conditions, including group conflict, almost to the exclusion of individual factors; while such may explain much in general, it often does not account for individual cases. Helpful to me in arriving at my conclusions on Lampião were James Chowning Davies, ed., *When Men Revolt and Why*, especially pp. 4–9 of Davies' introduction, and Jessie Crosland, *Outlaws in Fact and Fiction*, p. 7. Contemporary social science theories of "frustration-aggression" and "relative deprivation" in regard to criminal behavior and violent conflict might also be applied to Lampião's case, but they are so general in nature as to be more or less applicable to virtually all criminal and violent behavior. They contribute little to an in-depth understanding of individual cases, and they are difficult to test. Among the many writings on these theories, see Ted Robert Gurr, *Why Men Rebel*, containing an ample bibliography; pertinent criticism of Gurr is found in Howard Zehr, *Crime and the Development of Modern Society*, especially pp. 25–30.

3. Lampião

AFTER the death of their father, Lampião, Antônio, and Levino moved rapidly into professional banditry, accompanied by Antônio Rosa, a young friend who had lived with the Ferreira family in Alagoas. Since a band of only four persons was not very formidable, they allied themselves from time to time with larger groups. They may have stayed for a while with Antônio Matildes, but it was not for long. That old warrior soon departed in the face of fairly determined efforts by state police forces to suppress banditry. He fled to the state of Paraíba, where he lived in peace for the few remaining years of his life.[1]

The principal allies of the Ferreiras in this period were the Porcinos and their gang of Alagoas. This notorious band of hot-headed criminals, led by Antônio Porcino, had been building an evil reputation for at least five year. Now, joined by the Ferreira brothers and operating with a band of nearly forty men, they spread terror over the backlands of Alagoas and the adjacent area of Pernambuco. Their attacks on small towns and villages soon brought a sizable force of state police into the area, some of them commanded by the Ferreiras' enemy, José Lucena. On June 22, 1921, near the town of Espírito Santo on the Alagoas-Pernambuco border, Lampião, as a part of Porcino's band, had what was apparently his first major encounter with a state police force. It was no small one either, for the force totalled over a hundred men. There were several casualties on both sides, and at least one bandit and one soldier were killed. The soldier who was killed, it was said, was shot twelve times; he had been mistaken for Lucena. The Ferreiras left the scene of battle believing that they had eliminated one of their major enemies.[2]

[1] Genésio Ferreira, interview.
[2] *Estado das Alagoas*, June 23, 1921; *Jornal de Alagoas*, June 21 and 22,

The liaison of the Ferreiras with the Porcinos lasted for only a few weeks and may not have been constant during that time. Bands and individuals in that period often grouped together in order to accomplish specific tasks and then went their separate ways until there was a need again for greater strength. And, for that matter, the Porcino band was nearing the end of its days. Antônio Porcino, it was reported, died in an encounter with police in the neighboring state of Bahia in September, 1921. His brother, Pedro, was shot and killed in the same state by his own father-in-law.[3]

For several months following their raids with the Porcinos, Lampião and his small band of six or seven men worked chiefly with Sebastião Pereira and his cangaceiros. Alongside Pereira, Lampião picked up more valuable experience. The group met the police in several encounters, some of them major. In one of them, for example, the band, numbering some two dozen men, was confronted by a police force of similar size in a gun battle that lasted for five hours. Several bandits were wounded, including Antônio Ferreira. Somewhat later, Pereira and Lampião, with only 9 men, were surrounded by a force of 128 soldiers. In a remarkable display of bravery, the small band broke out of the encirclement and escaped. Still later, in another meeting with police, Lampião received his first serious wound. As Pereira told the story, Lampião was under heavy fire and, jumping around to avoid getting hit, lost his hat. Going back to recover it, he was hit in both the groin and shoulder. He was carried by Levino and another comrade to the house of an acquaintance of Pereira's. There he was treated by a physician acquired by the leader of the band and spent three weeks recuperating.[4]

Lampião gained more than battle experience in his months with Pereira. He undoubtedly also learned much about how a professional bandit operated, particularly in his relations with the larger community. He was introduced into Pereira's network of relatives, friends, and protectors, some of whom were to perform valuable services for him in the coming years. It should be remembered that Sebastião's

---

1921; *Diário de Pernambuco*, June 25, 1921, and March 31, 1926; Amorim, "O homem que chefiou Lampião."

[3] *Diário de Pernambuco*, September 22, 1921. The story of Pedro's death was told to me by his cousin, Maria Correia, interview.

[4] Amorim, "O homem que chefiou Lampião."

family was one of the most prestigious of backlands Pernambuco; they and their friends were worth knowing. Quite likely, the fledgling bandit also learned that the authorities, including the police, were not always to be considered implacable enemies. They could, on occasion, be bought.

Lampião spent only a few months with the celebrated cangaceiro, for Pereira in 1922 decided to abandon the area and seek a new life in some distant place. For a long time he had been urged to do so by relatives and friends, including the much revered Padre Cícero of Juàzeiro. Indeed, Pereira and Luís Padre, his cousin and close companion in the cangaço, had resolved to take the step. Armed with a letter of presentation from Padre Cícero to the vicar of a town in the far south of Piauí State, they had set out. Well into Piauí, however, they were attacked by police; disheartened by the experience, they returned to Pernambuco to continue the fight. But now, in 1922, Pereira decided to try again. He was, he has said, motivated, more than anything else by the fact that he had been suffering from painful bouts with rheumatism; thus, the hard, outdoor life of a bandit was becoming almost unbearable. This time, Pereira made the break successfully. After bidding Lampião farewell near the Pernambuco-Ceará border, he, with two of his band, journeyed to the distant and sparsely settled state of Goiás. Luís Padre had gone there earlier; together they lived to ripe old age.[5]

Lampião, with his own followers and remnants of Pereira's, now took his former comrade's place as the backlands' leading bandit. He established his preeminence almost immediately, and it was a position he was to hold until the end of his life. For several years other bands operated in the same area, but none could match him in skill and audacity.

The exploit that brought Lampião's name to the forefront occurred June 26, 1922. Appropriately, it took place in Agua Branca, Alagoas, a place of bitter memories for the Ferreira boys. It was a raid on the home of the baroness of Agua Branca, the aged widow of Joaquim Antônio de Siqueira Torres, who had been elevated to the nobility many years before during the time of the Empire. The choice of the baroness was understandable. It was believed, in the first place, that she had con-

---

[5] Ibid. Also see Nertan Macedo, *Sinhô Pereira: O comandante de Lampião,* pp. 36–37, 54–58.

siderable wealth in her home, a prime consideration for a bandit. In addition, her sons exercised the dominant political influence in the county and were thus allies of the police officials whom, among other things, Lampião held responsible for his father's death. If he was not avenging José Ferreira's death directly, he was striking close; moreover, there was the loot.

Lampião, with a band estimated at fifty, arrived in Agua Branca just before daybreak. There were only two or three soldiers in the town, so he had little to worry about from the authorities. The home of the baroness was a quaint but elegant structure located in the center of town on the side of a hill near the church. The robbers entered from the rear by breaking down a door in the lower part of the house and then went about their business of sacking the place. Going through the house and opening trunks and cabinets, the gang stole money, gold, jewelry, clothing, and household utensils. The take was considerable. The house was occupied at the time only by the ninety-year-old baroness and another elderly lady. The baroness, it is said, did not know what was going on, even when the bandits invaded her chamber and tore off a necklace she was wearing. When the townspeople learned what was happening, there was some feeble resistance from a nearby house, but none of the bandits was injured. It was Lampião's first major exploit on his own and it was eminently successful. For the first time, his name appeared in the region's newspapers.[6]

The daring raid on Agua Branca greatly alarmed the people in the backlands, who now expected other attacks. Even the normal lethargy of officials in the state capital was momentarily broken, for the Torres family was influential and well known. The reaction was not instantaneous, it must be said, but about ten days after the occurrence a contingent of forty police, commanded by a lieutenant, arrived in the backlands town. Lampião was still in the area and had launched another raid, this at Espírito Santo, a village just across the border in Pernambuco. Near there, on July 8, he attacked the police force, its size now doubled by civilian volunteers. Operating from a superior strategic position, the bandits succeeded in routing the police. Three

[6] Stories of the raid appeared in *Diário de Pernambuco*, July 5 and 7 and August 5, 1922; *Correio da Pedra* (Alagoas), July 2, 1922. Additional information was obtained from interviews with América Torres (Agua Branca, Alagoas, June 27, 1974) and Delilah Torres (Agua Branca, Alagoas, June 24, 1974).

soldiers were killed and two were gravely wounded.[7] Lampião continued to operate in the area for several weeks, even though the troops, now commanded by José Lucena, had grown to number about two hundred. A Recife newspaper in late August branded Lampião as "one of the worst criminals" who had yet appeared in the interior of Alagoas.[8]

That Lampião was becoming a fearsome bandit cannot be disputed. In sheer perversity, however, he was not as yet a criminal of the worst sort. Under usual circumstances, he neither plundered indiscriminately nor committed inexplicable murders. If reasonably complete information can be learned about a particular crime he committed during his early years, a rather clearly defined motive almost always emerges. Under usual circumstances, it was related to the concept of vengeance, either on his behalf or on behalf of a friend or ally. He normally did not choose his victims at random. This facet gave his early career a rationality that set it apart from that of the common criminal. Unfortunately, the clarity of the pattern was to be partly obscured in later years by the blood of victims of unusually vicious and irrational crimes.

Several additional crimes in the course of 1922 and 1923 further illustrate the early pattern. The first, on August 15, 1922, involved the killing of a man who was returning to his farm from the weekly market day in Agua Branca. A traveling companion recounted that Manoel Cypriano de Souza met Lampião and two of his band on a deserted stretch of the road in the early evening. The cangaceiros asked Manoel his name, and, upon learning it, ordered him to dismount and hand over his money. Recognizing Lampião and realizing that he might be killed, Manoel began to beg for mercy, pleading that he be permitted to live so as to rear his family. The bandit leader replied: "Now you recognize Lampião. You are the one who told the police where my father was so they could kill him. Now you will pay." Stepping back a few feet, Lampião shot Manoel three times in quick succession and, though the man was dead, ordered his companions to fire into his body a few more times. The witness then noticed that there were other cangaceiros nearby who had detained several other persons who were returning from town. The people had been held only so they could not

[7] *Diário de Pernambuco*, July 22 and August 5, 1922.
[8] Ibid., *Diário de Pernambuco*, August 29, 1922.

sound the alarm before the bandits had sufficient time to depart. On their departure from the area, the band passed by the home of Manoel Cypriano and sacked it, although they left unharmed the victim's son who was there. In later years, Lampião would be more thorough.[9]

A couple of months later, he killed again for vengeance, this time in Pernambuco. It was one of the most famous crimes of his early career, for the victim was a well-known political boss, Colonel Luís Gonzaga de Souza Ferraz.[10] Gonzaga, who lived in the Pernambuco town of Belmonte near the Ceará border, was not a personal enemy of Lampião's; rather, Lampião helped to kill him on behalf of a friend, Ioiô Moroto. Moroto was a relative of Sebastião Pereira, Lampião's former comrade in the cangaço, while Gonzaga was of the Carvalho clan, the Pereiras' traditional enemies. Gonzaga had been engaged in intrigue against the Pereiras for several years and had formerly lived in São Francisco, Sebastião Pereira's home village, but the immediate provocation for the event was the mistreatment of Moroto by a police force from Ceará. The police force had come to Pernambuco in pursuit of bandits and, while in Belmonte, its commander had made friends with Gonzaga. Leaving there on their return to their home state, the force passed São Cristovão, Moroto's ranch, and mistreated him and his family. In addition to vandalizing the house and its dependencies, they handled Moroto roughly and made obscene passes at the female members of his family. Moroto blamed the affront on Gonzaga.

Whether Moroto then asked Lampião for help to avenge the incident or whether Lampião, hearing of what had happened to his friend, came and urged him to take action is unclear, for both stories are told. A third version relates that Sebastião Pereira, when he renounced banditry, asked Lampião as a parting favor to kill Gonzaga. Whatever the case, Lampião and Moroto, at the head of seventy men, arrived in Belmonte, a picturesque town located on a high plain amid an area of low mountains, just before daybreak on October 20. Entering the sleeping town, they thought that they had little to fear, for only seven soldiers were in its police detachment. The group then proceeded to the home of Gonzaga, a large house located on the main plaza. The

[9] Criminal proceedings against Virgulino Ferreira et al., August 15, 1922, First Cartório, Agua Branca, Alagoas.

[10] The account of Gonzaga's death is based mainly on an interview with João Primo de Carvalho, Belmonte, July 30, 1975; the *Diário de Pernambuco*, October 21, 1922, carried a brief notice. Also see Wilson, *Vila Bela*, pp. 338–340.

intended victim was a wealthy rancher and businessman, and his general store, the town's largest, was located adjacent to his house. That this was revenge is evident, but that it was revenge with a profit is also evident.

Attempting to enter the house, the bandits were met by fire from inside. This alerted the police and others in the town, and a fierce gun battle of four or five hours' duration ensued. When it was over, Gonzaga was dead and his store had been sacked. Moroto had gotten his revenge. Its work accomplished, the band had to fight its way out of town, and not without casualties. Four or five of the bandits died. Moroto, incidentally, never paid for the crime. In the immediate aftermath, political conditions were such that he could not be prosecuted successfully, and he continued to live peacefully and well guarded on his ranch seven miles from town. When conditions did change and a criminal proceeding against him was initiated, he left the area and found refuge in the Inhamuns portion of Ceará with the Feitosa family, justly famous in the region for their protection of prestigious fugitives from the law. Some years before, beginning around 1905, the Feitosas also had protected various members of Antônio Silvino's family when they were being harassed by the Pernambuco police. Their descendants and those of Moroto still live in the Inhamuns. Moroto's offspring have been integrated into the Feitosa family.

Early in 1923, Lampião attempted to kill again for revenge, but in this instance the intended victim escaped while innocent persons suffered. On a night in late January, Lampião, with only four men, opened fire on a rural house in Floresta, one of the counties in Pernambuco where he used to live. The attack was for the purpose of killing a man known as Tibúrcio of Serra Vermelha, who, Lampião knew, was in the house. Tibúrcio was a former member of Pereira's band who had turned traitor and joined José Saturnino. Moreover, it was said, he had killed two of Lampião's group. When the firing started, all of the occupants of the house, including Tibúrcio, fled into the darkness and hid out until morning. One of them, a young man of twenty, was hit as he ran and was left wounded on the ground. The band then set fire to the house and departed. Tibúrcio escaped injury. It was, of course, not the first time nor the last that innocent persons were victimized by Lampião. If the targets for his major crimes were not selected indiscriminately, they often were attacked with such violence that innocent persons also suffered.

The year 1923 was a relatively quiet one in the career of Lampião, containing none of his better-known exploits. Yet, for one particular reason, it was a fateful year for him. It was then that he cemented his antagonism against a group that would become his most tenacious enemies. The people of Nazaré, the village near the Ferreira's ranch at Poço do Negro, never had much reason for liking Lampião. To them, the Ferreiras and their problems were a nuisance that disturbed the peace of their community. That they should arrive at such a conclusion was not surprising, of course, for they were tied to the Nogueira-Saturnino clan. Lampião and his brothers should have let well enough alone and stayed away from the village, but, in spite of the troubles they had experienced there earlier, they made a return visit in 1923.

The occasion of the visit was the marriage of a female cousin of Lampião's. Lampião, accompanied by a band of approximately fifteen, arrived on the last day of July to attend the dance on the evening of that day and the wedding ceremony on the next. He was fresh from new exploits in Alagoas, having, during July, chalked up several raids on ranches and a brief encounter with Lucena's forces. The presence of the now-famous bandit and his band in Nazaré was disturbing to most of the town's residents and potentially dangerous as well, especially if a police force should arrive. When various persons, including some of his cousins, complained about his coming, he became angry and left the village. He took with him the accordion with which the evening's music was to be made, saying that if he could not dance nobody would. In spite of this impetuous action, Lampião and his men returned the next day to attend the marriage ceremony in the village chapel. On that day, a large police force arrived while the wedding mass was in progress. Lampião, who had sentries posted, was warned and the fight began, the police being joined in the attack by several of the village's men and older boys. Given the occasion, it could have been more disastrous than it was, but Lampião and his band soon withdrew. The superior force may have led to his decision, but it is said also that the priest, Padre José Kehrle, talked to Lampião and convinced him to leave in the interest of the people's safety. Lampião had profound respect for priests and probably more for this one than most.

He was the same priest who had treated Levino's wound several years earlier, and was to become Lampião's chief confessor.[11]

The bandit never entered the village of Nazaré again. This final visit apparently cemented the enmity between him and the Nazarenos, as the people there were called. His character was well known to the Nazarenos, and it was a certainty that, given the opportunity, he would exact revenge for their participation in the attack on him. They did not wait for this but began to pursue him, first as private parties operating on their own and later as members of the state police forces. All told, it is estimated that at least sixty of Nazaré's men dedicated themselves to the pursuit of Lampião, many of them not much beyond puberty when they began. Of the sixty, fifteen or more died at the hands of Lampião and his band.[12] In all his career, Lampião encountered few who pursued him as faithfully as they did. Oftentimes, others pursued him only from a distance, out of fear of their lives, and others could be corrupted. But not the Nazarenos. They pursued him in Pernambuco, Alagoas, Paraíba, and Ceará, and when, in later years, he shifted the center of his operations to Bahia and Sergipe, they pursued him there. When Lampião died in the creek at Angicos, some of them were in the area, and, upon learning what had happened, were angry that others and not they had been privileged to bring his life to a close.

Such dedication in the fight against Lampião was rare. During this period there were occasional encounters with police forces, but they did not seriously hamper his operations. Being the pursued, it was he who usually chose the time and place for the battle and, as might be expected, it was he who usually inflicted the most serious damage. Moreover, most of the police were afraid of him and not anxious to do battle.

The reluctance of the police to confront the bandits is understandable when the difficulties under which they operated are recognized. They were, in the first place, undermanned. At any given time, there were no more than a very few hundred soldiers and officers of the state police stationed in the interior counties of each of the northeastern

[11] Venâncio Nogueira, Genésio Ferreira, and João Jurubeba, interviews. Also see *Diário de Pernambuco*, August 3, 1923. Noblat in "Lampião morreu envenenado," recounts Padre Kehrle's memories of the event.

[12] Estimates of João Jurubeba of the Nazaré clan. He was fifteen when he began to pursue Lampião in 1925 (interview).

states. Ceará, for example, had about four hundred troops in the interior counties during the mid-1920s.[13] Almost all state police were posted in towns and cities, and they were not expected to police rural areas. Had they tried to do so, the towns and cities would have been left defenseless. Many times, bandits might be robbing and killing within a mile or two of town, but, unless they threatened to enter the town, they had little to fear from police.

The main fight against the bandits was entrusted to the mobile police units known as *volantes*, meaning "flying squads." Despite their name, speed was not one of their characteristics, for, like the bandits, they usually went on foot. The police generally were not furnished with horses, since they were expensive, and trucks, which began to be used as transportation in the backlands during the mid-1920s, were not common, because roads were little more than cattle trails. Moreover, the bandits often traveled cross country where neither trucks nor horses could go very easily. The *caatinga* in many areas of the backlands is so thick and thorny that a man on horseback can pass through it only with difficulty. Thus, out of necessity, both bandits and police normally walked. The main disadvantage of the volantes, however, was inadequate manpower. The backlands of Pernambuco in 1922 and 1923, for example, had only one volante of twenty men and one officer devoted to the fight against banditry, and these were years in which not only Lampião but also numerous other bands were operating.[14] A state might put a much larger force than this into the field in response to a major attack, as Alagoas did after Lampião's raid on Agua Branca, but such an effort was rare.

Even among those police who did pursue Lampião, there was little enthusiasm for the task. Training was inadequate and provisioning and pay were scant and haphazard. Working conditions were rugged, to say the least—soldiers were expected to spend days and weeks on foot trailing bandits. Both men and officers often were corruptible, and, at times, they were one of Lampião's main sources of ammunition. Selling it to his agents, they would return to their base, claiming that they had expended it in combat.[15] Many of the forces in the field against

[13] Interview with José Moreira da Rocha, former governor of Ceará, *Diário da Noite* (Rio de Janeiro), November 28, 1931.

[14] Gueiros, "*Lampeão*," p. 60.

[15] Among others, Olympo Campos and João Jurubeba, both retired from the

Lampião simply avoided contact with him and fought only when forced to.

The general picture is one in which Lampião, as long as he confined his depredations to isolated ranches and villages, had little reason to fear police. The main exceptions were such soldiers as the Nazarenos who fought him, not from any incentive offered by the state, but for entirely private ends. This type of soldier was to prove to be by far the most effective combatant against banditry.

The state governments themselves exhibited scant interest in the problem of banditry in the backlands, as the lack of determined police effort shows. The administrations of governors during the period—such as those of Sérgio Loreto of Pernambuco and José Moreira da Rocha of Ceará—left the backlands in a state of virtual abandonment. The governors, sitting over lethargic administrations, played their cards in the game of national politics and had little interest in the interior counties other than maintaining their ties with the local political chieftains who delivered the votes to the state political machine.

The local chiefs, in turn, made their accommodations with the bandits, as they had long been accustomed to doing. When an agent of the bandits made a sizable purchase of ammunition in the town— large enough to attract attention—the chiefs and their officials either looked the other way or were party to the deal, for Lampião paid well. When Lampião asked for a contribution in money, they paid it in order to guarantee the safety of their rural properties. The more prestigious political chiefs might also be capable of guaranteeing Lampião freedom from police attack or harassment in their areas. The influence of the chiefs with the state authorities usually was sufficient to give them veto power over police actions. The relationship between the chiefs and the bandits was not always a one-way proposition. Lampião, it was widely believed, performed services for his highly placed friends, attacking, for example, a ranch of one of their enemies or killing someone they wanted dead. Specific instances of proof are difficult to obtain because the chiefs who requested the actions did not talk about them, nor did Lampião. Lampião's men, moreover, knew little or nothing about such matters, for their chief was extremely discreet with them

---

Pernambuco State Police, attested to the truth of the many charges that the police in this period were a major source of Lampião's ammunition (interviews).

regarding his relationships with prominent persons. Conversations with such people were conducted in private.

In this situation, the rural population was left almost completely defenseless. But many people in the rural areas also made their accommodations with the bandits. Prosperous ranchers paid Lampião the "taxes" he demanded, and on request they or their employees might reluctantly assist him with the purchase of provisions and ammunition. Others, of whatever class (property owner, cowboy, or tenant), might become his active agents and his friends as well, performing whatever services were needed. They served as messengers, for example, carrying his notes demanding money to ranchers and businessmen. They kept him provisioned on a regular basis and informed him of police movements when there was a need. For all of this Lampião paid well, for the cooperation of his protectors or *coiteiros*, as they were called, was indispensable to his well-being. All in all, it must be said that the rural population in general cooperated with Lampião because to refuse him a favor was an invitation to an almost certain reprisal. In doing so, they risked incurring the displeasure of the police, and many people did suffer at the hands of the *volantes*, who were feared almost as much as the bandits. But, when all was said, Lampão was a more real and persistent threat than were the authorities. The actions of the authorities and whatever protection they offered were erratic and temporary; they offered neither a permanent threat nor permanent security. In contrast, Lampião, as his fame grew, hung like the shadow of a cloud over the backlands, for his enmity, once incurred, was known to be dependable.

There were some backlanders who risked Lampião's wrath by informing on him or opposing him in other ways. Many of them, as a result, suffered miserably, losing their lives or having their property plundered and burned. Some of them, either on their own or as police, took up arms against Lampião. Many families simply deserted the backlands temporarily, returning only after the wave of banditry had passed.

The accommodation, uneasy as it was, between Lampião and backlands society was at its apex during the period from 1923 to 1926. It was in these years that he enjoyed the least police persecution and lived most openly in coexistence with the political chieftains. This is not to suggest that Lampião was free from police pursuit in this period, for, as will be seen, he had some serious encounters with the forces.

Such pursuit, however, was occasional and of insufficient strength to threaten the existence of the band. During much of this period, he based his operations in an area on the Pernambuco-Paraíba border, especially in Princeza County, Paraíba. He left Alagoas alone for the time being, apparently not bothering that state from mid-1923 until early 1925.

It was in the latter part of 1923 that Lampião settled in for a stay of several months in Princeza, which is located in a highly accidented area of unusually adequate rainfall and thick vegetation. The area offered an ideal setting for the bandits' headquarters. Their main base was the village of Patos, lying almost on the Pernambuco border. The choice was a natural one for Lampião, since Colonel Marçal Diniz, the owner of Patos and the nearby ranch of Abóboras, had long protected bandits. A portly man known for his friendliness, he also was hospitable to the forces chasing bandits, if they happened to pass his way. Colonel Marçal, like many other wealthy ranchers, was well schooled in the art of survival. He also had excellent connections; the most powerful political chieftain of the backlands, José Pereira Lima, was his son-in-law. Zé Pereira, as he was known, not only dominated Princeza County; his influence was a crucial factor in a vast area of Paraíba, as well as in adjacent counties of Pernambuco. In his home base of Princeza, his word was law.

Lampião had known Colonel Marçal since the days of Sebastião Pereira. Marçal had protected Pereira's band when Lampião was a part of it. However, it was with the colonel's son, Marcolino Pereira Diniz, that Lampião struck up the closest acquaintaince. Marcolino, about three years older than the bandit, was a young man of some culture, having completed a significant portion of the course in law in the state capital on the coast. In spite of this, he had little to recommend him in that period of his life. A heavy drinker and frequent barroom brawler, the wealthy colonel's son lived a life of dissipation. Of the two comrades—for Marcolino and Lampião became good friends—there were those who believed that the former had the edge on perversity.

With connections such as these, Lampião and his band lived virtually out in the open in Princeza. Cangaceiros, having no fear of police, went into the town and patronized the bars. At least some of the soldiers stationed there were offended by the open tolerance of bandits, but there was nothing they could do. Zé Pereira's power was such that in his county the state police had to do his bidding.

The town of Triunfo, lying in Pernambuco just a short distance from Patos, was, in the early twentieth century, noted for its violence, and it had been the scene of several murders and assassinations. One of these involved Marcolino and his bandit friend, Lampião. At a dance in the small mountain town on December 30, 1923, Marcolino got into an argument with the district judge over an alleged insult. Marcolino shot and killed the magistrate in the street and was subsequently taken into custody and placed in a local jail. He did not stay there for long. Within a short time, Lampião, accompanied by eighty or so cangaceiros, appeared on the outskirts of the town demanding his release. The authorities quickly complied with the request. Such was the weakness of justice in the backlands.[16]

The following year, 1924, was a fairly eventful one for Lampião. Early in the year, in February, he attacked a ranch in Santa Cruz, in Triunfo County, belonging to Clementino Furtado, the head of a large family. While the motive of the attack is not entirely clear, the intent seems to have been to kill Clementino and his family. The bandits surrounded the house with forty-five men, opened fire, and began a battle lasting six hours. The bandits were driven off by a small police force that fired a few shots from afar, not wishing to risk a major encounter. By that time, a brother and a nephew of Clementino were dead, and two others who had assisted in the defense were wounded. The bandits returned a few days later apparently to complete their job. This time a five-hour battle took place as Clementino and five companions defended the house. This time, too, a small police force was sent out from the town several hours after the firing began and only after Clementino had lost two more of his men, including another brother. The

[16] Information on the relationship between Lampião and Marcolino Diniz, Colonel Marçal, and Zé Pereira comes from interviews, of which the most valuable were Manoel Arruda d'Assis (Pombal, Paraíba, August 12 and 13, 1975), a retired colonel in the Paraíba police who was stationed in Princeza during the period, and Severiano Diniz, M.D. (Princeza, Paraíba, August 12, 1975), a cousin of Marcolino Diniz's. I also interviewed Colonel Marcolino Diniz in Patos on his eighty-first birthday, August 10, 1975. He acknowledged a relationship with Lampião but was unwilling to discuss many of the particulars of it.

intense firing, in both cases, could be heard in the town, but, as was so often the case, the police had little enthusiasm for confronting Lampião. Clementino (also known as Quelé), impressed by the lack of protection, went to neighboring Paraíba and enlisted in the state police as a sergeant. He became, like the Nazarenos, one of Lampião's most persistent pursuers.[17]

Only a few weeks after this, Lampião was said to be in serious difficulties. The newspapers reported that in an encounter in late March with a large Pernambuco force, he had been gravely wounded.[18] The battle, which took place near the Paraíba border in Vila Bela County, also resulted, the report continued, in casualties for the police. The commander of the police force in this case was Major Teófanes Torres, famous for his capture of Antônio Silvino ten years earlier.

Lampião, indeed, had been wounded. His horse had been hit, and he himself was hit in the heel of the foot. With his men putting up strong firing to cover his retreat, Lampião sought cover. The bandits then fled in all directions, trying to confuse the police, as was their custom. Armed only with a pistol, Lampião was left alone, hiding behind the trunk of a fallen tree. The soldiers were searching for him, led by a trail of blood, but, losing it, they departed. The bandits had little time to return to search for their chief. Regrouping about three miles away, they had another battle with the police. Lampião was left to fend for himself.

He had a hard time of it. Hours and then days passed, and he saw nobody. The food and water that he had been carrying ran out, and his swollen foot became badly infected. He could move only by crawling. Meanwhile, his brothers were searching for him. Antônio was accompanied by a well-known Paraíba cangaceiro chieftain, Cícero Costa, but their efforts were thwarted by an encounter with the police. Costa was killed and Antônio was wounded. Levino kept his eye out for vultures in the sky, assuming that, if his brother was still alive, the birds would be awaiting his death.

After twelve days, a woman passed by closely enough that Lam-

[17] Carvalho, *Serrote Preto*, pp. 199–206, tells the story of the attack on Santa Cruz. His discussion of the causes is hopelessly confused because of chronological inaccuracies.

[18] *Diário de Pernambuco*, March 27, 1927.

pião could call to her. At first afraid, she then took pity on the wounded bandit, and she and her husband came to his assistance. Through
them, Lampião sent word to Marcolino to come for him. Soon thereafter, a group of sixty men under Sabino Gomes, Marcolino's bodyguard, arrived and took Lampião to Patos. There he was treated by
two physicians, one of them a cousin of Marcolino's from Princeza. Antônio was brought there as well and soon recovered from his wound.[19]

Lampião spent several months recuperating, but his recovery was
complete. He walked thereafter with no noticeable limp. While he was
in Patos, a charming village resting in a green, narrow valley between
two mountains, his band in late July of 1924 raided the town of Sousa,
Paraíba. There probably were several reasons behind the attack on
Sousa, which was located some seventy-five miles to the north of Princeza. The main attack may have been intended against Cajàzeiras, lying
a few miles to the west of Sousa. Marcolino had a small business in
Cajàzeiras and knew the town well. It is said that he had given the
bandits information as to whom to attack in order to reap the maximum profits from the raid. Sabino Gomes, his bodyguard, accompanied the band. Hearing, however, that Cajàzeiras, a prosperous
town, was prepared for the attack, the group went on to Sousa.[20]

The attack on Sousa had motives other than plunder for some of
those who participated. Lampião's band, as it often did, had acquired
additional men for the trip, and, among these were Chico Pereira and
his followers. Pereira, then twenty-four years old, was the son of a
prominent rancher and businessman from a rural village in Sousa
County who had been assassinated three years earlier. The killing was
one of those classic cases of the backlands involving family rivalries.
When those accused of the crime were freed by the state tribunal,
Chico Pereira sought to execute justice on his own. On meeting one of
the formerly accused, he shot him. Pereira was arrested and tried, but,
having much sympathy in the community, was absolved by the jury.
Then, believing that justice still had not been adequately served, he
began to acquire a group of armed followers to exact further revenge.
Among the events that subsequently transpired was a conflict between

[19] The story of Lampião's wound was told to me by Manoel Arruda d'Assis
and João Ferreira (interviews).
[20] Manoel Arruda d'Assis, interview.

a friend of Pereira's, Chico Lopez, and an influential resident of the town of Sousa, Dr. Otávio Mariz, also one of Pereira's major enemies. The end result was an invitation to Lampião to participate in an attack on the town.[21]

Lampião himself did not make the trip. Still recuperating from his wound, he sent his band, led by Antônio and Levino. Sabino Gomes, Marcolino's personal guard, also went along. Chico Pereira was one of the leaders of the raid. The assaulters, numbering about seventy, arrived in Sousa before daybreak on the morning of July 27. This was a favorite hour for attack, since most people normally would still be sleeping and the bandits could arrive at their destination under the cover of night. However, movements of cangaceiros had been seen in the area and the people of Sousa were uneasy. On the eve of the attack, it was learned that the telephone lines out of the city had been cut. Nonetheless, the townsmen as a group had made no strong preparations for defense. The state had sent a small detachment of soldiers, about ten, to the town in anticipation of an attack, but little faith was placed in them. Only Pereira's enemies, including Otávio Mariz, were prepared to offer determined resistance; understandably, they were expected to be the main targets of the attack, if it should come.

The bandits made their move around four o'clock. First surrounding the town, they sent word to the soldiers to offer no resistance—a warning that apparently was heeded. Divided into small groups, the bandits then assaulted three business houses and about ten private homes, plundering and robbing. One of the most ferocious attacks was against the home of the district judge and was led by the cangaceiro known as Paezinho ("Little Father"), who had his own grudge against the magistrate. After heavy firing, the doors were broken down and the house and its contents were devastated. The judge was taken prisoner and, still clad in his night clothes, was forced to accompany the outlaws in a humiliating walk through the streets. Before the bandits left town, the judge's wife paid a ransom for his release. Dr. Mariz, at first offering resistance, succeeded in escaping, but his home was sacked. On their withdrawal, the cangaceiros stole numerous horses and mules. Three persons reportedly had been wounded by the ban-

---

[21] Chico Pereira's story is related in full in Francisco Pereira da Nóbrega, *Vingança, não: depoimento sobre Chico Pereira e cangaceiros do nordeste.*

dits. Once outside of Sousa, the gang continued its depredations and attacked two villages.[22]

The attack on Sousa was probably a mistake for Lampião and his men. They lost their haven of refuge in Princeza as a result of it. Zé Pereira, to this point, had tolerated the bandits in his county—although he may have done so only because of his ties to Colonel Marçal and Marcolino—but now he no longer was willing to do so. Whatever kind of man Zé Pereira was, he was not a simple harborer of bandits who used his county as a base for boldly attacking neighboring towns. Angered by the bandits' audacity, he ordered the police forces in his county to attack them and also put into the field a group of his own private gunmen. With these developments, Marcolino, Pereira's brother-in-law, told Lampião that it would not be prudent for him to remain in Patos, since his safety no longer could be guaranteed.[23] Sabino Gomes, Marcolino's bodyguard, joined Lampião's band. Recognized as a common criminal because of his participation in the attack on Sousa, he had little choice. Chico Pereira, for his part, was also outside the law and thus forced to live as a bandit. Arrested in 1928, he was the fatal victim of an alleged automobile accident as he was being taken to trial. Charges were made that his death was arranged by the police and that, in fact, the car was rolled over on him after he had been murdered.[24]

Lampião and his band were hotly pursued by the Paraíba police following the raid on Sousa. About a week after the event, on August 8, they were overtaken by the police in Princeza County in the home of an apparent protector. As one of the soldiers reported it, the troops were approaching the house when they heard the cangaceiros give the alarm. Gunfire came from within and near the house, as well as from a position to the rear of the force. Wily as he was, Lampião had set

[22] Ibid., pp. 107–137. Full firsthand accounts of the raid also are found in *A União* (Paraíba), October 3 and September 7, 1924.

[23] Marcolino Diniz said that he told Lampião to leave and denied that Lampião ever returned (interview). However, later news reports placed him on Marcolino's property.

[24] Pereira and his band, according to news reports, were seen with Lampião occasionally in the years following the Sousa raid. See, for instance, *O Ceará* (Fortaleza), May 18, 1927. The charges regarding the manner of Pereira's death are found in Nóbrega, *Vingança, não*, pp. 328–63.

the police up. One soldier was killed and another was wounded before the bandit leader and his seventeen desperados withdrew into the rainy evening. They left behind them twenty-one horses and mules and several saddles, part of the loot they had taken on their Sousa trip.[25]

In late August, the chief executive of Paraíba gave out the startling news that the notorious bandit and several of his followers had been killed in a battle with the police. The rumor had been circulating already; it was now officially confirmed, said the governor.[26] Lampião had not met his end—this was only one of several false reports of his death that were to circulate before he actually was killed a good many years later—but it does appear that he went into hiding for several months. Only after the end of the year did reports of his activities again appear in the region's press. Lampião obviously was waiting for the heat to cool off.

[25] Criminal proceedings against Lampião et al., August 8, 1924, First Cartório, Princeza, Paraíba.

[26] *Diário de Pernambuco*, August 27, 1924.

4. Captain Lampião and Padre Cícero

NEWS of Lampião's whereabouts began to reach the region's press again only in the early part of 1925, several months after the raid on Sousa. Apparently desirous of recommencing their operations, the bandits were reported in Piancó, Paraíba, and a few days later they began a journey across Pernambuco toward Alagoas.[1] In Pernambuco, they appeared at the town of Custódia, located about thirty miles from the Paraíba border. When the town awakened on a morning in late January, Lampião and a band of forty were in the main street, but apparently their intentions were honorable. Remaining in the town about twenty-four hours, they created no disturbances. They made some purchases, ate and drank, had clothing made, and then paid for everything and departed for Alagoas. Following a zigzag route, they took about three weeks to reach their destination, arriving there around February 20.

Lampião may have taken an indirect route because he was unhurried, but he may also have done so to confuse the police. Word of his appearance in Custódia had reached Princeza, and, in response, Zé Pereira sent a force in pursuit. This force in turn joined another group from Paraíba, and together they followed his trail. Further on, they were joined by soldiers from the Pernambuco police. All together, there were three officers and seventy-seven men on the bandits' trail. Both the bandits and the soldiers were walking.[2]

When Lampião arrived at the border, he rested for a few days on

---

[1] *Diário de Pernambuco*, January 18, 1925.

[2] The story of the march across Pernambuco is told in Carvalho, *Serrote Preto*, pp. 301–315. The attack on Algodões, related by Carvalho as happening at this time, evidently occurred in the following year (see *Jornal do Commércio* [Fortaleza], May 14, 1926).

the Pernambuco side in the village of Espírito Santo, the site of some of his previous raids. He then crossed over into Alagoas and paid a call on the place near Mata Grande where his father was buried. Arriving in Pariconhas in Agua Branca County, also the site of an exploit a few years earlier, he demanded clothing and money from the merchants and did not offend anyone physically.[3] Approaching the town of Mata Grande, he sent messengers ahead with notes demanding sizable sums of money from five prominent persons. When he failed to receive the money, he attempted to invade the town. Many of the people, upon learning that the celebrated outlaw was on the heights near the mountainous town, ran over each other in seeking to flee. Lampião fought a two-hour gun battle with the town's defenders but, finding the resistance stiffer than he had expected, withdrew. One of his men died and two others were injured.[4] Lampião then headed in the direction of Pernambuco.

The military forces that for so many days had been in pursuit caught up with the bandits at a ranch known as Serrote Preto ("Black Hill"), near the Pernambuco border. Having been told where the bandits were, the police took the initiative and attacked. They were met with fierce resistance from inside the house where the bandits had holed up. One of the Paraíba officers impulsively ordered his men to charge the house, whereupon he and some of his men were immediately cut down by the bandits' withering gunfire. The other Paraíba force continued to fire on the house, as did the Pernambucans from some distance back. Meanwhile, Lampião sent out Levino and twelve other bandits to flank the Paraibans; when Levino's contingent opened fire, the Pernambucans fired at them, subjecting their Paraíba comrades to the crossfire at the same time that they were being fired on directly from inside the house. The result was disastrous. With a dozen soldiers already on the ground dead and others seriously wounded, including the surviving Paraíba officer, the police withdrew. By that time, night had fallen, and from a distance the soldiers saw the outlaws come out with lamps in their hands to strip the dead bodies of their possessions.

[3] *Diário de Pernambuco,* March 15, 1925; *Correio da Pedra,* February 22, 1925.
[4] *Diário de Pernambuco,* March 15 and April 15, 1925; Pedro Barbosa de Melo, interview, Mata Grande, Alagoas, June 22, 1974.

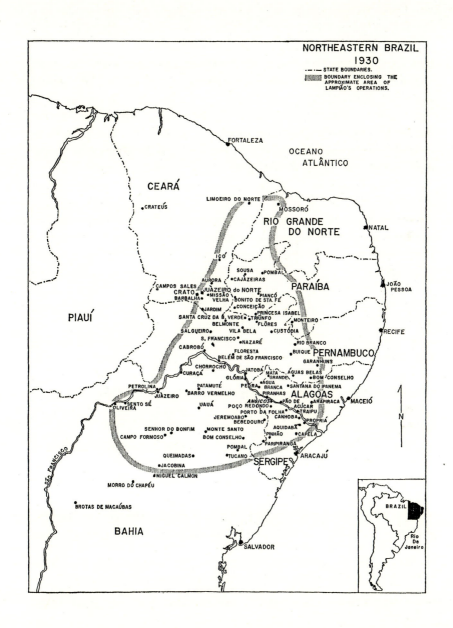

NORTHEASTERN BRAZIL
1930

STATE BOUNDARIES.

BOUNDARY ENCLOSING THE
APPROXIMATE AREA OF
LAMPIÃO'S OPERATIONS.

FORTALEZA

OCEANO
ATLÂNTICO

CEARÁ

CRATEÚS

LIMOEIRO DO NORTE

MOSSORÓ

RIO GRANDE
DO NORTE

NATAL

IÇÓ

SOUSA
POMBAL

AURORA   CAJÀZEIRAS
CAMPOS SALES
CRATO   JUAZEIRO do NORTE   PIANCÓ
BARBALHA   MISSÃO
VELHA   BONITO DE STA. FÉ
JARDIM   CONCEIÇÃO
SANTA CRUZ DA B. VERDE   PRINCESA ISABEL
BELMONTE   TRIÚNFO
FLÔRES   MONTEIRO
SALGUEIRO   VILA BELA   CUSTÓDIA
S. FRANCISCO   NAZARÉ
CABROBÓ   RIO BRANCO
FLORESTA   BUIQUE
BELÉM DE SÃO FRANCISCO   GARANHUNS
CHORROCHÓ
CURAÇA   JATOBÁ   MATA   AGUAS BELAS
GLÓRIA   GRANDE   BOM CONSELHO
PATAMUTÉ   PEDRA   ÁGUA
PETROLINA   BARRO VERMELHO   BRANCA   SANTANA DO IPANEMA
JUAZEIRO   PIRANHAS
SENTO SÉ   UAUÁ   ANGICOS   PÃO DE   ARAPIRACA   MACEIÓ
OLIVEIRA   POÇO REDONDO   AÇÚCAR   TRAIPU
PORTO DA FOLHA   CANHOBA   PROPRIÁ
JEREMOABO   BEBEDOURO
SENHOR DO BONFIM   MONTE SANTO   AQUIDABÃ   CAPELA
CAMPO FORMOSO   BOM CONSELHO   PINHÃO
PARIPIRANGA
POMBAL
QUEIMADAS   TUCANO   SERGIPE   ARACAJÚ
JACOBINA
MIGUEL CALMÓN
MORRO DO CHAPÉU

PIAUÍ

PARAÍBA

JOÃO
PESSOA

RECIFE

PERNAMBUCO

ALAGOAS

N

BROTAS DE MACAÚBAS

BAHIA

SALVADOR

BRAZIL

Rio
De
Janeiro

Lampião apparently went into hiding for a few weeks following the Serrote Preto battle, quite probably to recover from its effects. His band, it was reported, also suffered casualties. One news report said that four bandits had been killed and several had been wounded. Exact data on Lampião's losses were never easy to obtain. Only under the direst circumstances would he leave the bodies of his fallen comrades at the scene of their deaths. He took them with him to bury in hidden graves, so that no one would know of his losses. Lampião, when possible, ceded the police nothing, not even the satisfaction of counting the enemy dead on the field.[5]

Where Lampião was holed up was something of a mystery. Just after the battle, he was believed to be on a mountain not far away, and a force had arrived under José Lucena to flush him out. Later the police reported that he was traveling across Pernambuco toward Ceará.[6] It may well have been that he spent much of the time in Ceará, for he often used it as a place of refuge. He developed good contacts in the mountainous Cariri region, located in the southeastern part of the state on the Pernambuco and Paraíba borders. His contacts there dated from the time when he was with Sebastião Pereira, who also used the Cariri as a hideout. It had physical advantages, being of very rough terrain, and, in addition, many of its ranchers and local political bosses had long protected bandits. The state government, moreover, was quite tolerant of such activities. Short of some major mishap, the authorities took almost no notice of the frequent incursions of outlaws from neighboring states.[7]

Lampião's band, which had lost members through deaths and wounds in the battle itself, reportedly suffered several desertions after Serrote Preto. This may have been true, for during subsequent weeks three former members of the band were apprehended in eastern Pernambuco and another was reported killed.[8] Such a decrease in the size of Lampião's gang was not uncommon following a major test of valor

[5] Carvalho, *Serrote Preto*, pp. 317–322, tells the most complete story of the battle. Briefer accounts were carried in *Diário de Pernambuco*, March 3, 1925, and *Jornal de Alagoas*, February 26, 1925.

[6] *Diário de Pernambuco*, March 3, 1925; *Correio do Ceará* (Fortaleza), March 5, 20, and April 13, 1925.

[7] On banditry in Ceará, see Abelardo F. Montenegro, *História do cangaceirismo no Ceará*; Gustavo Barroso, *Heróes e bandidos* and *Almas de lama*.

[8] *Diário de Pernambuco*, March 13 and June 19, 1925.

such as Serrote Preto. Apart from this, Lampião may have pared down the group to his hard-core henchmen for ease of traveling and hiding. The size of his band often fluctuated according to the needs of the time. For a major effort, he would take on extra help; no longer needing it, he would dispense with the services of all but his most trusted followers.

Lampião apparently did not surface until early July in a meeting with the Paraíba police in the Flores area of Pernambuco, not far from Princeza. Police reports said that it was a fierce battle in which several bandits must have been wounded, for large quantities of blood were found in several places.[9] Then, two weeks later, the Paraíba police announced that Lampião's brother, Levino, was dead. He had been wounded, they said, in a battle with a force led by Sergeant José Guedes and had died a few days later. At the time of the battle, Lampião was accompanied by fifteen men.[10] Guedes, of the Paraíba police, justly earned the reputation of being one of Lampião's most competent pursuers. When Levino died, it is said that Lampião cut off his brother's head in a desperate attempt to prevent the police from learning of his loss.[11] The body might possibly be uncovered, but recognition would be rendered unlikely. Levino was the first of José Ferreira's sons to die in the cangaço.

From all indications, Lampião loved his brothers dearly and suffered much from Levino's death. Following the event, he apparently went into a period of inaction for a few weeks, a not unusual occurrence for him following a traumatic experience. He came out of seclusion in early September with a frenzy of activity and acts of almost inexplicable cruelty, also part of a pattern that increasingly was to characterize his behavior.

The first news of Lampião following Levino's death reported his ambush of José Guedes' volante in the Pernambuco village of Gavião, just across the border from Princeza County.[12] Heavy fire was exchanged before the police put the bandits in flight, and one soldier was killed. The police said that they found four bandits dead, two of them decapitated. The next day, Lampião and his band of nearly three

---

9 *Diário de Pernambuco*, July 8, 1925.
10 Ibid., July 21 and 29, 1925; Manoel Arruda d'Assis, interview.
11 Carvalho, *Serrote Preto*, p. 293.
12 *Diário de Pernambuco*, September 15, 1925.

dozen, dividing into two groups, attacked two small villages in Princeza County. The assaults, in Caboré and Alagoa do Serrote, left seven persons dead and others wounded. Among the dead were a twelve-year-old boy and a man of ninety-six. Witnesses to the events testified that the victims were all poor folk who had nothing Lampião wanted, that they had no known intrigue with him and his band, and that, being unarmed, they offered no resistance. The bandits had stated, witnesses testified further, that their actions were repayment to Zé Pereira and the Paraíba forces for the harm they had caused them. Not being able to give Pereira his due in person, one bandit had said, they could take it out on people in his county.[13] Shortly thereafter, another ambush of Guedes and his troops took place on Abóboras Ranch, one of the properties of Marcolino and his father. The police claimed that they killed one more bandit there.[14]

Lampião, under hot pursuit in Paraíba and the adjacent area of Pernambuco, turned up in a few weeks in Ceará. His burst of activity in and near Paraíba apparently had been in retaliation for the loss of his brother at the hands of Guedes' force. It is clear that the actions against the police came on his initiative. Both the ambushes of the police forces and the atrocities in Caboré and Alagoa do Serrote were motivated by revenge of a rather indiscriminate sort. When Lampião arrived in Ceará in October, the Paraíba police were still in pursuit.

In Ceará, it was believed that Lampião had come to visit one of his powerful friends in the Cariri, Colonel Isaías Arruda of Missão Velha and Aurora counties.[15] Colonel Arruda, who himself maintained a private army of cangaceiros, was one of the region's political bosses who had long been known as a protector of bandits. Whether or not Lampião did see Arruda was not reported, although the bandits were seen in several other places. Arriving in a village in Maurity County on market day, Lampião and his thirty-seven men left a good impression. They made large purchases and paid for everything. In a conversation with a merchant, the bandit leader said that he would not harm Ceará. This promise, which he often made and generally kept, arose from his reverence for Padre Cícero of nearby Juàzeiro. Lampião, like most

[13] Criminal proceedings against Virgulino Ferreira et al., September 2, 1925, First Cartório, Princeza, Paraíba.

[14] *Diário de Pernambuco*, September 15, 1925.

[15] *Correio do Ceará*, October 28, 1925.

backlanders, genuinely adored the padre. The bandits, onlookers said, were well armed and mounted on horses.[16]

Lampião also wanted to pay a visit to the county seat of Maurity, but, cautious as always, he sent a messenger ahead, asking if he would be received peacefully. Colonel Pedro Augusto, one of the town's political chiefs, replied that the bandits would be met with bullets should they try to enter.[17] Indignant, Lampião wrote the colonel a curious little letter:

Major Pedro Augusto.

Salutations. Just today I was with one of your boys. Look what he did. He told me I would be ill-received. This, after I talked with a son of the county police chief the other day and gave him all my opinions: that I have no ill will toward this state, as I have proved. I don't think it's right that you are gathering and arming men. This is not right. I have to go through this place and I don't want to alarm Ceará. I want to be the friend of you gentlemen and nothing else. I'm not an urchin who goes around telling lies.

> Virgulino Ferreira
> "Lampião"[18]

Lampião, in spite of the affront, remained in Ceará for at least a few weeks, doing nothing worse than sending notes to ranchers and merchants requesting sums of money from time to time. After all, he probably thought, bandits had to live too. He appears to have continued his relatively peaceful pursuits throughout the remainder of 1925.

During the first few weeks of the new year, most backlanders temporarily forgot about the cangaceiros in the face of a new and seemingly more formidable threat. Bands of a few dozen outlaws they were accustomed to, but a wandering army of hundreds of renegades, living off the land and reputedly bent upon revolution, was something else. The Prestes Column, which crossed the Northeast early in 1926, was an aftermath of the unsuccessful military uprising in São Paulo in July, 1924. In the hope of keeping the revolt alive and dramatizing their op-

---

[16] Ibid., October 27, 1925.

[17] Ibid., October 27, 1925, and April 23, 1926.

[18] Ibid., November 11, 1925. The translation from the Portuguese, here and elsewhere in the book, is my own.

position to the national administration of President Artur Bernardes, some of the insurgents embarked on a trek through Brazil's far interior. Led in part by Luís Carlos Prestes, who later became the chief of Brazil's communist party, the insurgents were ready to enter Ceará from Piauí by mid-January. By that time, the rag-tag rebel army had been in existence over the course of a year and a half and thousands of miles. Obviously, the federal government's efforts to extinguish the flame of revolt had been ineffective. Defense against the insurgents often was left to the state police and backlands political chieftains and their gunmen.[19] Ceará, similarly, moved to meet the threat.

The task of organizing the state's defense fell in part to federal Congressman Floro Bartolomeu of Juàzeiro. It was he, as we shall see, who decided to involve Lampião in the plans. Floro's considerable prestige, in both the state and nation, was based on his management of the political influence of Padre Cícero.[20] Following his arrival in Juàzeiro in 1908, he and the revered priest had built a political machine capable of virtually dominating state politics. They had been the leading participants in an armed revolt leading to the overthrow of the state government in 1914. That Floro would now play a major role in the state's defense against the "revolutionary hordes"—as a Fortaleza newspaper called Prestes' insurgents[21]—was a logical consequence of his and the padre's power.

Floro began to put together a hastily recruited defense force, drawn for the most part from the Cariri's large pool of gunmen. The recruits for these "Patriotic Battalions" were given new weapons from the army's stores; Floro had ample support in both materiel and money from the federal government. Once organized, the force was taken by Floro to Campos Sales in southwestern Ceará, where the invasion was expected. While waiting in Campos Sales, Floro sent a letter to Lampião inviting him to join the battalions. His action, taken in moments of intense preoccupation, should not be regarded as startling, especially in view of the fact that many of those already enlisted in the battalions were themselves outlaws of various kinds. Among them, for example, were the many gunmen who made up the private force of

[19] The story of the insurgents is told in Neill Macaulay, *The Prestes Column*.
[20] On Floro and his relations with Padre Cícero, see Ralph della Cava, *Miracle at Joaseiro*, pp. 102–105 and passim.
[21] *Jornal do Commércio*, January 15, 1925.

Colonel Isaías Arruda of Missão Velha, one of Lampião's Ceará friends. Since Lampião's admiration for Padre Cícero was well known, Floro's letter was sent to Juàzeiro, where, reportedly, it was approved and countersigned by the famous priest. Next, a messenger was sent to contact the cangaceiro chieftain in Pernambuco and deliver the invitation to him.[22]

A good many weeks passed before the letter received a response, and, in the meantime, the rebels marched through Ceará during the last two weeks of January and then went on, in turn, to Rio Grande do Norte, Paraíba, and Pernambuco. Except for the usual depredations of a large force that lived off the land, their trek across Ceará was uneventful; there were no major battles. At this time, Lampião, apparently unaware that influential persons planned to make a soldier of him, was in Pernambuco carrying on his usual operations. He was demanding money of ranchers and burning the homes and corrals and killing the cattle of those who refused to comply.[23] On January 14, by which time some of Prestes' insurgents were already in Ceará, it was reported that Lampião had met the police in a serious battle near Triunfo. Some of the bandits, the police said, had been wounded.[24] About a month later, the governor of Pernambuco announced that the famous bandit himself was dead. He had been killed near Custódia, the governor reported, in an ambush prepared by a force under Lieutenant Optato Gueiros.[25] The report, of course, was false.

On February 23, Lampião chalked up another assassination from his list of major enemies. On that day, he attacked Serra Vermelha and killed José Nogueira, a brother-in-law of José Saturnino. While Nogueira had been the bandits' enemy since the origin of the trouble with Saturnino, the immediate provocation was a letter that Lampião had found in the possession of a tenant of Nogueira's. The letter—taken off the tenant's dead body, for Lampião had just killed him—was addressed to the Flors of Nazaré. It informed those well-known enemies

[22] My account of Floro's call for Lampião follows closely Octacílio Anselmo, *Padre Cícero: Mito e realidade*, pp. 528–529. Padre Cícero later attempted to make it appear that he had not countersigned Floro's request to Lampião. He also made the doubtful statement that Lampião and not Floro had taken the initiative. See Padre Cícero's letter, dated April 27, 1926, in *Jornal do Commércio*, May 6, 1926.

[23] *O Ceará* (Fortaleza), January 15, 1926.

[24] *Diário de Pernambuco*, January 14, 1926.

[25] Ibid., February 14, 1926; and *Jornal do Commércio*, February 15, 1926.

of Lampião of the locations of his points of passing and hideouts in the area and offered ammunition and rifles to them. In the attack on the Serra Vermelha ranch, another person, in addition to Nogueira, was killed and two others were wounded. After warning Nogueira's widow to leave the house, the bandits set fire to it.[26]

Several of the persons who offered testimony on the killing of Nogueira stated that they heard the firing and arrived at the site only later, since they were hiding out in the *caatinga* for fear of Prestes' army. At the same time that Lampião was killing Nogueira, Prestes' insurgents were in the area. Lampião, in fact, had an encounter with the column on that same day, but he thought that he was fighting a regular force. During the firing he and his men, as was their custom, shouted derogatory words that they usually reserved for police. Earlier in Paraíba, it had been suggested to Prestes by a third party that Lampião be invited to unite with the column, but the insurgent leader rejected the suggestion.[27]

Floro's call to Lampião for help finally received a positive response during the first days of March, by which time the insurgent army was in Bahia. By then, Floro was no longer in Ceará. Already sick when the invasion scare first hit the state, he had worsened rapidly. He soon embarked on an ocean voyage to Rio, where he died on March 8. Lampião, by that time, was in Juàzeiro, and it was not Floro but Padre Cícero who had to deal with him.

Padre Cícero was an unusual man.[28] Denounced by many northeastern intellectuals as a wily manipulator of popular ignorance, he was revered by most of the area's people as a living saint. Although the Juàzeiro priest may have deserved his reputation as an exceptional man, the popular sanctification of religious figures in the Northeast was not uncommon. Those who preceded him in being so acclaimed, as well

[26] Criminal proceedings against Virgulino Ferreira et al., February 23, 1926, First Cartório, Serra Talhada, Pernambuco. The account of the letter is from Genésio Ferreira, interview.

[27] On the band's contact with the column, see: Lourenço Moreira Lima, *A Coluna Prestes*, p. 271; S. Dias Ferreira, *A marcha da Coluna Prestes*, pp. 183–184; interview with Lampião in *O Ceará*, March 17, 1926.

[28] Among the many works on Padre Cícero, della Cava, *Miracle at Joaseiro*, dealing especially with the cleric's relations with the Church and with national politics, and Anselmo, *Padre Cícero*, a biography, stand out.

as those who have followed him, comprise an assortment of charismatic clergy, sincere mystics, frauds, and crazed and sometimes dangerous fanatics. To the uneducated and superstitious masses of the Northeast, all these popular figures had one characteristic in common. They were all the possessors of magical powers or, to those whose thinking was more sophisticated, they were unusually effective intercessors with the power or powers that govern the universe. Popular religion in the backlands—nominally Roman Catholic, but essentially of a folk variety—is but little removed in distance from the primitive state.[29]

Cícero Romão Batista came as a young priest in 1872 to Juàzeiro, then an isolated village in Crato County. As the years of his tenure passed, he gained the respect and affection of the people, in part because of the mystical visions he professed to have experienced, but in part also because he was a conscientious clergyman. His larger fame, however, originates from 1889 when allegedly a miracle occurred in Juàzeiro. In the mouth of one of the members of his local sisterhood, the host from his hand was reputedly transformed into blood. Word of the event spread, and when, reports said, it was reenacted several times in following weeks, the Northeast was well on its way to having itself another saint and another holy place. While, in subsequent years, the padre wrestled with the hierarchy over the validity of the alleged miracle and the many others that followed—he was eventually excommunicated—Juàzeiro grew into one of the major population centers of the backlands. For long little more than a vast conglomeration of mud huts, it was peopled largely by *romeiros*, or pilgrims, who flocked there from all over northeastern Brazil to pay a *promessa* (payment in money or deed in hope of a reward) to Padre Cícero. Among those who, in 1926, had moved recently to the northeastern mecca were various members of Lampião's family, including his younger brothers and sisters.

Following the death of José Ferreira in 1921, João, the older of Lampião's two younger brothers, had taken the family to Pau Ferro, Pernambuco, where they lived for a short while under the protection of Colonel Chico Martins. After a police force came there in search of

[29] This opinion is based mostly on my own observations of religious life in the backlands. Abelardo F. Montenegro, *História do fanatismo religioso no Ceará*, and Eduardo Campos, *Folclore do nordeste*, are relevant studies. Also see chapter 11 of the present study.

them, Martins sent them to Bom Conselho, also in Pernambuco, to live with his brother-in-law, Colonel José Abílio. Both Abílio and Martins were alleged protectors of Lampião, and, when the police began to harass Abílio, João sought out his brothers with the intention of joining the band. But Lampião told him that he had to take care of the younger children and sent him back. Since João had a friend, a relative of Antônio Matildes, who was living in Propriá, Sergipe, under the protection of the powerful Brito family, he and his younger brother and sisters moved there. He married in Propriá and later took his family to Juàzeiro.[30]

In response to Floro's letter, Lampião arrived in the vicinity of Juàzeiro in early March, 1926. The exact story of how and where the cangaceiro chieftain received Floro's call for help may be mostly lost, but one account has it that it occurred on a ranch in Pernambuco owned by one of Sebastião Pereira's cousins. At first suspicious that the invitation might be a ruse to entrap him, so the story goes, Lampião became convinced of its sincerity by the presence of Padre Cícero's signature.[31] Lampião, accompanied by an officer of the Patriotic Battalions, arrived in Juàzeiro County on March 3. In their passage through the nearby town of Barbalha shortly before, reports indicated, the conduct of the bandits was exemplary.[32] The outlaws, upon their arrival, camped on a ranch of Floro's in preparation for their entry into the city. On the ranch, Lampião was visited by the prefect and by Colonel Pedro Silvino, one of Floro's Cariri stalwarts who had overall command of the Patriotic Battalions. According to newspaper reports, the celebrated brigand was promised a pardon and command of a company to combat the insurgents. The presence of the renowned cangaceiro so close to the city created a stir there, and many could not wait until his arrival to get a look at him. Estimates of the number of people who flocked to the ranch to see him ran as high as four thousand. When Lampião was asked if he had already fought the rebels, he replied that indeed he had, although he did not know if he had killed any of them, for his ammunition had run out and he had been forced to flee. Asked

[30] João Ferreira, interview; interview with José Abílio, in *Jornal do Alagoas*, August 10, 1938.

[31] Anselmo, *Padre Cícero*, p. 533. Anselmo indicates that his information did not come from firsthand witnesses.

[32] *O Ceará*, March 17, 1926.

his opinion of them, he answered, "They are bandits who go around killing and robbing. . . ."[33]

Lampião and his bandits entered the city of Juàzeiro on the evening of March 4. Surrounded by some of his men, he was housed in the home of a businessman and popular poet, João Mendes. His visit to the city was a busy one. As had been the case on the ranch, people overcame their fears and arrived in great numbers to see him. By all accounts, he was an impressive figure. A reporter who interviewed him for a Fortaleza daily gave the public his impressions.[34] Lampião was, he wrote, a thin, well proportioned man of medium stature, with dark skin and thick black hair. His clothing, of an ordinary type, included a felt hat of regular formation (not the highly decorated hat with turned-back brim that the cangaceiro often wore) and a pair of leather sandals of the type worn by area cowboys. Around his neck he wore a green scarf, held secure by a diamond ring. Six additional rings of precious stones—a ruby, a topaz, an emerald, and three diamonds—adorned his fingers. He was armed with a rifle, a pistol, and a long knife of close to twenty inches in length. Lampião—as was the cangaceiro ideal—was well adorned and well armed.

The gold-rimmed dark glasses worn by Lampião were, as the reporter supposed, to hide a defective right eye. Lampião's right eye had been injured some years before when a piece of tree branch had penetrated it, causing the development of a leukoma (white opacity) of the cornea. Over the years, the condition worsened, and he became almost totally blind in that eye. He frequently wore colored glasses, not only to conceal the defective eye, but also, apparently, because he suffered from an intolerance to light in the other eye.[35]

Lampião's manner, the reporter indicated, was calm and deliberate. Although his speech was uncultured, he spoke without embarrassment, eyeing his listener closely and seeming to measure the effect of

[33] Ibid., March 12, 1926. It is likely that Lampião had learned who the rebels were after his battle with them.

[34] The following description of Lampião and his men is based mostly on the interview in O Ceará, March 17, 1926. João Ferreira, who was in Juàzeiro when his brother came, also gave me an account of the visit (interview).

[35] The results of an examination of Lampião's eyes by an ophthalmologist, made after the bandit's death, was reported in Jornal de Alagoas, August 1, 1938. The origin of the problem in the right eye was told me by his brother, João Ferreira.

his words. He looked grave, never smiled, and spoke only when answering a question. He gave the impression that he was fully aware of his own importance and enjoyed being the object of popular curiosity. Lampião, it should be noted here, was not unconcerned with his image among the people. He read newspapers and magazines when they were available, or perhaps had them read to him, since he may not have been an accomplished reader himself. He was particularly interested in news about himself and could become extremely angry when he read something that he considered untrue or unfair.[36]

Lampião received his callers in Juàzeiro with grace. They came already awed by the stories of his exploits and went away impressed by his commanding manner. To some of them he gave alms, and from some of them he received small items—a crucifix, for example—as gifts or remembrances. To small boys, he threw coins in the street. When asked by a reporter if it did not bother him to extort money from property owners and destroy their wealth if they refused him, he answered that he never did that sort of thing! He only requested money from friends, he said.

Lampião's men were also objects of interest. While much was known about him, relatively little had been known about the members of his band. There were forty-nine of them, dressed much as he was dressed, except that they wore the traditional cangaceiro hat. Their scarfs were of various colors, though green was most common. All were armed with rifle, pistol, and knife, and, in addition, each wore three or four cartridge belts around the waist and across the chest. It was estimated that they had four hundred shells each. The men were described as, in the main, good looking, of Caucasian descent, well tanned, and from eighteen to thirty years old. Only three of them were Negroes. Although several of the northeastern states were represented, the majority came from the Vila Bela–Triunfo–Flores–Floresta area of Pernambuco, Lampião's home territory. They spoke in jovial fashion of their feats in the cangaço and none seemed to be repentant. They unanimously agreed that the profession was a good one.

Lampião presented his men one by one to the reporter who was interviewing him. Those who had been with him the longest, he said,

---

[36] Numerous references to Lampião's fondness for newspapers and magazines, especially those that contained news of him, can be found. For instance, see *Correio do Ceará*, February 13, 1926.

were Luís Pedro, Jurití, Xumbinho, Nevoeiro, Vicente, and Jurema. All of Lampião's men commonly had nicknames. *Jurití*, for example, is a field dove, *jurema* is an acacia tree, and *nevoeiro* is fog. The bandit chieftain named Antônio Ferreira and Sabino Gomes as his chiefs of staff and added that if he were killed either of them might succeed him. The reporter asked him for his autograph, and he wrote in a regular, firm hand, "In remembrance of me, Virgulino Ferreira da Silva, known as Lampião."

The bandit leader and his men quite obviously enjoyed being in Juàzeiro. Lampião spent much of his time visiting the members of his family who lived there and had his photograph taken with them. In fact, the pictures taken in Juàzeiro are among the best ones of him, and there are many others, for he would go out of his way for the opportunity to be photographed. For their part, his men gave the populace a rare treat by going around the city singing the band's special song, "Mulher Rendeira."[37] Sung to a lilting, traditional tune—the title means "The Lacemaker," the making of lace being a valued folk art cultivated by backlands women—the words apparently were put together by Lampião and his men, some of whom had considerable musical talent. The verses, ever more in number as the years passed, tell the story of the bandits' conquests and tragedies in both love and war. While the words lose much in translation and more without the accompanying music, the following are illustrative.

About love,

> The girls of Vila Bela,
> They're poor but full of action.
> They spend the day in the window
> In love with Lampião.

On the deaths of the bandits,

> Cícero Costa died,
> Batista was buried,
> Tubiba got shot,
> Midnight deserted.

[37] *O Nordeste* (Fortaleza), March 8, 1926. Several verses of the song are found in Oliveira, *Lampião*, pp. 183–185. On the origins of the music, see Wilson,

The high point of Lampião's visit to Juàzeiro was his audience with Padre Cícero. The bandit had come there because of the priest's association with the Patriotic Battalions, and now, in Floro's absence, it was left to the clergyman to receive him. Padre Cícero, then eighty-two years old, did not relish the responsibility that had fallen on his shoulders and he may have foreseen the ridicule and criticism that would later be heaped upon them for his part in the matter. He apparently gave little detail in early public statements about the meeting between himself and Lampião, being, in fact, quite sensitive on the subject. A few weeks later, when criticism was raining on him, he spoke in general terms.[38] He disclaimed responsibility, in the first place, for the bandit's coming. He thus seemed to contradict the accounts which say that he countersigned Floro's invitation to Lampião.[39] He stated that he had realized that as the political chief of the city he had the "moral obligation" to repel the bandit and his gang, but he could not do so in that instance, since it would have placed him in opposition to the wishes of his "greatest friend," Floro. The priest thus let the bandit come—and though Padre Cícero did not then say so, he prevented the state police in Juàzeiro from taking any action prejudicial to the band.[40] Padre Cícero continued, saying that, since Lampião was there, his main desire was to take the opportunity to counsel him, which as a priest he had the duty to do, "seeking to turn away from the evil path those who are in error, trying to regenerate them with the teachings of . . . religion, pointing out to them the path of salvation and the means to follow it." Lampião left, the priest concluded, "satisfied, promising to practice no more crimes nor depredations, swearing that, once the insurgents were expelled, he would leave the Northeast to live, honestly, away from his enemies."

The old padre did not include in his statement the full explanation of what he had done to make Lampião go away so satisfied, but the

---

Vila Bela, pp. 331–332. A song based on "Mulher Rendeira" achieved considerable popularity in the United States in the mid-1950s. Entitled "The Bandit," it was recorded by Tex Ritter and issued by Capitol Records in 1954. While the music was an adaptation of the original, the words referred only to an unnamed Brazilian bandit.

[38] Padre Cícero's letter, *Jornal do Commércio*, May 6, 1926.

[39] According to one report, Floro withdrew the invitation to Lampião, but, if this is true, Lampião apparently did not know of it (see *O Ceará*, March 27, 1926).

[40] Ibid., March 17, 1926; *Correio do Ceará*, March 30, 1926.

story has been told by another. Pedro de Albuquerque Uchôa, an agronomist who worked in Juàzeiro as an agricultural inspector for the federal ministry of agriculture, related that late one evening around ten o'clock he received a call to go see Padre Cícero. Arriving there, he found Antônio Ferreira and Sabino Gomes with the padre. The priest than asked him to write out in the name of the Government of the Republic of the United States of Brazil a document commissioning Lampião as a captain in the Patriotic Battalions. Uchôa did not remember the exact words of the document, but, in general terms, it was a kind of "passport," that gave "Captain Virgulino Ferreira da Silva" and his men the authority to move freely from state to state in the company of the Patriotic Battalions in pursuit of the rebels. Next, Padre Cícero instructed the agricultural inspector to sign it, pointing out that he as a priest had no official post, while Uchôa was an employee of the federal government. Surprised—for he thought he was serving merely as secretary—and somewhat under protest, Uchôa affixed his signature. He later said that he "would have signed even the dismissal of Bernardes" as president of the nation had Antônio Ferreira and Sabino Gomes asked him to do so. The two bandits then left to deliver the commission to Lampião, who already had gone to bed.[41]

The commission that the celebrated outlaw received may have been of questionable legality, but, as Padre Cícero said, Lampião left satisfied. And there was still another reason for the bandit's satisfaction. Padre Cícero arranged for him and his men to be outfitted from the stores of the Patriotic Battalions. They received uniforms, and one can imagine the glee with which they exchanged their old lever-action Winchesters for the new bolt-action army Mausers. Whatever they were now—cangaceiros or soldiers—they were well equipped to do battle.

There is little reason to doubt that when Lampião left Juàzeiro on March 8, he had the intention of fulfilling his promises to Padre Cícero. As we shall see later, he did think at times about leaving the

[41] The story of the issuance of the commission appears in several places. A brief account was carried in *O Nordeste*, March 20, 1926. Uchôa's story as told to Leonardo Motta appeared first, it seems, in *O Ceará*, July 26, 1929. These two versions are in essential agreement on the content of the document. An alleged transcription of it, bearing an erroneous date, such as is found, among other places, in Gueiros, *"Lampeão,"* p. 55, seems to be apocryphal.

cangaço, and Padre Cícero had offered him what seemed to be a very favorable opportunity.

Turning south from Juàzeiro, Lampião headed in the direction of the rebels, who were then in Bahia. He stopped off in passing at the village of São Francisco, near the ranch where he had lived as a boy. Genésio Ferreira, his cousin, remembers that the villagers were much impressed by the uniforms and rifles, not to mention Virgulino's new status as an officer.[42] It was in Pernambuco, however, that his enthusiasm for the new life began to be dampened. By the time he arrived in Cabrobó, a town that lies on the São Francisco River just across from Bahia, the Pernambuco police, refusing to recognize his commission, were after him. With disillusionment setting in, he and his men turned around and began to make their way northward.[43] They stopped and camped in Salgueiro County and from there sent to Juàzeiro two rebels whom they had captured. Questioned in Juàzeiro, the captives explained that they had joined the insurgents in Piauí and then deserted them near the São Francisco River. On their way northward, they had been captured on a ranch in Salgueiro County where they were working. They explained that the captain, after interrogating them, sent them on under escort.[44]

Breaking camp in Salgueiro, Lampião rode into Ceará, again in the direction of Juàzeiro, intending to pay another call on Padre Cícero. On his way, he and and the ten men who accompanied him arrived on April 6 in the town of Jardim, a few miles to the south of Juàzeiro. A witness said that they rode into town naturally, as if they were prominent citizens, and made their way straight to the home of the prefect. They remained as his guests for two days before departing for Barbalha, located near Juàzeiro.[45] They were reported as passing through Barbalha, but they did not go on to Juàzeiro. Padre Cícero did not want to see Lampião again. He later wrote that he had sent word to Lampião that he could not come into the city. The priest did acknowledge, however, that the bandit's intentions were honorable: that Lampião had said he wanted the padre's blessing before renouncing banditry and going to Bahia to live. The old priest did not explain

[42] Interview.
[43] *O Ceará*, April 24, 1926.
[44] On the captives, see ibid. and *Correio do Ceará*, April 15 and 23, 1926.
[45] *O Ceará*, April 18, 1926.

why Lampião could not pay another call on him; he limited himself
to saying that he could not permit him to do so.[46]

The harsh criticism that had been directed at him as a result of
Lampião's earlier visit may largely explain the clergyman's actions.[47]
During the days following the bandit's presence in Juàzeiro, and for
years thereafter, Padre Cícero was accused of being a protector of
Lampião and other bandits and of having brought shame and ridicule
to his state. These accusations were widely used by his critics and de-
tractors, many of whom looked on him as a crass manipulator of the
ignorance and unbridled fanaticism of the backlands. It is worth noting
that at this time in 1926 Padre Cícero was a candidate for the federal
Chamber of Deputies, a fact that may also explain his efforts to dis-
associate himself from the bandit. Not only revealing that he had turned
Lampião away, he also denied that he had taken any action ever to
impede efforts against him, a statement that contradicted the words of
the police. Padre Cícero's hard line also seemed contradictory to his
own earlier, more humane statements. Shortly after Lampião's visit,
when asked why he had not ordered the arrest of the bandit, he was
reported to have said: "Here I receive everybody who seeks me and I
remain satisfied to lend aid to a criminal . . . seeking to guide him to
the right path."[48] Whatever may have caused the cleric's ambivalence
on the matter—conscience, sensitivity to criticism, or political ambi-
tions—his supporters were pleased with his new attitude. The *Jornal
do Commércio* of Fortaleza, which was supporting his bid for congress,
quoted with approval a Juàzeiro source which gave assurance that police action now in Padre Cícero's county against Lampião would meet
with "not a single obstacle."[49]

There was an element of tragedy in Padre Cícero's refusal to see
Lampião again. If the priest was correct in his assessment of Lampião's

[46] This account of Padre Cícero's reaction to Lampião's desire for a return
visit is from Padre Cícero's letter, *Jornal do Commércio*, May 6, 1926.

[47] As examples of the frequent charges against Padre Cícero as a protector of
Lampião, see: *O Ceará*, June 14, 1927; *Correio do Ceará*, May 4, 1926; *Diário de
Pernambuco*, July 15, 1927, reprinting accusations from the *Correio da Manhã* of
Rio de Janeiro. The *Jornal do Commércio*, May 27, 1926, reported that Padre
Cícero had been called Lampião's first lieutenant by a Rio Grande do Sul deputy
in the national congress.

[48] Quoted in *O Ceará*, March 17, 1926.

[49] April 9, 1926.

intentions, the bandit was at least disposed toward giving up the life he was leading. Lampião's actions as well, after his "commissioning," seemed to indicate a desire to carry out the duties he believed to have been legally entrusted to him. The apparent absence of crimes ascribed to him following his visit to Padre Cícero further supports the supposition that his professed intentions were sincere. In view of the hostility he had met in the Pernambuco police, it seems natural that he would have wanted to return to Juàzeiro to seek additional assurances from his protector before actually committing himself to abandoning banditry. But whatever chance the patriarch had of further encouraging the bandit's aspirations for an honorable life was lost by his closing the door on another visit. Lampião, according to reports, was infuriated by Padre Cícero's refusal.[50] He did not renounce his reverence for the old clergyman—for most backlanders that would have been tantamount to renouncing the Virgin Mary—he simply returned to Pernambuco, threatening to attack Barbalha on the way, and resumed his usual activities.[51]

Lampião, in Juàzeiro with Padre Cícero, came the closest to redemption, in all likelihood, that he ever came in his career as a bandit. With the help of that powerful patriarch, it probably was not too late for him to follow his old comrade in arms, Sebastião Pereira, along the path of regeneration. As the years passed, however, and as his crimes multiplied—and as the region and the nation changed—it became less and less likely that he could successfully change his life. Padre Cícero's refusal to pursue the matter as far as Lampião wanted to may have been a sad loss not only for the bandit, but also for the professed ideals of the padre and for northeastern Brazil. The regeneration of Lampião —and the sparing of the region's inhabitants of over twelve years of his violence—would have been one of the brighter stars in Padre Cícero's crown.

[50] Padre Cícero in his letter reported Lampião's reaction (*Jornal do Commércio*, March 6, 1926).

[51] *O Ceará*, April 18, 1926.

5. Serra Grande

CAPTAIN VIRGULINO, as Lampião was to call himself for the rest of his life, quickly reverted to his old ways following his disappointment in Padre Cícero.[1] Whatever sincerity his professions to that old patriarch may have contained, he was now once again just a bandit. If anything, his perversity seemed to grow worse.

During the next few weeks of April and May, 1926, Lampião and his band were reported as operating mostly along the Pernambuco-Paraíba border. The news of their activities that reached the region's press dealt mostly with assaults on villages but occasionally also involved a killing or rape. The worst attack seems to have been on Algodões, a pitiful little conglomeration of houses to the side of the main westward highway from Recife. Arriving around April 20, the band sacked what commerce existed there and, according to a report, raped several girls and women. While there, they also ambushed a small convoy of two trucks of soldiers and then forbade traffic along the road for several hours while they rested.[2] The killing of a police deputy, whose body was then mutilated, and incidents of rape also were reported in an attack on another village.[3]

Reports of rapes and apparently unprovoked killings of law officers and soldiers grew more common during the period following Lampião's unfortunate experience with Padre Cícero, although any casual relationship between the events would be difficult to establish. Lampião and his band had been guilty of rape before and of course

---

[1] Lampião thereafter signed his name "Captain Virgulino Ferreira da Silva, vulgo Lampião," *vulgo* meaning "commonly known as."
[2] *Jornal do Commércio*, May 14, 1926.
[3] *O Ceará*, May 14, 1926.

had killed soldiers and law officials before.[4] But incidents of rape now seemed to increase in number, while, sometime during this period, Lampião began a policy of killing all soldiers and police officials, including former ones, who fell into his hands. It would seem prudent only to suggest that his anger and resentment—and, quite likely, genuine disappointment—may have contributed to an increasing level of perversity.

Following his crimes in Pernambuco, Lampião moved over into Alagoas. There he and his men went on a binge of robbery and violence that lasted for several days. On June 6, they arrived at Caraíbas, located a short distance off the road linking the towns of Mata Grande and Agua Branca. Caraíbas was the property as well as the home of José Vicente, a well-to-do rancher.[5] Located on his land in a picture-book setting on rolling hill country, it was composed of Vicente's ranch house and its outbuildings—including warehouses and a cotton gin— a chapel, a small general store, and the cottages of the tenants. It was something of a twentieth-century backlands approximation of the coastal plantations described in Gilberto Freyre's *Casa Grande e Senzala.*[6]

There were many people in Caraíbas on the sixth, for a holiday had been declared, and the vicar from Agua Branca was coming to celebrate a mass in the chapel. When, shortly before mid-morning, the festive crowd spied in the distance a cloud of dust rising from the road, they thought it was the cleric and his entourage. To their dismay, however, they recognized, as the fast-moving group came into view, that it was a band of cangaceiros. When it arrived, they saw to its rear the fearsome figure of Lampião. The celebrated outlaw was, of course, known well in the Agua Branca–Mata Grande region, and he had been in Caraíbas before. In just the previous year he had passed through, extorting money and provisions from José Vicente. Vicente and his family had reason to be afraid of Lampião. While they were not his

---

[4] For a discussion of Lampião's attitude toward women and the matter of rape, see chapter 8.

[5] The following story of the events at Caraíbas is based on *Diário de Pernambuco,* July 4, 1926, which reprints an account taken from *Correio da Pedra,* and an interview with Miguel Vicente da Silva, José's son, at Mata Grande, Alagoas, June 22, 1974.

[6] Translated into English as *The Masters and the Slaves,* Freyre's work is a study of life in the sugar-producing coastal plantations of northeastern Brazil.

declared enemies, neither were they counted among those many ranchers and businessmen in Mata Grande County who protected him. They
were regarded, rather, as being at least loosely allied with the dominant families of Agua Branca County, exactly those whom Lampião
identified as his mortal enemies. To Lampião, they were fair game.

When the outlaws arrived in the village, they had with them a
captive, a messenger who had been sent from Agua Branca to warn the
people that cangaceiros were in the area and to tell them that the
priest was not coming. That attempt had failed, and now the village was
under the control of the outlaws. Young Miguel Vicente, José Vicente's
son, grabbed his father and mother and tried unsuccessfully to flee.
Many others also sought to escape, but only a few succeeded. The
bandits had taken over with such surprise and speed that little, other
than passive submission, was possible. Lampião accused the owner of
Caraíbas of being an ally of the authorities of Agua Branca and, on
his order, the buildings and corrals were set afire. The bandits also
took advantage of the more affluent of the male visitors who had come
to enjoy the holiday, taking their money and stripping them of their
clothing, leaving them in their drawers. Before departing on the horses
they had stolen there, the outlaws demanded a sum of money from
José Vicente and, when he could not produce it, left with him in their
power, holding him for ransom. Those at Caraíbas that day had gone
through an experience they were not likely to forget. As for Caraíbas,
Lampião's raid dealt it a severe blow. Today, crumbling foundations
and more modest structures attest to the destructive powers of the terrible bandit.

When the outlaws left Caraíbas, with José Vicente as captive, two
hours or more still remained of the morning, and it became clear that
they still had work to do that day. On the road toward the village of
Inhapí, they took another captive, the brother of Colonel Ulysses Luna,
who several years before had befriended Antônio Matildes and the
Ferreiras. Lampião no longer, it seems, had much regard for the
colonel, and to ransom his brother he demanded 18:000$000—a very
sizable sum with which one could have purchased in Brazil at that time
a new seven-passenger Studebaker Phaeton. In Inhapí, the bandits
robbed and destroyed a business house, and, according to a news account, repeatedly raped a seventeen-year-old girl, leaving her almost
dead. The next day, in an attack on a ranch, they killed milk cows and

burned a storehouse of cotton. They took captive on the road the same day a lone soldier who was arriving from Maceió and, after holding him for the night, knifed and shot him, leaving him dead. Finally, receiving their ransom money—Miguel Vicente borrowed money in Agua Branca to pay for his father—they released the two captives. They then invaded the nearby county of Santana do Ipanema.[7]

While the bandits were in Santana do Ipanema, they afforded the manager of the Standard Oil Company branch in Maceió (Alagoas' capital) a memorable experience. Adolfo Meira was assaulted by them as he traveled along a road by automobile in that county. Members of the band stole his money and jewelry, smashed his typewriter, and then took him to Lampião, who was waiting some distance away. Lampião instructed him to write a letter to Standard Oil requesting money and told him not to divulge for what purpose it was intended. When the oil company's representative explained that deliveries of money required certain formalities, Lampião angrily sentenced him to burn in his automobile. The sentence might have been executed had a friend of Lampião's not asked for mercy for the condemned man in the name of Padre Cícero, whereupon he was released. Meira noted in telling his story to the press that Lampião and his fifty men wore images of the Heart of Jesus on their hats and that each had a small picture of Padre Cícero on his chest.[8] However angry Lampião may have been at Padre Cícero at one time, he quite clearly was not going to give up the magic that was associated by most backlanders with that venerable figure.

Lampião's violence in the backlands of Alagoas in June was of such intensity and so widespread that the state government apparently felt compelled to issue a statement. An official communication claimed that the invasion by the bandits had taken authorities by surprise and that they had not had time to react quickly and efficiently. They had sent, they said, more troops and equipment to the interior, including six machine guns, but rains had made travel difficult. They noted too that Lampião and his men were said to have been well armed with weapons of the Patriotic Battalions given them in Ceará.[9] The bandits, it seems, met no significant police resistance in Alagoas. A news report

[7] *Diário de Pernambuco*, July 4, 1926.
[8] Ibid., June 23, 1926, and *Correio do Ceará*, August 20, 1926.
[9] *Diário de Pernambuco*, June 23, 1926.

late in the month said that they had disappeared. It was presumed that they had sought a hideout where they could deposit their loot and rest.[10]

Lampião and his outlaws reportedly were hiding out in Pernambuco in the vicinity of Vila Bela County, and it was there that their next crimes were registered. On July 29, the band attacked a lone soldier, apparently one of Lampião's enemies from Nazaré. While traveling along a road, he passed a house in which the bandits were holed up, and they fired on him and killed him.[11] Three days later, they again assaulted Serra Vermelha, the ranch near Lampião's birthplace, where earlier in the year they had killed José Nogueira, Saturnino's brother-in-law. This time, presumably, they were seeking to assassinate José's son, Raymundo. Shortly before the assault, according to reports, Raymundo had fired at Lampião from afar when the bandit was in the village of São Francisco. When the attack on Serra Vermelha was over, two persons were dead, including a girl of fourteen, and two more were wounded. Raymundo, one of the wounded, had put up stiff resistance from inside the house with three companions. For some four hours, they had held off the cangaceiro chieftain and his sixty-five men.[12]

The events of late July and early August took place in the area of the village of São Francisco, where Lampião generally could expect a friendly reception. Several of his relatives lived in São Francisco, and the Novães, an important family there, were also sympathetic—a situation best explained by the fact that they, like the Ferreiras, were enemies of the dominant families of nearby Nazaré. Shortly before Lampião's attack on Serra Vermelha, a group of twelve Nazareno soldiers had gone to São Francisco and ordered its residents to abandon their homes and businesses, alleging that it was a major refuge of the bandits. As a result of these bullying, strong-armed tactics—not uncommon to the police in that era—Emílio Novães, a young but prominent landowner and businessman who lived in São Francisco, joined Lampião's band. Some of his relatives, however, soon persuaded him to re-

[10] Ibid., June 27, 1926.

[11] Criminal proceedings against Virgulino Ferreira et al., July 29, 1926. Second Cartório, Serra Talhada, Pernambuco.

[12] Criminal proceedings against Virgulino Ferreira et al., August 1, 1926, First Cartório, Serra Talhada, Pernambuco.

turn to legal pursuits, and the move had Lampião's approval. Several acts of violence between the peoples of Nazaré and São Francisco already had occurred, including killings and ambushes, and the São Franciscans let it be known that the Nazarenos were unwelcome in their community. Already in 1926, Lampião had killed five of the Nazareno soldiers who were pursuing him.[13]

Lampião's association with another member of the Novães family, most of whom lived in the neighboring county of Floresta, did not have such a satisfactory ending. Occasionally, the celebrated brigand met someone who was more perverse than he, and unquestionably Horácio Novães should be placed in that category. Horácio was not only a common horse thief, but he was also a very dangerous one. After being convicted *in absentia* in mid-1925 of stealing mules and donkeys in Floresta and transporting them to Ceará for sale, Horácio and his band of outlaws joined Lampião.[14] This event was to hold dire consequences for the Gilo family of Floresta, one of whose members, Manoel, had been among those accusing Horácio of horse thievery. Not long before his trial, Horácio and two cangaceiros had appeared one morning at daybreak at Tapera Ranch in Floresta, where the Gilos lived, and, after rousing the sleeping residents, searched the house for Manoel, saying they were going to kill him. Not finding him there, they threatened to kill his father, Donato, but departed without doing so.[15] During the next year, Horácio, after joining forces with Lampião, succeeded in taking his revenge several times over.

The Gilo massacre at Tapera Ranch, on August 28, 1926, is one of Lampião's most remembered deeds in Pernambuco, but it was one which brought him no credit. It was also one in which he was deceived by his comrade, Horácio. During the months in which Horácio and Lampião rode together—or walked together, as the case might be— Horácio had tried to poison the mind of his companion against the Gilos, in preparation for his move. His major stroke was a letter, written over the name of the Gilos, but allegedly penned by Horácio's wife. Addressed to Lampião, it was insulting in tone and questioned

[13] *O Ceará*, September 12, 1926.

[14] Criminal proceedings against Horácio Cavalcante de Albuquerque (Horácio Novães) and Aureliano de Sá Filho, April, 1925, First Cartório, Floresta, Pernambuco.

[15] Criminal proceedings against Horácio Cavalcante (Horácio Novães), June 27, 1925, First Cartório, Floresta, Pernambuco.

Lampião's bravery. It was, in short, designed to provoke an attack. The attack came at four o'clock on a Saturday morning when Lampião and Horácio, accompanied by ninety other cangaceiros, opened fire on the Gilo home. Inside the house were a dozen people, including Manoel, two of his brothers, his father and mother, and various other male relatives. The Gilos offered strong resistance—they had been warned that such an attack might be in the offing—and the gun battle lasted for several hours. Meanwhile, some of the cangaceiros were stationed along the road that passed by the Gilo ranch in order to intercept any passers-by who would be going to the market day in Floresta, in that way making any aid for the beseiged family unlikely.

Around ten o'clock, by which time firing from inside the house had ended—the elder Gilo—the only male left alive in the house—came out and confronted his attackers. Lampião pulled out the letter he believed to be from the man standing before him and began to read it. Gilo, protesting, denied authorship of the letter, pleading that he did not even know how to read or write. Lampião, so the story has been told, was almost convinced of Gilo's innocence when Horácio, standing to the side, raised his pistol and shot and killed Gilo. In all, thirteen people died at Tapera Ranch that day. According to witnesses, bodies were strewn all over the place. Of the twelve people in the house, all died except Gilo's wife. The only male left in the immediate family was a young teen-aged boy who had made a trip to Ceará to buy sugar and, thus, was absent when the attack occurred. Two people not in the house also were killed. One was one of the persons detained while passing, and the other was a soldier, a member of the police force from Floresta that had belatedly arrived. Lampião, trusting Horácio no longer, ejected him from the band. The horse thief and murderer, so it is now asserted in Floresta, still lives in Bahia, where he fled after the crime. He never legally paid for his part in one of backlands Pernambuco's most heinous crimes.[16]

Following the Gilo massacre, the "governor of the backlands," as a Pernambuco newspaper called Lampião at this time,[17] was closely

[16] The account of the Gilo massacre is based on Criminal proceedings against Horácio Cavalcante (Horácio Novães) et al., August 28, 1926, Second Cartório, Floresta, Pernambuco; Ana Maria Barros (Floresta, Pernambuco, August 5, 1975) Olympo Campos, interviews; *O Ceará*, September 4, 1926; *Diário de Pernambuco*, September 1, 1926.

[17] *A Tribuna* (Petrolina, Pernambuco), September 25, 1926.

pursued by the police. Among those chasing him were José Saturnino and Manuel Neto, the later reputedly the most fearless of the Nazarenos. The military effort came close to paying off when, in mid-September, Lampião was wounded in a major battle at Tigre Ranch in Floresta County. Hit in the chest, he apparently suffered a serious wound. Little was heard of him for the next few weeks as he recuperated on Poço do Ferro Ranch, owned by Colonel Ângelo da Gia, one of his long-time protectors in Pernambuco. Only in November, it seems, did authorities learn of his whereabouts. By that time, he was well and in action again.[18]

Lampião was operating in Vila Bela County, which at this time was the headquarters of the state military forces assigned to the campaign against banditry in the Pernambuco interior. Commanding those forces was Major Teófanes Torres, who, then in his late thirties, already had fought Lampião for several years but who was best known for his capture of Antônio Silvino a dozen years earlier. Teófanes, who like many other police officers was often accused of doing business in ammunition with Lampião, was now being given stronger support by the state government. The new governor, Estácio Coimbra, and especially his chief of police, Eurico de Souza Leal, were considerably more dedicated to the eradication of banditry than their predecessors had been. It has been said that Teófanes, however valid the accusations of misconduct against him may have been, gave his men in the field virtually complete freedom to pursue the bandits.[19] As far as his military prowess went, he was not much of a field commander, for he normally preferred the relative comfort of Vila Bela City.

With Lampião operating in the immediate vicinity Teófanes put together a major military force to pursue him. The force caught up with the bandits on November 28 near Serra Grande, a mountain about twenty miles from Vila Bela City. The battle pitted 295 soldiers against

[18] Reports of Lampião's being wounded appeared in *Diário de Pernambuco*, September 22 and 24, 1926. A cangaceiro, Quindú, arrested in 1928, told of Lampião's having recuperated in Poço do Ferro, located in the Tacaratú area of Pernambuco (*A Tarde* [Salvador], September 3, 1928).

[19] On the Coimbra administration, see *O Ceará*, November 12, 1926, and *Diário da Noite*, November 21, 1931, the latter containing an interview with Eurico de Souza Leal. Also Miguel Feitosa, a member of the Pernambuco police in that period, provided a valuable overview of the times in an interview. On Teófanes Torres, one of the written accusations that he sold ammunition to Lampião is found in Carvalho, *Serrote Preto*, p. 362.

Lampião's approximately 100 bandits. It was the bandit's largest battle
to that time and perhaps the most formidable of his career. As usual,
the police were chasing the outlaws, a situation that gave the latter
certain advantages. Crossing the rugged mountain, they set up an ambush in an area of large boulders and deep cracks that offered them
control of the approach to be taken by the force. It was a place, so the
soldiers claimed later, where the cangaceiros, at little risk to themselves, could kill the soldiers almost at will. Although the soldiers brave-
ly attacked the entrenched bandits, they said, they could not overcome
the resistance of the "terrible general of the cangaço," even with their
superior numbers. The battle began about nine o'clock in the morning;
when it ended, as darkness was falling, ten soldiers had died and a
dozen more had been wounded, among the latter Manuel Neto of
Nazaré. It had not been a massacre, but, in view of the superiority of
numbers held by the police, the cangaceiros had not done at all badly,
although their losses, relatively speaking, were also heavy. Six bandits
were reported dead. Major Teófanes, at his headquarters in town, had
heard of the battle and, taking cars and trucks with additional soldiers
and ammunition, had set out to join his troops, but, alas, the battle
ended before he arrived.[20]

The police falsely claimed that they had killed Antônio Ferreira,
Lampião's brother, in the battle. He did die not long thereafter in
Pernambuco on the Poço do Ferro Ranch of Ângelo da Gia, but his
death was an accident. He and four others of the band were playfully
wrestling for a hammock on the porch of a ranch house when they
knocked over a gun, which went off and killed Antônio immediately.
Luís Pedro was held responsible. With great fear of what might happen to them, the bandits took the body to Lampião and explained the
circumstances of Antônio's death. Lampião scolded them for playing
around, but, rather than punishing them, he told Luís Pedro that he
would take Antônio's place. Luís Pedro became Lampião's most trusted companion and was to die with him at Angicos.

The police received word of the fatal accident and Miguel Feitosa,
a soldier, went to investigate. He and his party found the grave and
dug up Antônio's body to verify the report. The date of the incident is

[20] The most complete story of the Serra Grande battle is found in the criminal
proceedings against Virgulino Ferreira et al., November 28, 1926, First Cartório,
Serra Talhada, Pernambuco.

uncertain, but the absence of the bandit's name in news reports, observers' accounts, and criminal proceedings indicates that it happened within a few months following the Serra Grande battle.[21]

Following Antonio's death, it is said, Lampião in mourning let his hair grow. Be that as it may, shoulder-length hair soon did become a cangaceiro trademark. Like the curious headgear, the colorful neckerchiefs, and the bandoleers, it helped to set Lampião and his bandits still farther apart from conventional society and, in a sense, may have indicated a deepening of their alienation.[22]

Present at the battle of Serra Grande was a reluctant observer by the name of Pedro Paulo Mineiro Dias. He worked for Standard Oil, for Lampião had captured another representative of that powerful North American company. He was taken by the bandits two days before the battle as he and a companion traveled by automobile between Vila Bela and Triunfo. When the two men could not deliver the several hundred dollars demanded by Lampião for their freedom, Dias' companion was released with instructions to procure the sum in Vila Bela. Meanwhile, Dias was held hostage and was given a rare, if risky, view of life in the cangaço. Remaining with the outlaws for three days, he slept on the ground, as did they, and ate their food, which he described as roast goat, *farinha*, and *rapadura*. *Farinha*, a meal made from the manioc root, and *rapadura*, a caked form of brown sugar, are staple food items in the backlands.

Dias succeeded in making friends with the bandits, which no doubt was the prudent thing to do, and they especially appreciated his ability to play the guitar. Following the defeat of the police at Serra Grande, the bandits held a victory dance for which Dias helped to make the music. There being no women present, the men chose each other for partners. When, on the day following the battle, the money to ransom Dias had still not arrived, Lampião decided to let him go. The bandits had taken the money he had on him, his watch, and his wedding ring; Lampião made them return the ring. The outlaw leader

---

[21] The story of Antônio's death is widely told in the area. A considerably garbled version of it appears in Leonardo Motta, *No tempo de Lampeão*, pp. 42–43. My version is based in the main on Miguel Feitosa, interview.

[22] On the reason for Lampião's letting his hair grow, see Oliveira, *Lampião*, p. 41.

then arranged for a rancher friend to take Dias to a place on the road where he could hail a car for Vila Bela.[23]

When the Standard Oil man left the bandits' camp, he was carrying with him a letter from Lampião addressed to the governor of Pernambuco. In it, the cangaceiro chieftain proposed a division of the state between himself and the governor. He would govern, he said, that portion of the state lying westward of Rio Branco (now Arcoverde); the governor could have jurisdiction over the eastern portion.[24] The seriousness of Lampião's proposal may be doubted, but it was not the last time that he was to make such a suggestion. Aware of his own importance, he no doubt knew that newspapers were referring to him as the "governor of the backlands." He also knew that Antônio Silvino, too, had been given that title. While his suggestion may have had a note of seriousness, he probably was mostly playing the role of the bandit chieftain taunting the authorities.

If there was an implicit challenge in Lampião's taunt, the Pernambuco authorities accepted it. Over the year and a half or so beginning with the battle of Serra Grande, Lampião was to have a hard time of it in Pernambuco, and by the time that period was over he would be fleeing from the state like a scared dog with its tail between its legs. Lampião's heyday in his home state was over before the end of 1926. His difficulties had originated late in that year with the new administration of Governor Estácio Coimbra and his chief of police, Eurico de Souza Leal. In addition to pushing the police in the interior into stronger action and providing them with greater support, they took several other moves as well. Souza Leal, for one thing, called a meeting of the chiefs of police of the neighboring states of Paraíba, Rio Grande do Norte, Ceará, Alagoas, and Bahia late in 1926 to consider joint action against banditry.[25] Meeting in Recife, the states pledged themselves to guard their borders more efficiently, to put more men into the field specifically to combat banditry, and to cooperate with each other when one of their number might have a special problem. Inherent in the agreement was the renewal of a key policy, already

[23] *O Ceará*, December 1, 1926; Carvalho, *Serrote Preto*, pp. 340–341, 346; Melchiades da Rocha, *Bandoleiros das caatingas*, pp. 124–131.

[24] Rocha, *Bandoleiros*, p. 131.

[25] Reports of the meeting are found in *Diário de Pernambuco*, December 28, 1926, and *Diário da Noite*, November 20, 1931.

in effect for several years, permitting troops to disregard state borders in their pursuit of criminals.[26] This was an oft-criticized provision, since local populations at times were terrorized by police from neighboring states. Such freedom of movement, however, was essential to police efficiency against bandits.

Souza Leal and the governor knew that simply putting more troops into the field was not a sure solution. Lampião had demonstrated his ability to overcome the disadvantage of being met with superior numbers. Thus, a major part of the problem of defeating him obviously lay elsewhere, and they correctly pointed to it. It was the support—voluntary or forced—that bandits received from the backlands population. Without their coiteiros, or suppliers and protectors, the bandits could be much more easily dealt with.

For Lampião, the several varieties of coiteiros served vital functions. Those who were the dominant political chiefs of counties or regions did favors for Lampião or arranged things for him because they feared what he might do to their rural properties. Some of this class also had personal ties with Lampião or his friends or they were enemies of his enemies. Cornélio Soares of Vila Bela, for example, had known Lampião's family well. When in earlier years José Ferreira and his sons had come into town for the weekly market day, they spent the night or ate dinner at the home of Cornélio's brother, who was Levino's godfather.[27] Personal ties were strong in the backlands—as they often are in traditional rural areas of restricted spatial mobility—and the paternalistic feelings of the Soares family toward the Ferreiras could not be easily erased. Moreover, a relationship with Lampião could also be profitable, and Soares, among many others, was accused of doing business with the bandit.[28] Lampião also could expect sympathy or support from the family of Sebastião Pereira or from other enemies of the Carvalhos or from enemies of the Nazarenos. Others may have served as coiteiros because they liked Lampião, as Marcolino in Princeza did,

[26] Meetings had been held before on the problem of banditry. The main one immediately preceding the 1926 meeting was held also in Recife in December, 1922. Montenegro, *História do cangaceirismo*, pp. 82–87, contains a good account of it.

[27] João Ferreira, Genésio Ferreira, interviews.

[28] Carvalho, *Serrote Preto*, p. 362; Miguel Feitosa interrogated a cangaceiro who made the accusation (Miguel Feitosa, interview); criminal proceedings against Lampião in the Serra Grande case.

or they may have expected to share in his loot, which also appears to have been one of Marcolino's expectations. Maybe some of them thought that they could employ Lampião as a weapon against their enemies or that he could perform other personal services for them. There were several reasons for protecting Lampião, but the most important probably was the simple desire not to incur his enmity. Given the nature of the society, especially taking into account the failure of the state to monopolize violence, often there was no real alternative to offering Lampião protection.

Below these prestigious and wealthy families, there were many others who were counted among Lampião's coiteiros. Almost all of them lived on rural properties, either as owners, cowboys, or tenants and, short of risking death, there was no choice but to do the bandit leader's bidding. Many of these became his more or less permanent agents, regularly purchasing his provisions when he was operating in their area. They also served as his spies, informants, and messengers and kept him aware of police movements. Some of them disliked him, while others became his friends. They all respected him, out of fear if for no other reason. Many of them earned a considerable amount of money from him, for he paid well for the services they performed.

Many backlanders received a certain satisfaction from associating with the renowned cangaceiro. Already by 1926 or 1927, Lampião was a famous man. It was easy to enter into a relationship with him. He stopped by your house for coffee or a drink of water or maybe ordered you to prepare a meal, for which he usually paid. Getting to know you better, he might organize a dance on your ranch or in your village, at which the cangaceiros would make music and dance with the local girls. On such occasions, the cangaceiro chieftain would furnish everyone with *cachaça*, the local strong drink (distilled from sugar-cane juice), in great abundance. Thus, getting acquainted with Lampião was not difficult, and, if he asked you to purchase something for him or to do some other favor, you hardly could refuse. Almost before you realized it, you had become a coiteiro.

Chief of Police Souza Leal, then, began to confront the problem of the coiteiros. He, of course, did not have full freedom to operate against the county political chieftains, who, as the deliverers of votes to the state administration, had a certain impunity. The state officials, for example, did not move against the Vila Bela chieftain, Cornélio

Soares, even though he was named repeatedly as one of Lampião's major protectors. Cornélio simply was too powerful in county and regional politics to be tampered with very much. But Souza Leal did call a meeting of the county prefects to tell them that the administration meant to break the back of rural banditry. If he could not gain their active cooperation, he apparently could obtain from them a degree of neutrality. The state officials could negotiate in private with the bosses, reaching agreements that left the bosses unmolested in exchange for their promise not to hinder the campaign against banditry. An arrangement of this type apparently was made with Cornélio. Souza Leal also ordered the transfer of a district judge and the arrest of commissioners in two counties, all of whom reputedly were among those who gave Lampião assistance.[29]

Souza Leal's major actions were directed against the middle-level and lower-class coiteiros who were essential to the bandits' survival but who did not have sufficient political influence to protect themselves. Large numbers of them were arrested and held in custody for as long as a year or more.[30] Few, if any, were ever brought to trial, the state being mindful of the sympathy and understanding manifested by local juries for such alleged criminality. Jailing the coiteiros for extended periods of time withdrew their services from Lampião and thus accomplished the state's aims more effectively in most cases than trials would have done.

Illustrative of the middle-level coiteiros was José Olavo of Vila Bela. This thirty-year-old storekeeper was arrested late in 1926, shortly after the Serra Grande battle. Accused of being a major supplier of ammunition for Lampião, he was kept in custody for several months. Information obtained by the police about the case revealed a complicated story of subterfuge designed to protect everybody involved. The ammunition was purchased in nearby Salgueiro by a third party on the written request of Olavo. The Salgueiro agent thought, so he told the police, that the ammunition was destined for the Pereira family of Vila Bela. It was paid for, he said, by way of Cornélio Soares and his brother, Benjamin, who lived in Salgueiro. The ammunition, hidden in kerosene cans, was transported to Vila Bela by donkey. There, it was left at the ranch of a prominent person. The transporter claimed that he

---

[29] Interview with Souza Leal in *Diário da Noite*, November 21, 1931.
[30] *Diário de Pernambuco*, February 3, 1927; Miguel Feitosa, interview.

thought that it was for the use of the rancher, who, he added, expected an attack from Sabino Gomes. The transporter then informed Olavo that the cargo had arrived, whereupon he was ordered to return to the ranch and withdraw a portion of it to take to another ranch. This order he carried out, hiding the ammunition under onions and garlic. So the story went. Finally, one informant stated that he saw one of Olavo's employees delivering ammunition to the bandits. José Olavo then protested that he had become a supplier for Lampião only under dire threats of death and the burning of his rural properties.[31]

With a story such as that told by Olavo and his accomplices, it is no wonder that state authorities were reluctant to seek convictions from local juries. All of the information offered cannot be dismissed as falsehood, for Lampião was quite capable of making threats and, if need be, of executing them. The view put forth by backlanders, however, that they were totally caught up in a web of circumstance which left them powerless to choose may be a valid generalization, but it does not reflect significant exceptions. The fact was that a portion of Lampião's coiteiros found themselves in that class because they liked the bandit or, more often, because doing business with him was profitable.

This was true in Pernambuco particularly during the years preceding 1927 when the threat of police recriminations against coiteiros was relatively light. After that period ended, backlanders often tried to adjust, with some success, to the new circumstances, employing techniques with which they were already familiar. It had been possible, after all—and for many it remained so—to placate both the bandits and the military sufficiently to avoid trouble with either, and to avoid the role of active coiteiro. When in late 1927, for example, Lampião and his band camped on the ranch of Herculano de Carvalho in nearby Mata Grande, Alagoas, that rancher thought that he knew how to deal with the situation. In order to satisfy Lampião, he sent him the sum of money he requested and also sent along cigarettes as a present. He knew, at the same time, that he would be endangered by the police if they should learn of his actions, since Alagoas also was taking harsh moves against those who aided bandits. Herculano, therefore, sent his son to town to tell José Lucena, of the police, that the bandits were

---

[31] The information on Olavo is found in the criminal proceedings against Lampião in the Serra Grande case. He was accused of furnishing the ammunition with which the cangaceiros killed the soldiers in that battle.

camped on his ranch. He then sent his cowboy to warn Lampião that the police were coming! In Herculano's case, things did not work out as satisfactorily as he had hoped—as his subsequent interrogation by the police reveals —but his story is illustrative of the ability of the backlanders to make the best of a trying situation.[32]

An unfortunate result of the campaign against coiteiros was the persecution of Lampião's family. Various members of the Ferreira family were arrested in January, 1927, on allegations that they were furnishing Lampião with ammunition or aiding him in other ways. João Ferreira, Lampião's brother, was taken into custody in Juàzeiro, on the request of the Pernambuco police. João, accused of supplying ammunition to the bandits, normally worked as a transporter of cargo, as had his father, and this seems to have caused him to fall under suspicion. Four others were arrested with him: two of his employees and his brother-in-law and cousin. During the trip to Salgueiro, Pernambuco, after the arrests, the sergeant in command of the escort told João that he had instructions to kill them on the way. He assured him, however, that he would not carry out the orders. According to João, Lampião intended to free them on the Ceará-Pernambuco border, but arrived only after they had passed. In Salgueiro, there were reports that he would try again, and the town prepared for an attack. It never came. Taken to Vila Bela under heavy guard, the prisoners were interrogated by Major Teófanes, whereupon all but João were released. He subsequently was sent to Agua Branca, Alagoas, where he was absolved by a jury for alleged participation in the Pariconhas raid of 1921. In all, he spent a year and a half under detention before securing his release. One result of João's troubles was the entry into the cangaço of Ezekiel, the youngest of the Ferreira boys. On João's arrest, he sought out Lampião and joined the band. Other members of the Ferreira family were arrested in Piauí, where they were living, and also taken to Pernambuco. They were put to work as convict labor by Major Teófanes in the construction of the church in Vila Bela. None of Lampião's relatives was convicted of any wrongdoing.[33]

[32] Paulo Afonso (now Mata Grande) police inquiry dated January 5, 1928, Arquivo Público, Maceió, Alagoas.

[33] Information on the treatment of the Ferreiras is from João Ferreira and Genésio Ferreira, interviews; Augustin Lopez (Belmonte, Pernambuco, July 30 and 31, 1975), interview; *O Ceará*, January 27 and 30, 1927; and *A Tarde* (Salvador), January 23 and March 1, 1927.

Lampião was frequently on the move during the months following the announcement of Pernambuco's campaign to eliminate banditry in the region. After apparently resting for a few days following the Serra Grande battle, some members of his band in mid-December resumed their operations by seizing a retired district judge in Paraíba and holding him for ransom. Another part of the band attacked a ranch in Floresta, Pernambuco, killing more than 120 head of cattle.[34] Lampião apparently had divided his band into smaller groups in order to confuse the police and force them to widely disperse their limited numbers, and he was to use this tactic frequently in the future. When Lampião arrived in Ceará at the end of the month, it was reported that his band was operating as five separate units.[35] It was soon reported also that the chief of one of them, a cangaceiro nicknamed Bom Deveras ("Truly Good"), had been killed.[36] Such reports were to increase as the police campaign intensified. In Ceará, the outlaw chieftain apparently reunified his band, for when he entered Pernambuco again in early January, 1927, traveling by night to avoid detection, reports indicated that he was accompanied by about one hundred men.[37]

When Lampião left Ceará, Major Teófanes and his troops were on his trail, and they continued to pursue him across Pernambuco into Alagoas. As the bandits moved rapidly across several counties in that state, in the course of eleven days, they left a trail of extortion, burned-out ranches, murders, and hostages held for ransom.[38] In their pursuit, the Pernambuco and Alagoas police were joined by other troops from Paraíba, Bahia, and Sergipe. On the nineteenth, a force of mounted Pernambuco police caught up with the bandits near the Pernambuco-Alagoas border and engaged them in combat. Following the battle, which lasted between two and three hours, the police reported that they had killed three bandits and wounded others. In addition, another bandit was captured by the police in Alagoas.[39] Before the end of the month, the bandits had recrossed Pernambuco and were along the Ceará-Paraíba border. One of Lampião's best-remembered

[34] *Diário de Pernambuco*, December 19, 1926.
[35] *O Ceará*, December 28, 1926.
[36] *Correio do Ceará*, December 30, 1926.
[37] *O Ceará*, January 8, 1927.
[38] Ibid., April 26, 1927, carried a summary from Alagoas of the events there. Also see *Jornal de Alagoas*, January 20, 1927.
[39] *Diário de Pernambuco*, January 21, 1927.

deeds on this trip to Alagoas involved his relations with three Alagoans who paid a high price for their courage. When Lampião sent them a request for money, they not only did not send it, but in their refusal retorted that if he wanted to breed some brave men he should send his mother to them. In retaliation for that insult to his dead mother, and for their failure to send the money, Lampião killed 102 head of their cattle. But he did not attack them.[40] The bandit had a profound respect for bravery. That was one of the reasons why his career lasted so long.

Back in Paraíba, Lampião was attacked by a combined Paraíba-Pernambuco force in early February and lost still another member of his band.[41] He then went into Ceará. Although he apparently still felt relatively safe in that state, he was not as safe there as he had been in the past, since forces from Paraíba and Pernambuco increasingly were pursuing him there. If Ceará newspaper reports were true, he still had little to fear from that state's police. According to *O Ceará*, the police in the Cariri could attack Lampião only with prior permission in each instance from the state chief of police.[42] Ceará authorities, it seems, were continuing their long-standing policy of offering Lampião refuge in exchange for freedom from his attacks. He did not refrain from operating there completely, but he normally did not launch major assaults or murder people there. He seemed to restrict himself to requesting money and occasionally seizing someone for ransom. Padre Cícero, meanwhile, was still trying to shake Lampião from his skirts, denying repeatedly that he ever protected him and offering to aid in his capture.[43]

Over a period from March to early June of 1927, Lampião was reported at various times in Ceará, Pernambuco, and Paraíba. In mid-May, he and his band attacked a village in the north of Paraíba, an area in which they normally did not operate.[44] Lampião may have been seeking relief from the police, for, unquestionably, he had not been as free to move as in previous years; reports of the arrest and killing of bandits by police continued. Reportedly, he was complaining that he

[40] Aldemar de Mendonça, *Pão de Açúcar: História e efemérides*, fact no. 190.
[41] *Diário de Pernambuco*, February 3, 1927.
[42] February 6, 1927.
[43] *O Ceará*, January 2, 1927.
[44] Ibid., May 27, 1927.

had never before been under such pressure nor suffered such reverses.[45] Still another report said that he appeared at a ranch in Vila Bela asking for food, saying that he had not eaten in two days.[46] No doubt, he was feeling the pressure of the police and had been deprived of some of his former support with the arrest of his coiteiros, but just how seriously he was suffering is a question not easily resolved.

Anyone listening only to the Pernambuco authorities would have concluded that the bandit king was not only down but almost counted out. Souza Leal told the Recife press in late March that Lampião's band was disintegrating into small groups, each going its own way. Lampião, the police chief continued, had suffered such defeats that he had almost no resources left; he had very little ammunition and was, in fact, reduced to hiding out in the bush, afraid to appear in public.[47] The next month, Souza Leal offered his opinion that the case of Lampião no longer had its former importance.[48] Certainly Pernambuco officials could produce some fairly impressive statistics to show that their campaign against banditry had been fruitful. Major Teófanes gave a list to the press in early June showing that 100 bandits had been killed or taken prisoner since the previous December. Names, dates, and places were given. Of these, some 25 percent were identified as members of Lampião's band.[49] Yet, in spite of the claims of the police, news also reached the press that Lampião was being seen with a large group. In mid-May, in the most impressive of the reports, 123 men were said to be accompanying him when he was visited by the Aurora County, Ceará, police chief. Lampião, it was said, had invited the official out to his camp for coffee.[50] If, in fact, Lampião did have 123 men with him on the occasion—the figure may have been exaggerated—he probably had been joined temporarily by one or more of the several Ceará cangaceiro bands with which he was on friendly terms, for it is doubtful that he had that many regulars even in the best of times.

Although the claims of the Pernambuco authorities were only partially valid, Lampião had restricted his operations in Pernambuco under their pressure, and he was never again to regain his former status

[45] *Correio do Ceará*, April 26, 1927.
[46] *Diário de Pernambuco*, April 12, 1927.
[47] *O Ceará*, March 30, 1927.
[48] *Correio do Ceará*, April 26, 1927.
[49] The list appeared in *A Província* (Recife), June 11, 12, and 14, 1927.
[50] *O Ceará*, May 18, 1927.

there. Indeed, within a year or so, Pernambuco officials would be able to claim justifiably that they had defeated him effectively within their borders. But making life difficult for him in one state did not mean that his threat to the region had been eliminated. Lampião still had considerable resources at his command, including the ability to recruit men. Down in one place, the bandit chieftain, several times over the years, exhibited the resourcefulness to bounce back somewhere else. He was to try exactly this in June of 1927 with his incursion into Rio Grande do Norte, one of the most famous but least productive episodes of his career.

6. Mossoró

LAMPIAO's decision to attack Mossoró, interior Rio Grande do Norte's most important city, was, as it turned out, a mistake. But in early June of 1927 the bandit chieftain obviously was receptive to the idea of trying something in a new area. His movements in Pernambuco and Alagoas were restricted by police pressure, and, except for the earlier protection of Zé Pereira and his relatives, Paraíba had always made his coming unwelcome. As to Ceará, he had exempted it from his violence because of his informal understanding with authorities there and also out of respect for Padre Cícero. Rio Grande do Norte, the remaining state of the immediate vicinity, was lying in wait, Lampião may have thought.

At least two differing versions have been offered as to why the specific target of Mossoró was chosen. On the one hand, a member of Lampião's band said that it was on the invitation of another cangaceiro, Massilon Leite.[1] Massilon, who had his own band, already had raided Rio Grande do Norte and was considered by Lampião to be trustworthy. The other version relates that the architect of the attack was Colonel Isaías Arruda, the Cariri political boss who had long protected Lampião and other bandits. When the raid was proposed to Lampião, it is said, he first backed off, arguing that the city was too large and that such an attack would require a band of greater size than his. Arruda then overcame the objections by offering to assist in raising men and agreeing to furnish arms and ammunition in addition to guaranteeing Lampião a large sum of money. Such assistance presented little challenge to the Cariri chief. He had excellent contacts

[1] Jararaca's account, based on police interrogation, from *Correio do Povo* (Mossoró), reprinted in *Diário de Pernambuco*, July 8, 1927 (cited hereinafter as Jararaca's account).

with gunmen, and the Patriotic Battalions had transferred large quantities of arms and ammunition to him. The account of Arruda's offer did not make clear whether the money involved a guarantee in loot or Arruda was to pay it. In whatever case, the amount was said to be over 100:000$000. The two agreed, so it was asserted, that Massilon and his group would furnish the needed extra manpower.[2]

Whether at the invitation of Massilon or in response to Arruda's offer—which seems more likely—Lampião prepared for the journey. At his base in Aurora County, where he had been camped for three weeks, he received a large quantity of ammunition, estimated to have a value of 35:000$000 (over $4,000 in the U.S. equivalent).[3] Aurora, it should be noted, was one of Arruda's two counties. On June 9, Lampião and his men moved out of Aurora into Paraíba and began their trip northward. Their whereabouts was not kept a secret, for they were spotted in various places in Paraíba, and, on one occasion, had light contact with a police force.[4] Moving rapidly on horseback, the bandits were in Rio Grande do Norte before the end of the journey's second day. Still they made little effort to conceal their progress, rightly surmising, it would seem, that no one would guess their ultimate destination.

Robbing and burning ranches along the way, they also took captives and held them for ransom. Among the hostages was sixty-three-year-old Dona Maria José Lopez, who was being held for the considerable fortune of 40:000$000.[5] Another of the hostages, Colonel Antônio Gurgel, was seized on June 12, just as the bandits were approaching the vicinity of Mossoró. Gurgel, a prominent Rio Grande do Norte merchant, was taken as he traveled by automobile to one of his ranches to get his wife. News of the presence of Lampião in the general area already had reached Mossoró, and Gurgel feared for his wife's safety.

[2] *O Ceará*, June 28, 1927, carried the charges against Arruda. Arruda is not mentioned by name but the implication is unmistakable.

[3] Transcript of the police interrogation of Casca Grossa, a member of Lampião's band in the Mossoró attack, reprinted in Raimundo Nonato, *Lampião em Mossoró*, p. 299. Nonato's book, chiefly a collection of documents and newspaper stories, is the major printed source on the Mossoró attack. It is presumed that the ammunition was acquired from Arruda, one of Lampião's main suppliers (see the interview with Gengibre, of Lampião's band, in *O Ceará*, October 3, 1929).

[4] *O Ceará*, June 10 and 12, 1927.

[5] Dona Maria's story is told in an interview, reprinted in Nonato, *Lampião em Mossoró*, pp. 185–191.

Assaulted by a contingent of the bandits on the highway, Gurgel was forced to hand over his pistol, wedding ring, eyeglasses, and wallet. Looking into the wallet, one of the bandits gleefully shouted to his companions that they had found themselves a big rich colonel. The colonel was then taken to a nearby ranch, where the main part of the band was resting, and Lampião decided that they would ask 21:-000$000 for him. One of the colonel's brothers, who had been previously seized, was sent to Mossoró to secure the money secretly from Gurgel's son-in-law, who was the manager of the local branch of the Bank of Brazil. The messenger was warned that if the band should be attacked Gurgel would be the first to die.[6]

News of the proximity of Lampião, as we have said, was reaching Mossoró even before Gurgel's brother arrived. With his arrival and with subsequent news that the bandits had sacked and burned a rural railway station only twenty-five miles distant, families of means began to send their women and children to their ranches on the coast. The male population worked through the night preparing for the city's defense.[7] Meanwhile, the bandits were camped not far from the burned-out station. Arising at five-thirty the next day, they resumed their journey and before mid-morning were only a couple of miles outside the city.[8] There, Lampião instructed Gurgel to write Mossoró's political chief, informing him that 150 bandits waited on the outskirts—the actual number was around 60—and requesting 500:000$000 to save the city from being sacked and burned by them. Advised by the colonel that the sum asked for was a lot of money, the outlaw considerately reduced the request to 400:000$000.

By mid-afternoon the outlaws had crossed the Apodí River, which flows by Mossoró, and were ready to attack. Mossoró's prefect, in response to their request, had told them that the money would not be sent and that the city was prepared to receive them.[9] Inside the city, a combined force of armed townsmen and police—estimates of their

[6] Gurgel's account, ibid., pp. 192–215.

[7] *Diário de Pernambuco*, July 8, 1927, reprints from *Correio do Povo* the story of the attack.

[8] The best accounts of the bandits' moves are given in Jararaca's account, and D. Maria's and Gurgel's stories in Nonato, *Lampião em Mossoró*, pp. 185–191, 192–215.

[9] The prefect's letter to Lampião, as well as Gurgel's to the prefect, is found in *A República* (Natal), June 27, 1927.

number ran from 150 to 300—was waiting at strategic points. Occupying the home of the prefect, the railway station, the telegraph station, a school, a hotel, and several residences and stores, in addition to church towers which overlooked the town, they were amply supplied with ammunition purchased by public subscription.

One wonders if Lampião, looking, at that defiant city, did not have a premonition of defeat. Rising from a flat coastal plain, the city offered none of the protection of the hilly and mountainous country to which he was accustomed. Never before had he assaulted anything of that magnitude. He must surely have realized the possibility, even the probability, of defeat. One of his companions indicated that Lampião had doubts about the enterprise but, having issued his ultimatum, resolved to go through with it rather than reap the shame that withdrawal would bring.[10] Around four o'clock on that Monday afternoon of the thirteenth, with a light rain falling, the bandits attacked. To the sound of a trumpet—for Lampião did things in style—and the rumble of thunder in the cloudy sky, the outlaws entered the city, on foot and divided into groups. Singing "Mulher Rendeira" and shouting their usual vivas and obscenities, they opened fire on several of the points defended by the townsmen. After a half hour, with no notable success in cracking the defense, one group tried to assault the prefect's home. Out in the open, they came under fire from one of the church towers and other points nearby. Withdrawing, they left one of their number wounded on the street; he was finished off by the defenders. Another bandit, Jararaca, tried to retrieve the arms and ammunition of his fallen comrade and was also hit, but he succeeded in getting away. Another group tried to take the train station, but, met with stiff resistance, they too were driven back. Within an hour and a half, the bandits withdrew from the city, their tactics of brazen boldness having failed them on this occasion.

Lampião reportedly lost five or six of his men as a result of the attack, although the deaths of only three were verifiable. In addition to the one who died in the street, the body of another was later found, and the third, Jararaca, died under mysterious circumstances. Jararaca, who was named for a small but aggressive poisonous snake, was one of the band's most feared cangaceiros. He was twenty-six-years old and

---

[10] Jararaca's account.

had deserted from the military before joining Lampião. The day following the assault, he was found in a house just outside the city and was arrested, placed in jail, and interrogated. Talking freely, he discussed the attack on Mossoró and named several of the band's alleged protectors. Among them was Major Teófanes Torres of the Pernambuco police, with whom, he said, Lampião had long had an agreement; Lampião did not bother the property of Teófanes while, in return, the major did not personally pursue Lampião nor order others to pursue him closely. Having gotten the information from Jararaca, the police loaded the wounded bandit in a car, saying they were taking him to the state capital. Later, they announced that he had died on the way. In Mossoró, reliable sources said that the police had taken him out to the cemetery, shot him, and buried him.[11]

Once out of the city, Lampião and the other bandits returned to their camp where, together with their hostages, they mounted their horses and quickly departed for Ceará, following the telegraph line. One of the hostages said that Lampião, as well as others in the band, returned from the city panic-stricken.[12] Another report stated that Massilon temporarily took command of the retreat because of Lampião's confusion.[13] Such reports, while they may be exaggerated, may contain a good deal of truth, for Mossoró had presented Lampião with an unusual, and in all likelihood frightening, experience. Lampião, of course, did not lack courage, but he was not foolhardy. Unless forced by circumstances, he normally did not meet the enemy except under conditions that favored his victory. In Mossoró, the cards were heavily stacked against him, as he quite clearly realized, but, either to protect his honor as a bandit or out of vanity, he tempted fate and lost. Mossoró, the most ambitious and most foolish undertaking of his career, was a mistake. He was not to make that kind of mistake again.

The immediate destination of the bandits was Limoeiro do Norte, located on the Juaguaribe River in Ceará. By the afternoon of the fif-

[11] Jararaca's account. His words on Major Teófanes are only one version of the relations between the major and Lampião. Another source relates that Lampião did not attack the cattle of Teófanes because they were pastured on the land of a person with whom he had an understanding (Miguel Feitosa, interview). The allegations concerning Jararaca's death are widely believed. See Nonato, *Lampião em Mossoró*, pp. 146–147, for one account.

[12] D. Maria's story, in Nonato, *Lampião em Mossoró*, p. 187.

[13] *O Ceará*, June 28, 1927.

teenth, Lampião and his men, together with their hostages—the band was somewhat reduced in number, a small contingent having been left on its own in the hurried departure—had almost covered the fifty miles from Mossoró and were approaching the town. Probably not expecting trouble but, nevertheless, wishing to avoid it, Lampião sent a messenger ahead to tell the townspeople of his imminent arrival. He counseled the police to leave and warned the town that if any resistance was offered he would attack without pity. The small contingent of police obligingly departed, followed by some of the women and children of the more prosperous families. The political chiefs, presuming that the bandits would be hungry from their journey, ordered a steer slaughtered. Limoeiro do Norte was prepared to offer the desperados Ceará's traditional hospitality.

The outlaws rode into the city in mid-afternoon, shouting vivas to Ceará, Governor Moreira da Rocha, and, of course, Padre Cícero. Lampião was greeted warmly by the head political chief, and the bandit told him there was no cause for worry. His men were well disciplined, he said, and he offered his personal guarantee of safety for all. As to the tax that he almost always levied, it was agreed, after some negotiation, that the town would be charged the reasonable sum of only 2:000$000. Going then to the telegraph station, Lampião placed it under guard and examined the correspondence. Meanwhile, his men were being offered the comforts of the town's hotel, including dinner. Lampião partook of the meal only after some of his men had eaten, as was his custom. Always cautious, he feared poisoning. Having eaten and rested a little, the bandits walked around the small town, looking into shops and buying decks of playing cards and whatever else struck their fancy. The townspeople, for their part, overcame their initial fears and began to come out into the streets to meet their renowned visitors. Lampião's men especially made the small boys happy, tossing handfuls of coins to the ground for them to scramble after. About five o'clock, Lampião went to church to pray, accompanied by the priest. When the padre presented him with the collection plate, he dropped in a large bill for himself and ordered his men to contribute. Sometime before dark, Lampião and his band, along with their hostages, lined up for a local photographer to snap some group pictures. Reports out of Limoeiro were in unanimous agreement, it seems, that the visit was a success for the townspeople as well as for the bandits.

The band left the town around ten o'clock in the evening, after a round of goodbyes. They might have stayed longer, but an hour earlier the telegraph operator had learned that a police force had arrived in the neighboring town of Russas. Limoeiro's leaders then persuaded Lampião that he should withdraw in order to save the town from becoming the scene of a battle. Lampião reluctantly agreed. Early the next morning, troops did arrive in Limoeiro. Also by unanimous agreement, it seems, the town's citizenry preferred the cangaceiros to the troops. The force, which came from Paraíba, showed little sympathy for the warm welcome the town had given Lampião. They seized various small objects given by him and his men to the people as remembrances and threatened to arrest several persons, accusing them of being the bandit's accomplices. Overall, news from Limoeiro indicated the police were poorly disciplined and had made a bad impression.[14]

Having departed from Limoeiro, Lampião and his bandits headed southward up the Juaguaribe in the direction of Aurora, probably hoping to get back under the protective wing of Colonel Arruda. On this occasion, however, neither Arruda nor the normally neutral soil of Ceará was to offer refuge to Lampião. Before he was able to escape from that state into Pernambuco, he was to pass through as trying an ordeal as had yet beset him. Not only were there troops from Rio Grande do Norte and Paraíba after him, but Ceará's forces also began to pursue him. Arruda, for his part, was to prove a fickle ally. Whatever the colonel's reasons may have been, Ceará's seem to have been in reaction to the bold attack on Mossoró.

Within a few days of the attack on Mossoró there was a tri-state force of close to five hundred troops in pursuit of Lampião.[15] The first contact with him apparently took place on June 20, and it was Lampião this time who fell into the ambush. A Ceará force in early afternoon opened fire on the bandits on two sides, sending them into a state of confusion. Terrified, the horses and mules began to buck and wheel wildly, and the riders dismounted in the best way possible to seek cover and put up a fight. After an hour and a half, with the police fire be-

[14] On Lampião's Limoeiro visit and related events, see news stories and interviews in *O Ceará*, June 16, 19, and 21, 1927. In addition, *O Povo* (Fortaleza), November 26, 1948, carried an interview with the man who was the Limoeiro political chief at the time of the visit.

[15] *O Ceará*, June 21, 1927.

coming less intense, the bandits succeeded in getting around a hill and fleeing. While they suffered only one casualty, a serious wound to the arm of a cangaceiro called Moreno ("Black"), they lost their mounts and all provisions and ammunition except what they personally carried. If the bandits were terrorized by the attack, one can imagine the feelings of the hostages, Colonel Gurgel and Dona Maria, who were still in their company.[16]

The day of the attack, the bandits marched until midnight in search of safety. Now tired and hungry, with no one daring to sleep, they rested for a few hours. Before daylight the day following, they were on the trail again, but by mid-morning, still tired and hungry, they found a high spot affording a view of the surroundings and camped. Lampião dispatched some of the bandits to scout the area for water, food, and police. They encountered no police, but one returned with water while another, stripping down to plain clothing to hide his identity, had been able to purchase cheese from a rancher. The group remained there all day and night, making no noises above a whisper and lighting no fires. The next day, again on the trail by sunrise, the party had a chance meeting with a cowboy during the morning. Taking his horse for the wounded Moreno, Lampião was going to kill him to prevent his spreading the word that the band was in the area. But, thinking better of it, he forced the frightened man to serve as guide. The band was then led to an isolated place near Vaca Morta ("Dead Cow") in the County of Riacho do Sangue ("Blood Creek"), still in the basin of the Juaguaribe River. The band spent the next day vigilant and hungry, having been able to find only a little *farinha*, cheese, and one turkey to satisfy the hunger of so large a group. By evening, fear was reigning in the camp, for a scouting party reported that the place was surrounded by a numerous force. No one slept during the night, but the silence was broken only by the sounds of nature. Gurgel later wrote that he commended his soul to God that night, certain that his appointed hour was approaching.

At six-thirty the next morning the police attacked, sounding their bugle and opening fire on the bandits from a distance of over two hun-

---

[16] Gurgel's account, in Nonato, *Lampião em Mossoró*, pp. 205–206, tells the story of the battle. This account, together with that of D. Maria (ibid., pp. 185–191), is the best source for the moves of the bandits until the hostages were released.

dred yards. The bandits returned the shots sparingly, saving their ammunition, but more than compensated for their weak firepower with vivas to Padre Cícero and a host of saints. Gurgel, from a gully in which he and Dona Maria had been placed for safekeeping, also heard his captors hurl insults at the police in a language that, he said, was "very dirty."[17] Lampião, after an hour, passed the word to his men to cease firing and keep quiet in their positions. The police fell for the ruse, thinking the bandits had fled, and began to advance. When the police were near, the cangaceiros opened fire again, causing several casualties. A half hour later, the soldiers having extricated themselves from the bandits' deceit by withdrawing, Lampião and his band began their own withdrawal toward safety. Even though they fell under fire once more before getting out of the area, they suffered not a single casualty. In spite of the fact that there were 50 cavalrymen among the forces, not to mention the 350 foot soldiers, the bandits were not immediately pursued.

The Battle of Macambira (taking its name from the hill where it was fought), pitting fewer than 50 cangaceiros against 400 soldiers, was a failure of considerable magnitude for the police. The commanding officer of the forces, Major Moysés de Figueiredo of the Ceará police, was much criticized for the failure, especially by the press, which had reported that the Ceará police had the bandits completely surrounded and that escape was impossible.[18] Major Moysés defended himself by charging that his orders had not been carried out.[19] He had planned the attack in the field, he wrote, and then, as befitted his status as commander, returned to camp to await the results. He blamed the failure on his second in command, saying that his orders to surround the bandits and then rush them had not been followed. When the police attacked, his second in command, he charged, had, before completing the encirclement, ordered the bugle sounded and commenced firing from afar. The likely explanation here is that the police, not knowing exactly where all the bandits were—for Lampião kept his men widely dispersed when there was danger—made contact with them before the

[17] Gurgel's account, ibid., pp. 207–208. This is the best account of the battle. Also see *O Ceará*, June 26, 1927.

[18] *O Ceará*, June 24, 1927.

[19] Moysés de Figueiredo defended himself in his book, *Lampeão no Ceará: A verdade em torno dos factos (Campanha de 1927)*, pp. 26–30.

encirclement was accomplished. Hence, the police attack was premature. It may have been, too, that the police, as Ceará's newspapers continually charged, preferred to fire at Lampião from a safe distance and, if possible, give him adequate warning of their approach, so that he could withdraw. If that was their attitude, it was one shared by many a soldier who fought Lampião at other times and in other places.

When Lampião withdrew from Macambira, he apparently decided that his hostages no longer had much value. With his band hiding out and on the run, any chance now of collecting ransom money was unlikely. Killing the hostages was not contemplated, since both Lampião and his men liked them and enjoyed their company. Thus, shortly after the battle, Sabino informed Gurgel that he and Dona Maria should say farewell to the captain, for they were free to leave. Their goodbyes completed, the hostages were guided by Sabino and four other bandits to a road leading out of the bush. Each was given a sum of money, in addition to some cheese that had been bought on the way, and bidden farewell. Both Gurgel and Dona Maria indicated that the bandits generally had treated them kindly. Dona Maria, understandably, had been treated well, and she reported that one of the bandits attached himself to her, waiting on her with care.[20] Gurgel had one complaint. Sabino had taken the hostage as his eating companion, not so much out of friendship, perhaps, as out of perversity. The cangaceiro heavily laced his food with hot pepper sauce, which Gurgel found uncomfortable. As he ate, tears ran from his eyes, much to Sabino's obvious enjoyment.[21]

During the week following the Battle of Macambira, the bandits were reported as still making their way southward toward Aurora. The soldiers were after them, the press said, and news of victory at any moment was expected. Sources from the Juaguaribe River valley, moreover, indicated that the band was being rapidly depleted by desertions and that those left were exhausted, suffering from extreme hunger, and out of ammunition.[22] In fact, such reports exaggerated the seriousness of the band's situation. As always when under pursuit and on the run, they slept and ate little, since vigilance was ever a necessity and the obtaining and preparation of food entailed chances of being detected,

[20] D. Maria's and Gurgel's accounts of their release are in Nonato, *Lampião em Mossoró*, pp. 189–190 and 209–213.

[21] Ibid., p. 204.

[22] *O Ceará*, June 28 and 29, 1927; *Diário de Pernambuco*, June 28, 1927.

as well as loss of time. Moreover, a cowboy who was recruited to guide them to Aurora said that they were well armed and had a large supply of ammunition, carried on ten mules that they had lately secured. He added that all of the men, but especially Lampião and Sabino, had ample quantities of money. The size of the band seems to have remained stable since Limoeiro, for the cowboy indicated that it was made up of about fifty men. There were some, he said, who had the desire to desert but were afraid to try it out of fear of Lampião and Sabino.[23]

The fleeing outlaws succeeded in reaching Aurora without further serious difficulties by the first days of July. There, on the land of Colonel Arruda, they expected to find protection and rest. Unbeknownst to them, however, their former friend was planning a betrayal. A believable explanation of why Arruda turned on Lampião seems difficult to obtain, and the bandit himself was perplexed by the political chief's actions.[24] One might speculate that the failure in Mossoró had something to do with it, if credence is given to the view that Arruda helped to plan that venture, but building a case to support the speculation might be difficult. Of all the aspects of Lampião's career, the relations between him and the political chieftains are the least susceptible to enlightenment. But, be that as it may, Lampião met unexpected trouble in Aurora.

It is known that Arruda planned his betrayal with Major Moysés of the Ceará police. According to the story as told by the major and his friends, Arruda offered his services to the military. A plan was then agreed upon and put into effect. Lampião and his band were invited to dinner by the cowboy of the ranch where they were camped. Lampião accepted the invitation, not knowing that the house was to be surrounded by fifteen police and one hundred of Arruda's gunmen. Nor did he know that the food was to be poisoned. Lampião, when he and his men arrived at the house on July 7, was wary as usual and permitted some of his men to eat before him. When they detected a strange taste to the food and soon thereafter became sick, Lampião realized

---

[23] *O Ceará*, July 7, 1927.

[24] Interview with the cangaceiro, Rouxinol, in *O Ceará*, July 26, 1928. Rouxinol talked as well about the former close relationship between Arruda and Lampião, as did two other captured cangaceiros, Balão and Cansanção, in *O Ceará*, February 14, 1928.

that he had been double-crossed. The cangaceiros then attacked their hosts, and the troops and gunmen nearby, hearing the shots, opened fire on the house. When the attackers set fire to the surrounding brush in an attempt to seal them in, the bandits realized that they had to make a break. With all who could do so firing fiercely—some of them were beset with vomiting and diarrhea—they succeeded in getting away, aided by the smoke from the burning vegetation. None of the bandits apparently died from the poison, perhaps because it was too weak to kill them or because they had eaten very little of the food.[25]

Major Moysés again fell under heavy criticism. Twice, he had planned attempts to exterminate Lampião and his men under conditions that seemed to favor success, and twice he had failed. Especially critical were the commanders of the troops from the other states, for they had not been informed of the arrangements made with Arruda. They charged that Moysés, after the Macambira failure, dispersed the other forces widely over the area in order to leave Lampião to himself and the Cariri chieftain.[26] Moysés offered the explanation that he had planned to include other forces in the venture but was unable to do so because the attack came two days before it was planned. He gave no adequate explanation of why it was two days early, referring only vaguely to unnamed circumstances that necessitated a change of orders.[27] One of the Paraíba officers reflected the general sentiment in his opinion that Moysés wanted for himself all the glory of eliminating Lampião.[28] Perhaps glory was not all Moysés and Arruda hoped to obtain. The money Lampião normally carried and the precious stones and gold objects he and his men wore were themselves sufficient motivation. Generally, the police did not invite other units to accompany them when they thought they had a good chance of putting the bandits away, and the wealth the outlaws carried was no doubt the reason.

Arruda, incidentally, did not long survive the Aurora attack. The

---

[25] Figueiredo, *Lampeão no Ceará*, pp. 23–47, 100–101. Figueiredo's book does not mention the attempted poisoning. This information comes mainly from the interrogation of Casca Grossa (see Nonato, *Lampião em Mossoró*, p. 300), and police officials who later talked to cangaceiros who were present at the event. Manuel Arruda d'Assis, João Jurubeba, and David Jurubeba, interviews. Also Gueiros, "*Lampeão*," p. 97.

[26] Manuel Arruda d'Assis, interview.

[27] Figueiredo, *Lampeão no Ceará*, p. 67.

[28] Manuel Arruda d'Assis, interview.

next year, he was shot and killed on the Crato-Fortaleza train as it passed through Aurora. His assassins were two members of a rival family that he had long persecuted.[29] In the annals of political violence in the Cariri, Isaías Arruda secured a prominent place for himself. The manner of his death was an appropriate commentary on his way of life.

Shortly after the Aurora battle, Lampião and his band fled into Pernambuco with a large force on their trail.[30] Lampião probably no longer had the kind feelings for Ceará that he had so long entertained. That state promised no longer to afford him freedom from persecution. It seems reasonable to assert that his loss of Ceará as a secure supply point and place of refuge played a significant role in his continuing decline over the succeeding year. In fact, Pernambuco's earlier predictions that he was nearing the point of extinction were to come perilously close to being realized. Lampião's revival from his earlier difficulties there, as evinced by his daring venture into Rio Grande do Norte, was temporary. That thwarted effort, moreover, brought down around him severe, if inept, persecution from the military forces of several states. Seen in retrospect, the attack on Mossoró was a mistake not only because it failed; it might have been an even greater mistake had it succeeded. It was one thing to prey on isolated ranches and small villages; it was entirely another to threaten important towns where people of influence lived.

On a positive note, Lampião's spectacular success in eluding his pursuers in the face of greatly unfavorable odds did nothing to harm his heroic image. He proved conclusively once again that he and his men were more than a match for the police. Of course, that meant little to the men themselves as they fled into Pernambuco, tired, hungry, and still fearing for their lives. There is evidence that the band diminished rapidly in size over the next few months. Reports reached the press regularly of members or, more often, former members of the band being arrested or killed or, frequently, turning themselves in.[31] Being a cangaceiro in such trying times was not like being one when oppor-

[29] *O Ceará*, August 10, 1928.

[30] *O Ceará*, July 13, 1927.

[31] See, for example, *Diário de Pernambuco*, August 2, 18, and 30, September 3, 6, 15, 17, 22, and 24, 1927. *Diário da Noite*, November 24, 1931, gave the names of forty cangaceiros, allegedly associated with Lampião, killed in 1927 and part of 1928. Gueiros, *"Lampeão,"* p. 31, states that Teófanes Torres claimed in 1928 that over six hundred men associated with Lampião at one time or another

tunities for plunder were abundant and life gay and easy and not exceptionally dangerous. A considerable number of Lampião's young recruits may have repented of joining the band and taken the first available opportunity to leave it. The chief may have intentionally reduced the size of his followers, simply because he no longer needed large numbers. Over the next year, he attempted to maintain a fairly nonaggressive, low profile. He could do this much more successfully with a small group than a large one. Lampião, in his fight for survival through the years, demonstrated a remarkable capacity for adapting to changing circumstances. His actions at this time were indicative of that ability. The fact that former members of the band turned themselves in or were arrested or killed may also be, in part, proof of their inability to survive outside the law without his leadership.

By September, two months after the flight from Ceará, reports in Pernambuco stated that Lampião was demoralized and that his followers were reduced to fourteen.[32] Only widely spaced encounters with the police were being announced. In early October, the prefect of Vila Bela opined that Lampião could be considered defeated and his group extinct.[33] News later in the month said that he had only six men with him, although, the report noted, they were well armed and supplied with ammunition. They were, it was added, constantly on the run.[34] His band, rather than being reduced to six men as the report indicated, may have been divided into two groups. The same source reported, interestingly, that Lampião had said that he would give himself up if he could get a guarantee of his life. This may have been true, for Lampião occasionally did have such inclinations. However, even if he made the statement, it is probable that no one in a position of high authority was interested, for the problem posed by Lampião was thought to be almost over.

Through the end of 1927 and into 1928, news of Lampião and his activities was scarce. Sources in Alagoas said that he was there in January with a band numbering between sixteen and twenty but was not posing much of a threat. Although he was requesting money as always,

over the bandit's career had been killed or arrested over a period of several years. While that figure is probably inflated, the number, no doubt, was large.

[32] *Diário de Pernambuco*, September 13, 1927.
[33] *O Ceará*, October 6, 1927.
[34] *Diário de Pernambuco*, October 12, 1927.

he refrained from committing violence. He was compared to an old lion, "tame and humble." The police were after him, nonetheless, and at one point it was claimed that he was surrounded by a force of four hundred Pernambuco and Alagoas troops.[35] No subsequent news of the encirclement appeared. Lampião had gotten away again. By late January, he had returned to Pernambuco and was in the Vila Bela area, much to the apprehension and embarrassment of the police authorities. State Chief of Police Souza Leal was coming to the area to make a personal inspection of the campaign against banditry—probably to ascertain whether Major Teófanes' bragging contained much truth. On his trip to Vila Bela, the state official was scheduled to pass through Custódia, but the police persuaded him to take another route, alleging that the road was practically impassable. The road may have been bad—all roads in the backlands were bad—but the actions of the police were motivated by fear that the high official's party might have a meeting with Lampião. On the same day that Souza Leal would have traveled the road, Lampião and his band, mounted on horses, were riding along it creating havoc. They encountered two mailmen and stole the money from the satchels and burned the correspondence. Later in the day, they sacked two convoys, one of merchandise and the other of grain. The Recife journal that reported the news averred that the chief of police just missed being captured.[36]

In February, the outlaws were in the Pernambuco-Paraíba border area, apparently under heavy police pursuit. A rancher in Paraíba said that when they stopped at his house they had a lot of money, ammunition, and hair—all of the men were wearing long hair and beards.[37] With a police force after them, the bandits had too little time to care adequately for their personal appearances. During the following month, their situation worsened. In Ceará, they continued to suffer from the actions of the police. Residents of the Cariri who saw Lampião and his fourteen men said that they were hungry and almost naked and that their ammunition was running short.[38] A meeting with the police was reported on the ranch of Antônio Piçarra, long known as one of the out-

[35] O Ceará, February 15, 1928, reporting news from Maceió.

[36] Jornal do Recife, February 5, 1928. In the February 7 issue, the informant named by the newspaper denied that he had furnished the story. On February 17, in an editorial, the paper defended the story it had related.

[37] Diário de Pernambuco, February 21, 1928.

[38] O Ceará, March 14, 1928.

laws' coiteiros. The battle, which took place on March 27, was said to be a tremendous one of prolonged firing.[39] Sabino Gomes was killed at about this time, reputedly on Piçarra's ranch, and it seems likely that his end came in one of these battles.[40] Sabino had been with Lampião since the Sousa raid of 1924 and was one of his most trusted companions. A short, stocky, dark-skinned man who talked a lot, he was often described as one of the band's most perverse members. Some of his former comrades, however, said that he was a "fine fellow."[41]

Sabino's death was a loss that must have been felt deeply by Lampião as his situation during the immediate succeeding months continued to be precarious. In May, after several weeks of inaction, he reappeared in the Mata Grande–Agua Branca area of Alagoas with a band variously described as numbering between nine and twelve. Two battles with police took place there, and in one of them two coiteiros, who had brought food to his camp, were killed.[42] He was in Pernambuco near the Alagoas border in June, extorting money from small farmers.[43] In early July, he assaulted two trucks on rural roads in Alagoas, and reports said that he had only six men with him.[44] Coming out in the open again late in the month, after having been hidden for several days, he met Sergeant José Saturnino, his old enemy, at the head of a volante. The bandits, unwilling to pit their small numbers against the larger police force, fled at the first shots.[45]

In view of the extent of his difficulties, Lampião was doing reasonably well in keeping his small band together. They may not have been enjoying life, as in the old days, but they were staying alive and out of the hands of the state. Those things alone are no mean accomplishments for outlaws. There was one thing that Lampião never seemed to lack, no matter how low his luck sank, and that was money. In early

[39] Ibid., March 27, 1928; *Diário de Pernambuco*, March 29, 1928.

[40] Manuel Arruda d'Assis, interview; Carvalho, *Serrote Preto*, pp. 165–167. Ângelo Roque, a cangaceiro, relates in Estácio de Lima, *O mundo estranho dos cangaceiros*, pp. 269–271, that Sabino was killed on Piçarra's ranch. But it is unclear whether Roque was a witness to the event or not, since it seems that he joined the band only later. If he was not there, it may be assumed that he heard the story from Lampião or someone else who was present.

[41] Interview with Balão and Cansanção, *O Ceará*, February 14, 1928.

[42] *Diário de Pernambuco*, May 19, 1928.

[43] *O Ceará*, June 24, 1928.

[44] *Diário de Pernambuco*, July 10, 11, and 18, 1928.

[45] Ibid., August 1, 1928.

August, he and his band of six went into the village of Entre Montes, Alagoas, a small port village on the São Francisco River down from Piranhas. There they bought food supplies and paid with excessive generosity. The residents were very appreciative of the bandit chieftain's exemplary behavior, since early in the previous year his men had burned three houses in a visit to the village.[46] Near Entre Montes, at a house on the river, Lampião saw a large boat pass by with police on board, and he threatened to fire a few shots at it. He was persuaded to desist by the lady of the house, who explained that it carried soldiers from Sergipe, a state that had never taken action against him. The lady's information was correct—among the boat's passengers was the Sergipe state police chief.[47]

Lampião, soon thereafter, decided to abandon the area north of the São Francisco River, at least for the time being. He was accompanied by his brother, Ezekiel, known as Ponta Fina ("Fine Point" or "Sureshot"); his brother-in-law, Virgínio, known as Moderno (meaning "quiet" or "easy going"); Luís Pedro; Mariano; and the bandit known as Mergulhão ("the Diver").[48] Under close pursuit by police, he and his men crossed the São Francisco River to the Bahia side from a point in Pernambuco just to the north of the Alagoas border. The date was August 21, 1928.[49] A woman who saw them shortly before they crossed told a police force which arrived on their trail that they did not give the appearance of constituting much of a danger. Dirty, thin, and exhausted, she said, with dark circles around their eyes, they looked almost dead.[50]

For Bahia, their crossing was a tragedy, but for Lampião and his weary band of five desperados, it was a new beginning.

[46] Ibid., August 24, 1928; Antônio Correia Rosa (a resident of Entre Montes), interview, Piranhas, Alagoas, August 19, 1975.

[47] *Correio de Aracajú*, August 22, 1928.

[48] José Fernandes de Vieira, interview, Salvador, Bahia, November 30, 1973.

[49] The Bahia police, knowing that Lampião was in the area, were watching the river closely and learned almost immediately of his crossing. See various telegrams of the Secretaria de Segurança Pública, Bahia, dated August 22, 23, and 24, Arquivo Publico, Salvador (telegrams of the SSP cited hereinafter as telegrams, Bahia).

[50] Miguel Feitosa, interview. Feitosa was in the force.

7. Queimadas

MANY reasons have been given in explanation of why Lampião and his band of five men crossed the São Francisco River in late August, 1928. There was the distinct possibility that they were simply seeking refuge from police persecution in Pernambuco. Lampião had talked of leaving the Alagoas-Pernambuco area when he was in Entre Montes in the early part of August, affirming that he was tired of killing and wanted peace.[1] Since he had never operated as a bandit in Bahia and Sergipe, the states on the southern banks of the river, he could reasonably expect to find there a lesser degree of police persecution. He already was somewhat acquainted with northeastern Bahia, having traveled there as a youth with his father in the transportation business.[2] He knew that the area offered vast expanses and sparse population. Obviously, it would be a good place to lose his pursuers.

The Bahia police suspected also that Lampião wanted to unite with a band of Bahia cangaceiros led by Antônio de Engracia. That may have been true, for Engracia soon joined Lampião's group. A former member of Lampião's band, Quindú, gave another reason when he was arrested in Bahia in early September. He told police that the outlaw leader had come to the state on the invitation of Horácio de Matos, the powerful chieftain who dominated the Lavras Diamantina region of central Bahia. Quindú had heard Luís Pedro, he claimed, say that Lampião had received such an invitation.[3] Horácio did maintain large numbers of gunmen, or jagunços, but Lampião's failure to seek out the area—even though he had ample opportunity—would seem to

[1] Diário de Notícias, October 3, 1928.
[2] João Ferreira, interview.
[3] A Tarde, September 3, 1928; O Ceará, September 26, 1928.

place in doubt Quindú's claims.[4] Moreover, there is little reason to believe that Matos needed Lampião; he had sufficient manpower of his own.

There were still others who asserted that Lampião had been invited to Bahia by Colonel Petronilo Reis of Santo Antônio da Glória County.[5] It is true that Glória was the county to which Lampião crossed over from Pernambuco, and it is also true that he met Petro, as the colonel was called. When Lampião came into Glória, he stopped first at Salgado Ranch. There he presented himself as Sergeant Manuel Neto of the Pernambuco police, a deception which he could manage, since the volantes dressed like cangaceiros. Resting and conversing with his host for a while, he asked if there were any criminals about. The rancher assured him that there were none but soon learned differently. Lampião, before leaving, revealed his identity and asked for a guide. He told the rancher that he had come to Bahia on the invitation of a friend but did not mention his name.[6] From Salgado, Lampião went to the settlement of Várzea da Ema, one of Petro's many properties. Petro was there at the time and greeted the band when it arrived. Lampião again introduced himself as a Pernambuco sergeant, but later, taking Petro aside, revealed the truth. Just what the two talked about is disputed, but Petro, in his story, limited himself to saying that he agreed to furnish horses and a guide for Lampião, who wanted to go to Bonfim.[7]

Other versions of the story include the strong suspicion that Petro agreed to furnish a good many other things as well; in essence, it is said that he set himself up as the bandits' main source of supplies and protection in the area. Whether or not there is any truth in this charge would be difficult, if not impossible, to determine, for political chieftains did not speak candidly of their relations with Lampião. That

[4] On Horácio de Matos, see: Walfrido Moraes, *Jagunços e heróis*; Américo Chagas, *O chefe Horácio de Matos*; Eul Soo Pang, "The Politics of Coronelismo in Brazil: The Case of Bahia, 1889–1930" (Ph.D. diss., University of California, Berkeley, 1970).

[5] José Fernandes de Vieira, interview; Severiano Ramos (Jeremoabo, Bahia, August 17, 1975), interview.

[6] Letter, dated September 24, 1928, from Adelino Ferreira, of Santo Antônio da Glória, published in *Diário de Notícias*, December 28, 1928.

[7] Interview with Petronilo Reis, published in *A Tarde*, September 8, 1928.

Lampião's first main base in Bahia was Petro's properties is known. How warmly, if at all, Petro welcomed him is not generally known.[8]

If the truth were known, it quite probably would reveal that Lampião came to Bahia seeking freedom from the police and that the friend who had invited him was his fellow cangaceiro, Antônio de Engracia. That Lampião was seeking a measure of peace is clear from his conduct during the first few months in Bahia. However, the police from Pernambuco were not inclined to give Lampião the rest he was seeking. Manuel Neto and his Nazareno volante picked up the bandits' trail on the Bahia side of the river a few hours after they crossed and tracked them to Petro's main ranch. Petro was not there, being at Várzea da Ema, but his head cowboy described what happened.[9] He was at the creek, he related, when one of his family summoned him to the house, saying that a large group of bandits had taken it over. He went there and found that it was Manuel Neto and his volante, indistinguishable in both dress and conduct from cangaceiros. They demanded that he guide them to Lampião's location and assaulted him when he denied any knowledge of the matter. After taking a beating, the cowboy agreed to lead them to Bonfim, where Lampião had gone. When they arrived there on August 26, a brief exchange of gunfire ensued before the bandits fled into the bush. Incidents similar to the beating given Petro's cowboy—he displayed his wounds to the press in Salvador a few days later—combined with Lampião's inaction led Bahia to ask Pernambuco to withdraw its volantes.[10] The Pernambuco police have enjoyed pointing out that it was not long before Bahia sent urgent appeals for them to come back.

The Bahia police were not prepared in this early period to enter a major contest with Lampião. Banditry had not been as widespread a problem in that state as it had been to the north of the river, and, consequently, the police lacked the numbers and experience, as well as the desire, to give him close chase. They did occasionally pursue him, probably from a safe distance, but a backlander from Uauá told the press in September that while the police might keep Lampião on the run,

[8] The strongest charges against Petro are found in Prata, *Lampeão*, pp. 49–50. The cangaceiro Volta-Sêca also named him as one of the band's coiteiros. José Izidro, interview, Salvador, Bahia, November 24, 1973.

[9] Interviewed in *A Tarde*, September 8, 1928.

[10] João Jurubeba, Miguel Feitosa, Olympo Campos, interviews. Gueiros, "*Lampeão*," p. 101.

they would not catch him. Lampião and his small band, he said, were ranging widely over the area. They would ask for directions to one location and head that way, but then, finding a rocky area to hide their tracks, would veer off toward another place, leaving the authorities confused.[11]

That Lampião was not causing much trouble may explain better than anything else the state's slow start in meeting the threat. The bandit was saying that he had come to Bahia only to rest and had no intentions of hurting anyone.[12] Moreover, he was building the reputation of being a kind and generous man. In September in Barro Vermelho and Patamuté, he gave money to the poor and passed out drinks to the thirsty. He traveled by car between the two towns, generously paying the chauffeur and his assistant.[13] On ranches and in villages, he attended wedding parties, on occasion purchasing a pretty dress for the bride or furnishing the drinks. In Canché, he drank with the small contingent of soldiers that manned the police station there and exchanged a rifle with one of them.[14] Lampião was on good behavior. He was also doing a good job at public relations. The visits of the legendary bandit thrilled the backlanders. No doubt, too, he and his men were enjoying themselves. At the same time, the knowledge of the region that Lampião was gaining and the contacts and friends that he was making would serve him well in the future. Lampião's inactivity did not indicate that he had decided to go straight, but that he was preparing himself for the time when he would resume his operations.

After September, little was heard of Lampião until near the end of the year. There was speculation that he might have gone on to Goiás or Mato Grosso.[15] Apparently, however, he was resting in Santo Antônio da Glória on one of Petro's ranches.[16] He began to make public appearances again only in December. Early in the morning on Sunday the sixteenth, he and his men came on foot into the town of Pombal, located approximately 110 miles to the south of the point where the band had crossed the São Francisco in August. His coming was not un-

[11] João Borges de Sá, interviewed in A Tarde, September 27, 1928.
[12] Ibid.
[13] A Tarde, September 20, 1928.
[14] Miguel Feitosa, Severiano Ramos, interviews. Gueiros, "Lampeão," pp. 104–107.
[15] A Tarde, December 20, 1928.
[16] Prata, Lampeão, p. 49.

expected, since, during the preceding days, he had been seen in other places in the area. His travels were relatively open, as if he expected little or no trouble from police. Arriving in Pombal at six o'clock in the morning, Lampião went directly to the house of the prefect, who received him at the door. Lampião assured the official that he came in peace and asked him to tell the four soldiers in the police station not to interfere. A man was sent to so inform the soldiers, and the cangaceiros were invited into the house to eat. After a hearty meal, Lampião went to the police station and surrounded it. He called on the corporal in charge to come out, telling him that he only wanted him to accompany the band to a nearby town. Before leaving Pombal some two hours later, Lampião took time to acquaint himself with the townspeople who, it was said, treated him as if they were his vassals. The bandit, wishing to leave the people a remembrance of his visit, asked if there was a photographer in the town. As it turned out, the tailor had a camera. When it was secured, Lampião and his eight men lined up on the town square for a picture. Soon thereafter, with the corporal in attendance, the cangaceiros rode out of town in a borrowed automobile.[17]

Later in that same week, Lampião had his first meeting with Colonel João Sá of Jeremoabo.[18] The chance meeting was, for the outlaw chieftain, a fortuitous circumstance. Sá, as northeastern Bahia's most important politician, was a man with whom he needed to reach an understanding. The encounter between the two took place as Sá, a member of the state legislature, was traveling to Salvador. Stopping at Sítio do Quinto to spend the night, he and his companions were surrounded by the bandits, who were there resting. Once their identities were established, Lampião invited Sá and his party to drink with him. In the ensuing conversation, he gave the assurance once again that he bore no ill will toward Bahia, saying that he had come there only to rest. As long as he had money for his expenses, he said, he would inconvenience no one, but once his money ran out he would be compelled to request aid from citizens of means. The two men talked for two hours or more and, since a part of their conversation was away from the ears of others,

---

[17] The account of Lampião's visit to Pombal is based on an interview with Pedro Nolasco dos Santos of Pombal, in *A Tarde*, December 21, 1928.

[18] Sá gave his version of the meeting in *A Tarde*, December 20, 1928. A more complete story was given by one of his traveling companions, José da Costa Dorca, in *O Ceará*, January 11, 1929.

it presumably included matters they preferred to keep confidential. It was the beginning of a relationship between the two men that was to be long lasting and mutually satisfactory. Sá apparently became one of Lampião's most trustworthy protectors in Bahia; in return, Lampião always respected Sá's twenty or more ranches. The political chieftain's friends claim that he was never a willing coiteiro, that he did what he did only to protect his properties.[19] That may have been true, but Lampião was at least willing to make their relationship a more mutually helpful one. On parting in Sítio do Quinto, the bandit was overheard offering his services to the wealthy politician and rancher. Lampião told Sá that if he had any enemies all he need do was name them and they would be dealt with.[20] Lampião apparently saw here the opportunity to make a worthwhile friend.

Lampião was soon to need friends. The meeting with Colonel Sá coincidentally came just before the bandit's period of relative peace in Bahia began to come to an end. Near the end of that same week, as a matter of fact, Lampião had his first serious encounter with the Bahia volante of Captain Hercílio Rocha, who for some months had been charged with commanding the troops against him. The Bahia police received an unhappy introduction to Lampião's tactics. The force learned that he was on a ranch near Massacará and trailed him to it. Arriving there, they surrounded the house in which he and his men supposedly were holed up. When they opened fire on it, they were answered with gunfire from inside the house, but they were also fired on from the rear. Knowing the police were after him, Lampião, as he so often did, had sent out some of his men to attack from behind. The police force fled in disarray, but not before two of them were killed.[21]

About two weeks later, on January 7, the police met Lampião again. This time they followed him to the village of Abóboras in an isolated region well to the north of the town of Bonfim. It was the day of the local market, and the bandits were in the village enjoying themselves. When the police arrived and surrounded the town, Lampião and four of his band were on the porch of a house dancing with the local girls while the four remaining bandits stood guard. Lampião and

[19] Felipe Borges de Castro, interview, Salvador, Bahia, November 25, 26, 27, 1973; José Fernandes de Vieira, interview.
[20] Dorca in *O Ceará*, January 11, 1929.
[21] *A Tarde*, December 31, 1928.

his men on the porch disappeared, according to the police, when some women shouted to them that the volante had arrived. The four bandits on guard put up effective resistance to cover the retreat of their comrades and then tried to extricate themselves. After a heavy exchange of shots, they fled, carrying one of their number who left a pool of blood behind. The wounded bandit, Mergulhão, died shortly thereafter. The police found his grave and dug up his body to verify his identity. He was the first of Lampião's band to be killed in Bahia. Two of the police force—they numbered eight, one less than the bandits—were killed and two more were wounded. The police reported that the resistance to their attack was directed by a fair-haired cangaceiro who displayed rare courage under fire.[22] That young man was Christino Gomes da Silva, soon to be better known as Corisco or the Diabo Louro ("Blond Devil"). Of all those who followed Lampião, Corisco stood out for both his courage and his cruelty.

Lampião went into hiding for several weeks following the battle at Abóboras. He now had killed four Bahia soldiers, and he realized, no doubt, that his honeymoon with that state was over. After the battle, he was reported as fleeing toward Santo Antônio da Glória. When the police in late February learned of his whereabouts again, he was extorting money near the border with Sergipe, and a few days later he entered the town of Carira in that neighboring state.[23]

Lampião's visit to the Sergipe town was, for the bandits, pleasant and not extraordinary. For the town's residents, it was, of course, a noteworthy occasion. They learned that the celebrated cangaceiro was near when, shortly before five o'clock in the afternoon, the police chief received a note from him requesting permission to enter the town. No reply was sent, for confusion reigned in the town. A few minutes later, Lampião and his band of seven came riding in on mules. There had been six soldiers in the town, in addition to the police chief, but four of those had fled in terror by the time the outlaws arrived. Lampião directed himself to the home of the police chief, and after introductions were made, he asked him to prepare supper for the band. While that

[22] A *Tarde*, January 9, 15, and 17, 1929; Bahia, Secretaria da Polícia e Segurança Pública, *Relatório de 1929*, p. 84. See also Felipe de Castro, *Derrocada do cangaço no nordeste*, pp. 27–29.
[23] A *Tarde*, March 4, 1929.

was being done, the cangaceiros walked around the small town, making purchases and drinking beer and cachaça. When Lampião learned that two soldiers had remained in the police station, he sent them beer and cigars and, somewhat later, paid them a visit. He praised them for not having fled, saying they were a credit to their profession, and assured them that he had no desire to fight against the Sergipe police. He added that he had come to the state only to become acquainted with it and intended to offend no one.

The bandits remained in the town for several hours, drinking, singing, and visiting. Few of the town's citizens left in fear, and, wherever the bandits went, they were accompanied by a crowd of people. Lampião, in particular, was the object of attention and admiration. Especially striking, it was said, was his cartridge belt. Some two hands in width, it contained four rows of cartridges and two more of gold and silver buttons. As to Lampião himself, he was in a happy mood, and it was noted that he spoke well though rather caustically. He talked of his past, explaining that he became a cangaceiro only because the police killed his father. Speaking of the Sergipe police, he said that if they were like the forces of other states he had little to fear from them. Usually they did not arrive, he said, until three days after he had left. Lampião also made some inquiries about neighboring towns, particularly as to how many soldiers they might have in them. The bandits offended no one, although Lampião did request cash contributions from the merchants. At one o'clock in the morning, after a futile search for an accordion to make music for dancing, the band mounted their mules and left town. It was well for all concerned that they did, for two hours later—not three days, as Lampião had bragged—a force of fifty soldiers from Bahia surrounded Carira, thinking the cangaceiros were still there.[24]

Over a period of several months following the visit to Carira, Lampião and his band ranged over a broad area of Bahia, with an occasional visit to Sergipe. The bandit's actions, especially in Bahia, were

[24] Alexandre Barreto, a resident of Carira, gave a full story of the bandits' visit in *O Paulistano* (São Paulo, later Frei Paulo, Sergipe), March 3, 1929. A briefer account was contained in a report from County Chief of Police Dionysio dos Santos to the State Chief of Police (Arquivo Público, Aracajú, Sergipe, Packet SP1 37).

now falling back into the normal pattern—there was no longer any pretense that he was in Bahia just to rest. It was now the main base of his operations. In a typical action, in mid-April he assaulted the small village of Pedra Branca, located on the São Francisco River in Juàzeiro County in northern Bahia. There, the band sacked a ranch and the village's businesses, taking money and jewelry.[25] The robbery of jewels and objects of gold and silver helps to explain how the bandits were able to to adorn themselves so elaborately. One might think that in the often barren and impoverished Bahia backlands, such indications of wealth would have been rare. Of course, great wealth was rare, but, among the small class of substantial landowners and merchants, a large part of the family's patrimony consisted of precious stones or objects of gold and silver. The instability of the paper currency and the scarcity and unreliability of banks made such objects the safest form of property of enduring value.

Only a few days after the Pedra Branca raid, Lampião made another visit to Sergipe and appeared in several widely separated counties. He raided Canindé, on the São Francisco River, and, in Poço Redondo, he and his men attended mass.[26] On a ranch, Lampião, in conversation with the owner and some of his friends, expressed a desire to visit Aracajú, the state's capital on the coast. He became quite angry, it was said, when one of the ranchers told him that such a visit would be impossible.[27] Just out of Pinhão, where they extorted money, the cangaceiros were overtaken by a Bahia volante and a twenty-minute battle took place.[28]

Battles between the bandits and the police continued to occur during the months immediately following, although police actions remained weak and generally ineffective. When damage was done, the police bore the brunt of it. This was particularly true in an encounter with the bandits in July. On that occasion, a volante of nine soldiers, commanded by a corporal, had been sent out from Bonfim to search for criminals who, having escaped from jail, were expected to try to

[25] *A Tarde*, April 15, 1929.
[26] Francisco Rodrigues, interview, Piranhas, Alagoas, August 19, 1975; *Correio de Aracajú*, April 22, 1929.
[27] *O Paulistano*, April 28, 1929.
[28] *Correio de Aracajú*, April 22 and 23, 1929.

join the bandits. Four of the soldiers and the corporal were resting in
the village of Brejões on July 4 when they were surprised by Lampião.
Not having time to put up a fight, the five were captured and killed.
Lampião himself shot the corporal at close range through the ear.[29]

The surprise attack at Brejões pointed to a major police difficulty.
They seldom knew where the bandits were for any substantial period
of time. The bandits, traveling widely over Bahia and Sergipe on horseback, were able to cover fifty to sixty miles a day. Compounding the
problem, people in the country and villages were afraid to inform on
Lampião, usually for fear of retaliation, and when they did appear to
cooperate they often gave erroneous information. Moreover, rumors of
sightings of Lampião's band were numerous, for it generally was assumed that any small unidentified band was his. It is no wonder that
the police often felt frustrated. On June 14, the commander of the volante in Uauá wired the state police chief that during the past two days
he had received widely divergent information on Lampião's whereabouts. One official source reported, he said, that the bandit was on a
mountain near Juàzeiro and was unable to travel, having been stricken
with malaria. The police chief urged the volante to attack with haste.
A second officer told the chief that Lampião had been seen in Sergipe,
while a third one informed him that Juàzeiro was in terror, momentarily expecting an attack from the bandits. A fourth officer, guarding a
highway crew, said that the third officer's report was nonsense.[30] The
fact that Lampião might appear almost anywhere at some unexpected
moment caused the police to disperse their limited numbers widely.
In June, for example, Captain Rocha reported that the ninety soldiers
under his command—the entire force expected to pursue the bandits
through the countryside—were divided into four volantes.[31]

The officer guarding the highway crew had a difficult task on his
hands. Lampião was proving himself to be inimical to progress as represented by improved transportation facilities. The bandit knew that
improved motor roads and other modern means of communication destroyed the isolation on which his continued existence largely depended,
and, specifically, that they facilitated the movement of troops. In Au-

[29] A Tarde, July 9, 1929.
[30] This telegram is in special packet on Lampião, Arquivo Público, Bahia.
[31] A Tarde, June 26, 1929.

gust, the officer supervising the construction of a road from Juàzeiro to Santo Antônio da Glória—a route which passed through the northern reaches of the Raso da Catarina, a barren region often used by the bandits for refuge—received several messages from Lampião. In one, the cangaceiro chief counseled the officer to halt construction, stating frankly that the road would make his operations difficult. If it did not stop, he threatened, he would tear off the officer's head and cut off the feet of the workers. When that message was received, construction was suspended temporarily, for the workers fled in terror.[32]

Lampião also had little use for railroads, though his violence against them, strangely enough, seems to have been limited to burning train stations. There is no evidence that he ever tried to wreck or rob a train. In early July, he burned the station and cut the telegraph wires in Itumirim, situated to the north of Bonfim on the Salvador-Juàzeiro route, and robbed the stationmaster. Humanely, however, he permitted him to remove his personal possessions from the building before setting the fire. In reaction to the burning, the state police chief ordered contingents of from ten to thirty soldiers to be sent to guard each of the stations in the area frequented by the bandits.[33]

While in Itumirim, Lampião visited the local grammar school. The schoolmarm was not charmed by him, as were so many less sophisticated women in the backlands. She was offended by the cangaceiro chief, not only because he invaded her school and told her it would be a good place to hold a dance, but also by his appearance. Quite unlike the photographs she had seen of him in the newspapers, she said, he was ugly, had long matted hair, and was very dirty. She lamented that the circumstances of the moment had forced her to offer him her hand. The teacher was in Salvador when she talked about his visit to the press. The shock of it all had led her to take a leave of absence from her post.[34]

Before the end of 1929, there were alarming reports that Lampião's band was growing in number. The police were told in late September

---

[32] The officer, Colonel Ademiro Gomes dos Santos, was interviewed in *A Tarde*, August 27, 1929, and *Diário de Notícias*, September 17, 1929.

[33] *A Tarde*, July 9, 1929. A report, dated July 9, 1929, from Itumirim to Governor Vital Batista Soares, on the incident is found in the special packet on Lampião, Arquivo Público, Bahia.

[34] *A Tarde*, August 8, 1929.

that it had reached eighteen.[35] Some of Lampião's former companions in Pernambuco were crossing the river to join him, and he was also securing new recruits in Bahia. Among the latter were Antônio de Engracia and his brothers, already known as bandits in the Juàzeiro area. Over the months some confusion resulted from a fluctuation in the band's number, until it became clear that they did not always stay together. As he had done in Pernambuco, Lampião was dividing his following into separate groups at times, Corisco and Engracia acting as subchieftains when necessary.[36]

Lampião's group, of course, attracted the most attention. On September 17, he invaded Riacho Seco in Curaçá County, a small port town on the São Francisco River down from Juàzeiro. There, he robbed various stores, and, in one of them, he called the crowd together and distributed the merchant's wares to them.[37] If this was a generous act—the question is debatable—Lampião soon thereafter exhibited the other side of his personality. In October he made good on his threats along the Juàzeiro–Santo Antônio da Glória road, on which construction had resumed. Near Carro Quebrado ("Broken Cart"), he surprised a crew of road workers and killed all nine of them.[38]

Late in the next month, Lampião and his band returned to Sergipe. On this trip, they made one of the better-known public appearances of their career. It was in the county seat of Capela, located less than thirty miles from the state capital. Around seven o'clock in the evening of November 25, the prefect received word that Lampião and his band were near the town and wished to talk with him. They had not been able to come all the way in, the messenger explained, because one of the cars in which they were riding had a flat tire. Passing through the nearby town of Dores earlier, Lampião had obtained the services of four automobiles for the trip to Capela. Capela's prefect was not disposed toward refusing the celebrated brigand's request because, two days earlier, most of the soldiers stationed there had been sent further inland to join the search for the bandits. The prefect forbade the four

[35] Auto de perguntas, dated September 28, 1929, Alcino da Silva Duarte, in special packet on Lampião, Arquivo Público, Bahia.

[36] A Tarde, October 9, 1929.

[37] O Ceará, September 22, 1929. For a discussion of Lampião as a Robin Hood–type bandit, see chapter 11 herein.

[38] A Tarde, October 21, 1929; O Ceará, November 5, 1929; Ângelo Roque in Lima, O mundo estranho, pp. 193–94.

remaining soldiers to appear in public and then went to await his guests. An hour later, the eleven bandits entered, and Lampião explained that they would do no harm.

Lampião, moving quickly to take control of communications to the outside, sent one of his men to guard the town's telephone and another its telegraph station. The telegraph agent was attending the moving-picture show, and when the cangaceiros went there to get him they created something of a stir. With the appearance of Lampião in the theater, it was said, the operator broke the film and the orchestra played some discordant notes. Some of the patrons attempted to leave, but Moderno told them to keep their seats unless they wanted to get shot. Lampião also dispatched four of his men to wait for the train, which was soon expected.

Those immediate necessities cared for, Lampião and his men directed themselves to other matters. As he had in nearby Dores, Lampião requested a contribution from the town's citizens, in this case the considerable sum of 20:000$000. The prefect explained that, just having passed through three years of drought, the town would have difficulty raising that amount. Lampião obligingly reduced the figure to 6:000$000 because, as he said, he too knew what droughts were, having suffered through one for the past fourteen years. The figure agreed upon, the police chief made the rounds to collect the money from the leading citizens. He had no trouble making the quota; as one observer said, it was known that Lampião was "nobody to fool around with." When the train arrived, the bandits were waiting. A soldier descended and was questioned by them. Upon learning that he was in the Sergipe force, they told him that he was lucky. Had he been a Bahia soldier, they said, they would have killed him.

Lampião and his men, having attended to the main business matters, then settled down to several hours of pleasure. They went to stores and purchased various items, including jewelry. Lampião bought clothing and a pistol, and, in gratitude for his business, the merchant presented him with a copy of Ellen G. White's *Vida de Jesus*. Everywhere the bandits went, they were accompanied by a throng of admirers, who were thrilled to be in the presence of the famous cangaceiros and, even more so, to hear the stories they told of their feats. The priest visited the band, and, when two of the men requested his blessing, he asked them to give up the evil life and regenerate themselves. In reply, they only smiled. Around eleven o'clock, Lampião tried to telephone the state chief of police, but, since the intermediate operators had quit for the night, he could not get through. Nonetheless, he gave the Capela operator a handsome tip for his efforts. The bandits also ate in the hotel—the telegraph operator tasted the food before they ate—and drank, and rode around in automobiles, and visited the "district," without which no backlands town would be complete. The men took turns standing guard while others of their number enjoyed the ladies' attentions. It was 3:00 A.M. before Lampião called the band together to depart. They left, headed toward Dores, in the same automobiles in which they came. At an intermediate point, however, they sent the cars on home and transferred to horses.

Lampião left a very favorable impression in Capela. The local correspondent of a newspaper in the capital wrote that although the bandit was uncultured he left no doubt of his shrewdness and intelligence. Moreover, he was a courteous and attentive listener, as well as a good conversationalist. For both Capela and the bandits, the visit was an unqualified success.[39]

Lampião's visit to a town in Bahia slightly less than one month later was not to be so fondly remembered. His actions there, a macabre mixture of murder and pleasure, also form one of the most talked about episodes in his career. Queimadas is a small town on the Salvador-Juàzeiro railroad about fifty-five miles southeast of Bonfim. Lying on the eastern bank of the Itapicurú River, the town begins at the railroad station on the margin of the river and stretches up the hill for a few blocks. When bathed by the afternoon sun from the west, its white and pastel-colored buildings and red tile roofs light up the rather drab countryside of low hills and scrub vegetation. The sun had completed more than half of the afternoon portion of its arc on Sunday, December 22, 1929, when some of the townspeople saw a group of men crossing the narrow river in a small boat.[40] Although the men in the boat

[39] The story of Lampião's visit to Capela is told in several works, among them, Prata, *Lampeão*, pp. 126–134, and Goís, *Lampião*, pp. 64–68. The basic narrative I have followed comes from a long article by a Capela correspondent in *Correio de Aracajú*, November 29, 1929. The quotation is also from that source. *A Tarde*, November 30, 1929, carried a briefer account.

[40] The following account of the Queimadas incident is based in the main on two sources: a report of an investigation of the events by Lieutenant Geminiano José dos Santos, dated December 5, 1929, in special packet on Lampião, Arquivo

appeared to be dressed like cangaceiros, the people believed them to be a Pernambuco police force. By the time Queimadas' citizens learned they were mistaken, Lampião and his band were taking possession of the town.

The bandit chief dispatched two of his men to seize the railroad station and its telegraph facilities while he and five others went up the hill to the police station. The town's eight soldiers were taken by complete surprise. Some were playing cards, while their commander, Sergeant Evaristo Carlos da Costa, was resting in a hammock, dressed in pajamas.[41] The cangaceiros were in the station before its occupants knew what was happening. They easily overpowered the soldiers and locked them in the jail. The jail's six prisoners were set free; two of them, unbeknownst to the assaulters, were soldiers who were being disciplined. The liberated soldiers left quickly and returned the following day. The cangaceiros demanded the arms and ammunition, which the sergeant had stored away under lock and key in reaction to an earlier shooting of a defenseless man by one of the soldiers. In answer to the sergeant's plea that he could not comply with the request, since he was responsible for the weapons and ammunition, Lampião settled the matter by declaring himself to be both the governor and chief of police. By that time, additional cangaceiros had entered the town, bringing the total to eighteen.

As elsewhere, Lampião levied a tribute on Queimadas' leading citizens. Having seized the district judge, Lampião forced him to prepare a list of probable contributors, and by each name was placed the sum demanded. The task of collecting the money was entrusted to three men who, when the bandits entered the town, had been going house to house raising money for a Christmas party. Working until six o'clock, the fund raisers turned over to Lampião a little more than 23:000$000. Visiting the general store and warehouse of one of the men, Umbelino Santana, Lampião instructed him to furnish the cangaceiros with whatever they wanted, saying that he should keep a list of the costs. That was generous, Umbelino supposed, since his portion of the tribute had

---

Público, Bahia; my interviews with Umbelino Santanna (Queimadas, Bahia, July 12, 1974), a participant in the events, and, of lesser importance, Hermenigildo Barbosa (Queimadas, Bahia, July 12, 1974). *A Tarde*, December 24, 1929, and January 2, 1930, carried lengthy reports.

[41] Felipe Borges de Castro, interview.

been 1:000$000. The store owner invited Lampião to drink with him and he accepted, requesting a mixture of vermouth and a favorite Brazilian soft drink. Lampião even drank first, leaving his host feeling proud that the famed desperado had trusted him. Before leaving the store, Lampião took some medicines, saying that one of his men was sick. When the bandits came to shop, the young merchant noted that socks, soap, and perfume were among the most requested items.

Just before sunset, Lampião and two of his men returned to the police station. Their actions there are what is most remembered about their visit to Queimadas. Taking a soldier out of his jail cell, the bandits escorted him to the door of the station and shot him twice in the head. They then returned for another and repeated the scene. This continued until the seven soldiers were all lying dead in a bloody heap. The last one was told to raise his head, that he was going to die. In reply, he called the bandits cowards. They not only shot him but, as he was dying, also stabbed him. One of the executioners wanted to kill the jailer as well, but Lampião refused his request, saying that he was a civilian and not a *macaco*, a word meaning monkey which the cangaceiros derisively applied to soldiers. Sergeant Evaristo, who was under guard in the judge's house, escaped the fate of his men. He seems to have been liked by the people in Queimadas, and several of them earlier had requested that his life be spared when Lampião spoke of killing the soldiers. The sergeant was a protestant—he refused Lampião's invitation to drink—and one woman of his persuasion seems to have been especially instrumental in saving him. In gratitude, the lady gave Lampião her wrist watch. Lampião had explained to the sergeant why he was going to kill the soldiers. He had lost a man at Abóboras, he said, and if he killed every soldier in the Bahia military force, the account would still not be settled. It was a clear, if chilling, statement of Lampião's implacable hatred for the state police forces that pursued him and an equally clear indication of his intention to kill them, at least when the risks to him and his men were minimal.

Leaving the police station, the bandits joined their comrades at the hotel for supper. Afterwards, they began to prepare for an evening of entertainment. Lampião had told several people during the afternoon that there would be a dance that night. He had invited Evaristo, but the sergeant had told him that he did not dance. To ensure a successful event, Lampião instructed one of the young women to see that a sufficient number of girls attended, with preference, he added, for those from the more common classes. The young lady understood this to mean that his men would not feel comfortable with the daughters of the town's leading citizens.

The dance was held, half of the men participating while the others stood guard, and on Lampião's request, a movie was shown in conjunction with it. The girls were treated with respect because Lampião threatened to castigate any men who might get out of hand. None apparently did, although when one of the young ladies thereafter turned up pregnant there was considerable wonder in the community as to whom the father might be. At any rate, the evening was a success for the bandits—some of them also visited the whorehouses down near the river—and it was near three o'clock in the morning before Lampião called his band together to depart. Before leaving, he left a message on the wall of the building where the dance was held. Addressed to the governor and written in crude grammar and spelling, it was taunting in tone. He told the governor that he had come into Queimadas to enjoy himself, and, in spite of the state's persecution, he was getting fat and thinking about getting married. He signed it: "Your superior, Capt. Virgulino Ferreira Lampião."[42]

The band left Queimadas at four o'clock. Lampião departed on a borrowed mule but assured its owner that it would be returned. True to his reputation as a man of his word, the bandit sent the mule back home in a few days.[43] Two hours after leaving the town, the band stopped at a ranch to sleep and rest. By the time word of their stopping reached Queimadas, forty soldiers under the command of a lieutenant had arrived on the train from Bonfim. When the force learned that the cangaceiros were camped not far away, a sergeant who knew the country well urged the lieutenant to march after them. The officer, however, followed his original plan of leaving some soldiers in Queimadas and sending the remainder on to another point on the tracks.[44] The lieutenant's action was typical of what many commanders did in the campaign against banditry, and in Queimadas it was taken to be cowardice.

The cangaceiros, after having rested from the festivities, headed eastward. Arriving in the small town of Mirandela, about sixty miles

[42] A transcription of the message is found in Lieutenant Geminiano's report.
[43] Umbelino Santanna, interview.
[44] Ibid.

from Queimadas, Lampião sent a message to the commander of its small contingent of soldiers requesting permission to come in to drink. The sergeant, who had six soldiers in his detachment, replied that if the bandits tried to come into the town they would be greeted with bullets. The bandits then launched a two-hour attack on the community, but, with civilians aiding the soldiers, they were held off. One cangaceiro was wounded; two civilians among the defenders died. It was Christmas morning.[45]

After leaving Mirandela, the bandits passed within a few miles of the county seat of Tucano. Lampião sent a letter to the town demanding 6:000$000 and threatening to sack the town if he was turned down. There was a detachment of ten soldiers in the town, and its commander refused to let the money be sent. Acting on his own, he sent word to Lampião that if he wanted the money he would have to come into town to collect it in person. Lampião did not come, for he almost never faced that many soldiers needlessly, but he did send a reply. The bandit chieftain's letter, according to a report, was replete with gross obscenities.[46]

By the closing of 1929, Lampião had been in Bahia for almost a year and a half. It seemed obvious that his crossing of the São Francisco River had signaled a permanent move. He now gave every indication of being well established in his new territory. He possessed an effective network of suppliers, protectors, and informers, and his efforts at extortion were successful enough that he never lacked money. His band, moreover, was growing, a fact which in itself was an indication of his success. He had learned the lay of the land and seemed to be able to disappear almost at will for weeks at a time from the public view. He was acquainted with Sergipe, where he had encountered but scant resistance from the police. In Bahia, to say the least, the police appeared to be manageable. Lampião had made a new beginning.

[45] *A Tarde*, January 3 and 8, 1930.
[46] *A Tarde*, January 3, 1930.

8. Maria Bonita

AFTER Lampião's appearances in Mirandela and Tucano in late December, 1929, there was no public word of the bandit's whereabouts for three months. The Bahia police were mystified, fearing some disagreeable surprise.[1] For the Salvador newspaper readers who avidly followed the bandit's career there was a break in late January when the police announced that the head of a cangaceiro had arrived in the capital. It was from the body of Gavião ("Hawk"), who had been killed by an intrepid backlander shortly after the Queimadas incident. The cowboy, who accompanied a police physician to Salvador with the trophy, explained that he had been forced to accompany Lampião's band as a guide, and at one point he and Gavião, falling back some distance from the others, had gotten into an argument. When Gavião started threatening him, the cowboy grabbed the bandit's knife and killed him. The police, hearing of the occurrence, had sent the physician to exhume the body and bring back the well-decayed head.[2] In those days, the study of the alleged relationship between criminality and physical type was in vogue in Brazil, especially in Salvador, where the Nina Rodrigues Institute of Legal Medicine was located. After being examined, measured, and classified, the skull later was put on display in the institute. It sat there as a grim forerunner of several others that were to join it in later years.

The Bahia volantes, meanwhile, were in the *caatinga* searching for the bandits. The troops commanded by Lieutenant Odonel Silva were in the area of Juàzeiro when they received word on March 23 that

[1] SSP to Captain P. Neves, February 25, 1930, telegrams, Bahia.

[2] A *Tarde*, January 25, 1930. Oliveira, *Lampião*, p. 167, asserts that one of the cangaceiros killed Gavião and that the guide took credit for it, but she gives no indication of her source.

Lampião, with a band of fourteen, had been sighted not far away. For the next two days, the bandits and the police seemed to be playing hide-and-seek. On the twenty-third, the force found their trail but lost it at nightfall when the bandits went into the *caatinga*. After resting for the night, the soldiers resumed their search on the twenty-fourth. A few hours later, they arrived at a ranch where Lampião had passed around sunrise, and, forcing their march, set out after him. At another ranch, they were told that the bandits had seized the mail courier, taking 3:000$000 from the bags before burning them. They arrived about midnight at Periperi Ranch, about seven miles distant from the city of Juàzeiro, and there learned that Lampião had departed four hours earlier. While there, he had sent four letters to prominent citizens of the city demanding money for a guarantee of the safety of their ranches. From there, the police were told, he had gone to Favelas Ranch and had ordered that *cachaça* and other drinks be brought there for him and his men. Lampião was leaving a clear trail, and the police should have been suspicious.

Although they were tired and weary, the volante arranged for a guide and shortly after midnight set out for Favelas, less than two miles away. Mounted until this time—as were the bandits—Lieutenant Odonel and his nineteen men went quietly on foot. After a half hour, the guide told them they were approaching the cangaceiros' camp. Moments thereafter, the bandits opened fire, before the volante had time to establish positions. Once again, Lampião had set up an ambush, and, unwittingly, the police had fallen into it. In the fight, the bandits were well spread out and attacked the police from various positions. Lieutenant Odonel and his men might have suffered heavy losses had they not received unexpected assistance from the arrival of another force which, unknown to them, was in the area. The bandits, their rear guard now under attack, regrouped and fired fiercely from behind a wall of rock before abandoning the field. The battle had lasted about twenty minutes; two of the soldiers were wounded seriously, and one of them later died. No bandits apparently had been hit. When, after daybreak, a few soldiers were sent back to inspect the battleground, they found canteens and one rose-colored, perfumed neckerchief.[3]

It was several months before the Bahia police had another major

[3] Lieutenant Odonel's report on the battle to his superior is in *A Tarde*, April 5, 1930. Also see the same journal, March 25 and 26, 1930.

encounter with Lampião. In the meantime, he and his men continued to operate over a broad area of Bahia and Sergipe. Much of the time they were divided into three bands, led, respectively, by Lampião, Corisco, and Antônio de Engracia. After the battle, Lampião moved quickly across ncrtheastern Bahia to Santo Antônio da Glória, where he remained for a few weeks. In late April, he was sighted in one place at the same time that Engracia was ambushing a police force in another.[4] Lampião and his men, in late May, attempted a surprise attack on Patamuté but were chased away by a police force. They then fell on a group of road workers near there, killing one of them.[5] In late July, they entered various villages and small towns in the Bahia-Sergipe border region, including Pinhão, Sergipe, where they sacked various businesses on the twenty-second. A minor skirmish occurred there on the arrival of a Bahia force; in anticipation of it Lampião had warned the schoolteacher to order her pupils to lie flat on the floor.[6] A week later, Corisco and his group seized the Calumby sugar plantation and mill near Capela. They ordered its owner, Luís Matos, to go to town to seek 10:000$000 while they held his family as hostages. When Matos returned in early morning with an armed force of police and civilians, the bandits were drinking and making music. The force attacked at daybreak, putting the bandits to flight. Matos noted, in telling his story to the press, that the hostages had been treated with respect and that Corisco, recognizing the possibility of an attack, had permitted Matos' wife to send the children to another house.[7]

The Bahia police soon learned again that Lampião was an extremely cunning and dangerous foe. After the trip to Sergipe, he disappeared for a few weeks but then surfaced in late July in Bahia, near Cipó. Cipó was a thermal station that, in spite of its isolation and the difficulties of travel, attracted bathers from afar because of the supposed curative qualities of its water. On July 30, when it was learned that Lampião was near—on that same day President-elect Júlio Prestes was being feted in Salvador, only 130 miles distant—panic reigned in the town, especially among the guests. However, with eighteen soldiers present, the resort prepared to resist. Civilians, including some of the

[4] *Diário de Notícias*, April 23, 1930; *A Tarde*, April 25, 1930.
[5] *A Tarde*, June 30, 1930.
[6] José Melquiades de Oliveira, interview, Pinhão, Sergipe, June 30, 1974.
[7] *Correio de Aracajú*, August 1 and 2, 1930.

bathers, joined in the defense. Lampião and the cangaceiros passed within a few hundred yards of the town at about ten o'clock but did not enter. Although no exchange of fire took place, there was one casualty; one of the civilian defenders fell, and his rifle accidentally discharged, mortally wounding him.[8] Following the threat to Cipó, several volantes were ordered to the area to search for the outlaws. One of them was led by Lieutenant Geminiano José dos Santos; his meeting with Lampião at Mandacarú shortly thereafter would be his last battle.

Lieutenant Geminiano and his volante of fifteen men picked up the bandits' trail twelve miles out of Tucano on July 31. Through the day and well into the night, the soldiers searched. At two o'clock in the morning they were told that they had overshot their mark, and the bandits were now behind them. Turning back, they arrived at daybreak at Mandacarú Ranch, located at the foot of Serra do Urubú ("Vulture Mountain"). There, they were told by a cowboy that the bandits were nowhere around. The cowboy was lying, and moments later the volante was attacked. The opposing sides were very nearly matched in number, but, as was usual, the advantages lay with the bandits. Taking the police by surprise, they fired on them from all sides. Jumping through the air and rolling on the ground, they subjected the force to a withering fire while, at the same time, shouting obscenities at the police and vivas to Padre Cícero and singing "Mulher Rendeira." The dexterity of their performance, one of the soldiers said, was unbelievable. The police force never organized any effective resistance. Lieutenant Geminiano was killed in midbattle, as was his second in command, a sergeant. Terrorized and without leadership, the survivors fled. Total casualties were reported as five dead and five wounded.[9]

A grim sight awaited the party that returned later to survey the scene of the massacre. The lieutenant's head was missing and his body had been knifed repeatedly in the stomach and groin. All of the bodies, in fact, had been stabbed numerous times, and the sergeant's eyes had

---

[8] The story of the threat to Cipó is told in a reprint of a newspaper story in Pedro Vergne de Abreu, *Os dramas dolorosos do nordeste*, pp. 19–22, 31–32. Abreu, a former state and national legislator from Bahia, published this volume as a propaganda tract, hoping to encourage a more determined effort against Lampião. A curious little book, it also contains Abreu's opinions on the curative qualities of the waters in the baths and an analysis of their chemical composition.

[9] *A Tarde*, August 2, 1930, and Abreu, *Os dramas dolorosos*, pp. 37–42.

been poked out.[10] The atrocities were very likely in retaliation for what the bandits considered to be the desecration of Gavião's body by the police. The taking of Gavião's head to Salvador in all likelihood had not gone unnoticed by the bandits, especially since Lampião was an avid reader of the *Diário de Notícias*, the Salvador newspaper that was most lurid in its reporting on the cangaceiros.[11] At any rate, these events apparently set off a series of beheadings by both sides, a grisly practice that in time would bring Lampião's head to sit there in Salvador among the other trophies.

The ability of Lampião, as shown at Favelas and Mandacarú, to lose the police and choose the time for battle was a skill many people found remarkable.[12] By 1930, of course, Lampião was a seasoned campaigner, thirteen years having passed since he first began to fight. As the one who was pursued, he had certain tactical advantages as well. It was he who could most easily set up an ambush, especially since his spies and informers kept him knowledgeable of police movements. When the police were attempting to pursue him, he could lead them into an ambush not only by leaving a clear trail of physical evidence such as tracks, but also by telling people in the area where he was going. When the ambush was sprung, the men, after a few minutes of battle, might flee in all directions in apparent wild disarray. The police would believe they had routed the bandits, but the bandits would regroup a short time later for another ambush when it was least expected. When, on the other hand, Lampião sought to avoid conflict or to put his pursuers at ease (so as to more easily attack them), he would order people in the area to furnish the police with erroneous information.

Essential to success in such tactics was what many police considered to be his uncanny ability to cover his tracks. Lampião's means in this regard were several. The most common was traveling over areas of

10 A *Tarde*, August 2, 1930.

11 Lampião's fondness for the *Diário de Notícias* is referred to in Auto de perguntas, Alcino da Silva Duarte, September 28, 1929, special packet on Lampião, Arquivo Público, Bahia.

12 The following account of Lampião's use of deception is based mostly on my interviews with soldiers who pursued him, especially Miguel Feitosa, João Jurubeba, David Jurubeba, and Severiano Ramos. Also see the published works of other soldiers: Goís, *Lampião*, especially p. 241; Gueiros, "*Lampeão*," especially pp. 80–81, 107–108, and passim; João Bezerra, *Como dei cabo de Lampeão*, p. 96.

rocky surface where his men could gingerly leave behind little or no evidence of their passing. Even before reaching the hard surface area, the bandits might drop out one by one. They would take long leaps to the side of the trail where their tracks might not be noticed, then regroup at a designated location. This was a procedure which they sometimes used when they wished to set up a rear-guard attack on a pursuing volante. They also used leafy branches of trees to obliterate their tracks, or they put sheepskin (with the furry side out) on the bottoms of their sandals to make their tracks less easily distinguishable. They were also known to arrive at a place and then walk backwards in the same tracks until they could leave the track by recrossing a hard surface or leaping to the side. To the police, the bandits had disappeared into thin air.

The police, of course, soon learned of Lampião's trickery, and the volantes employed skilled trackers to lead them. Some of the trackers, understandably, were better than others; many of the best ones had years of experience tracking wild beasts that preyed on backlands cattle. To them, the bandits' methods were not such a mystery, but to the ordinary soldier they bordered on the inhuman. For that matter, many of the skilled backlands soldiers who pursued Lampião for years believed that he possessed an almost superhuman ability to avoid his enemies. On the darkest night, they said, he would veer widely around an ambush that had been prepared for him. Even when beset by extreme hunger and thirst, he would walk many miles to avoid soldiers before seeking relief. That Lampião was an uncommonly astute human being cannot be denied; the skills he possessed, however, were those of a careful, observant, and intelligent man who had survived in the wilds while under pursuit for many years. Much of his success can be attributed to pure ingenuity, as in one case where he reportedly escaped from a police encirclement in Bahia with the use of cowbells. Divided into groups, the band crawled through the police lines tinkling their bells to the same rhythm as that of a slowly walking cow. Much of his success in addition was due to extreme care. When, for example, the band was hiding out, they buried the skins and inedible portions of animals they killed for food so as not to attract vultures, whose presence circling overhead might give away their location.

In actuality, Lampião's basic key to success was simple. He normally preferred to run and hide rather than confront the police. For this, the police often taunted him as being cowardly, but for Lampião it was a tenet of survival. His aim was not to engage the police in open and sustained warfare, for, given the inequality of forces, he could not have long survived. However much he hated the police, he sought to engage them only when the advantages lay heavily with his side. He murdered them when there was no immediate risk, as in Queimadas, or he attacked them when he could scarcely lose, as in Favelas and Mandacarú. And, in the latter instances, he attacked only when they were closely pursuing him, interfering with his operations and posing a direct threat to him. By the 1930s, it was becoming clear that he preferred not to do battle at all. He would have been happier had the police just left him alone. The mature Lampião probably would have been content to settle down as a backlands sultan, doing only what was necessary to keep his subjects in line and the tribute flowing into his coffers.

Of course, Lampião, continuing his fight for survival, never found the opportunity to settle down. Mandacarú, however, was his last major battle with the Bahia police in 1930. Although he continued his operations—a few days after Mandacarú, he killed three more road workers[13]—important events in the nation at large soon relieved the pressure on him. Significant news of him reached the press again only in October when it was announced that the revolutionary forces had captured him in Sergipe.[14] The report of Lampião's capture had no basis in fact, but the revolutionary forces were a reality. In October and November of 1930, Brazil experienced a major governmental upheaval. Led by Getúlio Vargas of Rio Grande do Sul, who had support from other sections of the nation and segments of the armed forces, the rebels overthrew the incumbent administration of President Washington Luís and ended Brazil's First Republic. In this way, they thwarted the planned presidential inauguration of Júlio Prestes, whose election in the preceding March, they charged, had been fraudulent. The Revolution of 1930 created a government, with Vargas as its head, that lasted well beyond Lampião's death in 1938.[15]

[13] *A Tarde*, August 4, 1930.
[14] *O Povo*, October 23 and 24, 1930.
[15] A convenient summary of the 1930 Revolution is found in Thomas E. Skidmore, *Politics in Brazil, 1930–1964*, pp. 3–12.

Although the governmental changes of 1930 in time resulted in a heightening of the campaign against banditry, the short-run effect was to pull military forces to the capital areas in order to meet immediate political needs. The backlands, meanwhile, were abandoned to Lampião. He took advantage of the lull in police activity to make a trip into Pernambuco and Alagoas. This was apparently the first time he had returned to those states since his departure over two years previously. Crossing the São Francisco, he invaded Floresta County in Pernambuco on November 26 with a band of twenty. After taking two hostages whom they encountered on the road, the bandits arrived at Ambrósio Ranch. There, they demanded 3:000$000 of the owner, and, not getting it, assaulted him and several other males who were present. They then invaded the house and, emptying trunks, found jewels and clothing and 1:000$000 in paper and silver. Returning to the yard, Lampião demanded to know the name of one man, and, when the others told him they could not identify him, the bandit searched the man's pockets. Upon finding papers which stated that he had formerly been a soldier in Nazaré, Lampião ordered him tied to a wooden post. The man was then knifed, his throat was slit, and his head was cut off. The bloody body was left tied to the post, the head lying nearby on the ground. When the band left Ambrósio Ranch, they took its owner and one other man and held them for ransom. The next day, they received the money and released them. On that day also they captured a former police deputy and murdered him after the same fashion as the ex-soldier on the ranch. Before leaving the area, the bandits entered the town of Jatobá (now Petrolándia), extorting money and robbing business houses.[16]

Moving eastward, the band attacked Mariana and in Aguas Belas County made a surprise attack on the undefended ranch of Colonel João Nunes, the commander during a part of the 1920s of the Pernambuco State Police. Since the colonel, by then retired, presumably was worth more alive than dead, they crossed over into Alagoas with him, demanding 15:000$000 for his release. During the walk into Alagoas, however, the old soldier's bravery and affability impressed the cangaceiros, several of whom learned to like him. When, after some days, the ransom had not arrived, they persuaded Lampião to turn him

16 Criminal proceedings against Virgulino Ferreira et al., November 26, 1930, Second Cartório, Floresta, Pernambuco. Also *Diário de Pernambuco*, November 28 and 29, 1930, and *A Tarde*, November 29 and December 1, 1930.

loose.[17] By then, it was early December and the band was in Sergipe on the southern side of the São Francisco.

The Revolution of 1930 may have immediately afforded Lampião greater freedom from police activity, but its long-range effects were detrimental. Among those who participated in the Revolution were many, particularly younger military officers, who wished to transform the nation into a progressive and prosperous unitary society. To these modernizers, the historical abandonment of the backlands to autocratic political chieftains (and their private armies) and to bandits was an anachronism. However, after the Revolution, they participated in a government that, beset by problems on all sides, largely perpetuated the condition. The extent of their accomplishments in changing the structure of backlands society fell short of their desires, since, in many ways, the new regime turned out to be much like the old.

The government eventually did bring a strengthened determination to the campaign against banditry, but, unfortunately, that took time. Meanwhile, the new government's representatives in the northeastern states demonstrated that they had no quick cure for the problem. The obstacles faced by their predecessors were still present. The fight in the years immediately succeeding the Revolution was centered in Bahia, as it had been since Lampião first crossed the São Francisco. In reality, the postrevolutionary campaign was a continuation of the one begun—however haltingly—in 1928.

Police action in Bahia against Lampião, as we have noted, had been ineffective. The bandits roamed the area almost at will, and when the two sides met it was the police who suffered the most heavily. Indeed, disaster had followed disaster. The first commander of the campaign against the bandits, Captain Hercílio Rocha, had lasted until September, 1929. By then it was evident that, instead of suffering reverses, Lampião was regaining the kind of influence he had enjoyed earlier in Pernambuco. Rocha was replaced by Captain José Macedo, and under him efforts were made to broaden the campaign. Additional men were sent to the area and trucks were furnished for transporting

[17] *Diário de Pernambuco*, December 3, 1930; *A Tarde*, December 4, 1930. The ex-cangaceiro Volta-Sêca told the story of the Nunes capture years later to a reporter, Bruno Gomes (*Diário de Notícias*, May 6, 1959). This was one of a series of articles under varying titles, running from April 25 to May 22, 1950, in which Volta-Sêca related his life in the cangaço (hereinafter cited as Volta-Sêca's story as told to Gomes).

them, although the lack of passable roads greatly limited their use. Measures were taken as well to disperse the troops in order to match Lampião's wide-ranging travels. While the command post remained in Uauá, strong contingents were also placed in Coité (located in the south of the area), Juàzeiro, and Santo Antônio da Glória. By this time, volantes from Pernambuco were again permitted in Bahia, in spite of continuing complaints about their cruelty. By this time, too, the Bahia volantes were imitating their Pernambuco colleagues by adopting the cangaceiro mode of dress. Although it was disapproved of by many civilians, the practice was an attempt to infuse into the forces the same kind of esprit d'corps exhibited by the bandits. The expanded efforts notwithstanding, Captain Macedo had a short tenure; he was replaced in late December as a result of the disaster at Queimadas.[18]

On Christmas day, 1929, three days after Queimadas, Colonel Teréncio dos Santos Dourado, an ex-commander of the Bahia State Police, was entrusted with the command of the campaign. The choice of Dourado, of obviously far greater prestige than the two previous commanders, was evidence again of the resolve of the state to meet Lampião's challenge. The colonel divided the area inhabited by the bandits into six regions, placing an officer in charge of each one. Three sets of radio equipment were sent to provide much needed intercounty communications. One was set up in the command post, now moved to Bonfim, while the others went to Jeremoabo and Uauá. All told, 1,200 soldiers and 36 officers—over one-third of the Bahia force—were within the command.[19] Such an impressive statistic was deceiving, however, as Dourado pointed out when, after eight months of failure, he relinquished the post of commander in August, 1930, following the defeat at Mandacarú.[20] While critics seemed to think, he said, that 1,200 soldiers were combing the backlands for Lampião, that was not true. In addition to chasing the bandits, the force had full responsibility for normal police duties. Moreover, it was common practice in Bahia, as it had been in other states, to concentrate the overwhelming majority of the soldiers in the towns, not only to exercise routine policing but also

[18] Bahia, Secretaria da Policia e Segurança Pública, *Relatório de 1929*, pp. 79–87. At least some Bahia volantes were using cangaceiro dress by September, 1929 (*Diário de Notícias*, September 13, 1929).

[19] Ibid., pp. 81, 88.

[20] Dourado was interviewed in *A Tarde*, August 8, 1930.

to protect the major population centers from attack. Less than 150 troops, he said, were available to man the volantes that actually pursued the bandits in the field. Each volante normally having from 20 to 30 men, 150 troops provided for five or six units charged with pursuing from one to three bands of criminals over an area of not much less than 50,000 square miles.

Although Dourado did not conceptualize the problem in such terms, the difficulties that he faced in Bahia were closely related to the fact that his force was engaged in a struggle against guerrilla warriors. Lampião, after all, was a skillful tactician in that type of warfare.[21] He had learned much, no doubt, during his apprenticeship to Sebastião Pereira, and, during the succeeding years when the campaign against him was not particularly intense, he had had the opportunity to gradually develop his skills. By the time he came to Bahia, following those last trying years in Pernambuco, he was a veteran campaigner. In addition to having to contend with the quality of Lampião's command, the Bahia effort was burdened by the usual disadvantages that military forces confront in fighting guerrillas. Typically, as in Bahia, small bands of guerrillas, moving with stealth and speed, force the military not only to disperse its strength but also to use its scattered forces mainly in population centers, thus leaving the countryside virtually unprotected. As a result, the rural population is forced, unwillingly or not, into the camp of the guerrillas, since, in the absence of police protection, they normally have no other recourse. Bahia and most of the rest of the backlands, it should also be noted, offered near ideal conditions for the successful use of guerrilla tactics. Highly accidented in many parts, widely covered with thick and difficult vegetation, and sparsely populated, the area afforded plentiful places to hide and store supplies. Moreover, a well-developed transportation system, with which the police might have overcome some of their difficulties, did not exist. Since even relatively efficient and well-financed governments have often failed to counter guerrillas successfully, it is no wonder that so often

---

[21] There might be some quarrel with the designation of Lampião as a guerrilla, if guerrilla is defined as one who fights for political motives. In terms of the modes of warfare that the word suggests, however, Lampião is a prime example. On guerrilla warfare, see James Eliot Cross, *Conflict in the Shadows: The Nature and Politics of Guerrilla War*, especially pp. 4–39.

the effort in the northeastern Brazil of the 1920s and 1930s did not succeed.

Indeed, Colonel Dourado, in pointing to other difficulties that had hindered the campaign, illustrated the poverty and inefficiency of the police force itself. The soldiers' pay was often late in arriving, he said, and uniforms were frequently unavailable. Many a volante returned from days and weeks in the bush with its men practically naked. On their meager pay (approximately forty cents per day in the U.S. equivalent), soldiers had to furnish their own food except when they were on march. Then, volante commanders had authorization to purchase food and furnish it to them without cost. Food for troops in the field usually consisted of *rapadura*, *farinha*, and meat. The first two items could be purchased in villages and ranches. Meat, in the form of cattle, sheep, and goats, was taken wherever it might be found. If the owner appeared, he was paid or maybe promised payment, but, if he was absent, most commanders made no effort to meet their obligation to compensate him.[22] Although Colonel Dourado did not mention this, it was all too common for the commanders to charge their men for the food and to pocket the profits for themselves. This was a long-standing abuse also common in Pernambuco and other states. Other difficulties, the colonel mentioned, were created by Lampião's tactics. Chased in one area, he would flee to another; hotly pursued in Bahia, he would soon turn up in Sergipe. Even when he set up an ambush, he would flee after a few moments of battle, giving the police insufficient time to offer effective resistance. If Lampião would accept combat, Dourado said, he would have been defeated months earlier. The colonel was suggesting, of course, that Lampião abandon his guerrilla tactics.

Upon Dourado's resignation, command of the northeastern region was offered to Colonel Alberto Lopez. He accepted the post, provided that a list of conditions be met.[23] Included on his list were requests for additional supplies and services, including adequate uniforms, increased pay, and medical assistance for the troops, as well as more trackers, pistols, binoculars, and transportation facilities. Crucial to his plan was the freedom to operate unhindered by the local political chief-

[22] José Izidro, interview.
[23] The conditions are set forth in SSP to Senator Pedro Lages, August 4, 1930, in telegrams, Bahia.

tains who traditionally had exercised veto power, if not actual command, over troops in their dominions. Understandably, given the political and financial conditions of the times, Lopez's demands were found to be unacceptable.

Dourado was replaced by Major Domingos Dutra, who had distinguished himself in 1924 when he helped to suppress an attempted revolt in Sergipe at the time of the abortive São Paulo uprising. Subsequently, he had combatted the Prestes Column. His campaign against the bandits was delayed for a few weeks while the headquarters was being moved from Bonfim back to Uauá.[24] Meanwhile, the government of Bahia offered a reward for Lampião. Wanted posters, bearing the bandit's likeness, declared that 50:000$000 would be paid to whoever—civilian or military—should deliver him in whatever manner to the police.[25]

Before Dutra could carry out any effective resumption of the campaign, the Revolution occurred in October and November of 1930, and, for a time, the struggle over power and the resulting political reorganization took precedence over suppressing banditry. The incumbent state administrations were swept away and replaced by presidentially appointed interventors. In Bahia, there was a series of them before much stability was achieved. The main immediate interest the new regime had in the backlands was in disarming the populace, especially the more powerful political chieftains who had opposed the Revolution.[26] Such a move was urgent in order to consolidate the power of the new government; the fight against banditry could wait. Although the new politicians were prepared to amass a force of over 1,000 troops, together with machine guns, gas, and airplanes, to neutralize Horácio de Matos, one of the backlands Bahia colonels who had opposed the Revolution, they showed no such determination in the fight against Lampião, according to one government critic.[27] The criticism was true, of course, but to the new regime the actions reflected the order of its priorities.

Disarmament of the backlands left the natives with scarcely more

---

[24] *A Tarde*, August 11 and September 12, 1930.
[25] A photograph of the poster is in *A Tarde*, September 12, 1930.
[26] Pang, "Politics of Coronelismo," pp. 304–305.
[27] Pedro Vergne de Abreu, ed., *O flagello de "Lampeão,"* p. 26 (another propaganda work by the author of *Os dramas dolorosos*).

than muzzle-loading shotguns for hunting. Critics cried that the measure left the backlanders defenseless against the bandits, and that was true. The Commercial Association of Morro do Chapeu of the Bahia interior, for example, complained to the state police that with no soldiers and no private arms, the town was defenseless against bandits.[28] The importance of the disarmament effort is questionable, since those who had the means to possess modern weaponry usually had made their peace with Lampião. If the disarmament of the backlanders was thorough, its effects did not reach Lampião. He continued as usual with plentiful weapons and ammunition equal in quality to those of the federal army.[29]

The new government got off to an extremely slow start in its campaign against the bandits. The newly created regional police chief for northeastern Brazil, Captain Juarez Távora, announced a reorganization of the effort in February, 1931, but nothing much seems to have come of it.[30] Arthur Neiva, a scientist who served as interventor in Bahia from February to August of that year, listed among his accomplishments the intensification of the campaign against banditry. As evidence, he pointed to the deployment in the area of 1,200 troops.[31] That was no more than had been there under the old regime. Money to finance any extraordinary effort was a chronic problem in Brazil, and in those especially dark days of the early 1930s it probably was insurmountable. In the meantime, the forces in the field had to work under the usual extreme deprivation. The headquarters at Uauá sent a telegram in February to Salvador stating that a request for troops from one area could not be met for lack of money. A contingent had just arrived from the field, the message continued; it was suffering from hunger.[32]

While officials in Bahia were stumbling along in the usual fashion, major attention of the campaign momentarily shifted to Rio de Janeiro. There in the nation's capital, far removed from the backlands, the Vargas regime early in 1931 was concocting its own plan to eliminate Lampião. At the center of it was Captain Carlos Chevalier, a popular avia-

---

[28] A Tarde, January 12, 1931.

[29] For a discussion of Lampião's sources of ammunition, see chapter 10 herein.

[30] The text of Távora's plan was carried in Sergipe-Jornal (Aracajú), February 24, 1931.

[31] Found in Interventor, Bahia, 1931–1934, Arquivo Nacional, Rio de Janeiro.

[32] Receipt reported in SSP to Bonfim, February 11, 1931, telegrams, Bahia.

tor who also entertained Cariocas (natives of Rio) with his daring parachute jumps. The possible use of airplanes in the fight against Lampião had been suggested before, and now, under Chevalier, they would be tried out, the press reported. According to plans developed in mid-February and thereafter under Interior Minister Oswaldo Aranha, the Chevalier Mission would make extensive use of radio communications and would involve some one thousand military personnel. Chevalier indicated that he wanted at least two hundred Carioca policemen among them. As to the availability of the airplanes—or, as seemed more likely, an airplane—there was some doubt among officials as they wrestled with the troublesome problem of finances. It was announced that the Ministry of Agriculture would make a study of places suitable for the construction of airstrips; presumably, planes would be made available later.

In the course of the development of the plans, Chevalier gave numerous interviews in which he expressed great confidence in his ability to vanquish the bandits.[33] He also said that he would take along a well-known Rio film maker to preserve the scenes of the adventure for posterity. Just when the aviator would get his mission underway became something of a question. He first announced that he would leave soon after Rio's annual Carnival was over, and *O Globo*, a popular Carioca newspaper, reported that a gala going-away party would be given for him. But Carnival ended and the weeks passed, and still Captain Chevalier was in Rio, granting interviews.

In early April, it was announced that he was almost ready to depart, but two weeks later, when he still had not left, the press wondered if he ever would.[34] The suspense came to an end late in the month when Major Juarez Távora wired Bahia that the proposed venture was, for the time being, "paralyzed for the lack of funds." The states, he said, were to conduct a campaign against Lampião using their own resources.[35] That was the effective end of the Chevalier Mission, although the captain was still granting interviews concerning it

[33] On Chevalier's plans, see: *A Tarde*, February 14, 21, and 25 and March 3; *Diário da Noite*, February 24, 1931.

[34] Continuing news on Chevalier was reported in *A Tarde*, April 8 and 17, 1931, and *O Globo* (Rio de Janeiro), March 21, 1931.

[35] The telegram is in *A Tarde*, April 28, 1931.

late in the year. He made the interesting claim in one of them that, by way of Bahia ranchers, he had succeeded in infiltrating Lampião's group with two spies who were to have revealed the band's hiding places.[36] Nonetheless, the cancellation of the Chevalier Mission probably was just as well. There seems ample justification for doubting that the Carioca police could have succeeded where backlanders had failed. And an airplane or two searching the vast and often rough expanses of the Northeast would not have made much difference. The whole proposal must have seemed rather ludicrous to perceptive observers.

Following the failure of the Chevalier Mission to get off the ground, a reorganized campaign against Lampião was again delayed for several months. Not until September, with the decision of the federal government to allocate 400:000$000 to the campaign in Bahia, did things take a turn for the better.[37] In that same month, the state acquired a new interventor with the naming of twenty-six-year-old Captain Juracy Magalhães to the post. Pressing Rio to make the allocated funds available, he was given an assist by Corisco's perpetration of a monstrous atrocity. The story of the event and its causes are fairly well known.

Corisco, years before, allegedly had been unfairly treated by a police deputy, Herculano Borges, in the village of Santa Rosa in the Bonfim area. The incident involved, it is said, an attempt by the village officials to force Corisco to pay a tax on meat he was selling in the market. When Corisco refused to pay, claiming that the officials were trying to collect a tax he had paid already, he was jailed. Upon his release, he bought a rifle and swore to avenge the dishonor. Soon thereafter, and presumably for these reasons, he became a cangaceiro and joined Lampião's band. Later, when the band invaded Santa Rosa and laid waste to his store, Borges moved to Bonfim, returning to the village only occasionally to take care of business matters. On September 22, 1931, he was returning from Santa Rosa, where he had attended the market day, when he was seized by Corisco and nine of his henchmen.

[36] *Diário da Noite*, December 17, 1931.

[37] A handwritten note (apparently by Getúlio) on an appeal from Magalhães authorized the expenditure (Juracy Magalhães to Chefe, Governo Provisório, September 18, 1931, in Interventor, Bahia, 1931–1934, Arquivo Nacional, Rio de Janeiro).

Corisco, on the following day, suspended him by his feet from a pole between two trees—in the manner in which animals are slaughtered—and skinned him alive. He then cut off his head, ears, and feet and quartered him. Exhibiting the various parts of the body on stakes as a public demonstration of the power of his vengeance, he threatened with death anyone who should bury them.[38]

Magalhães sent a full account of the atrocity to President Getúlio Vargas and, stating that it was repugnant to govern a state in which such savagery was practiced, again appealed for federal help for the campaign against banditry.[39] A few days later, in early October, it was announced that the money previously authorized by the federal government had been made available.[40]

The campaign was initiated in that same month with considerable fanfare. Captain João Facó, the state chief of police, asserted that the bandits already were under constant pursuit by a large force that would surround the area and gradually close in. In addition, Paraíba, Pernambuco, Alagoas, and Sergipe would be cooperating. To strengthen communications, additional radio equipment was being made available to the forces.[41] The campaign, it was optimistically said, should not have to go beyond sixty days.[42] In the meantime, a Rio newspaper was running a contest, allegedly to offer assistance to Facó's campaign. The *Diário da Noite* offered a prize to the best suggestion of how to eliminate Lampião. One contestant suggested that he be bombed from the air, while another urged that a policeman dressed as a monk be sent to assassinate him—a plan that was sure to work, its author said, in view of the bandit's piety.[43]

Throughout 1931, while plans for his demise were being bandied about in Rio and Salvador, Lampião was pursuing his normal courses

---

[38] *Diário de Notícias*, October 2, 1931; Volta-Sêca's story as told to Gomes, *Diário de Notícias*, May 9, 1959; Felipe Borges de Castro, interview. In Lima, *O mundo estranho*, pp. 67–68, a different story of the entry of Corisco into the cangaço is given.

[39] Magalhães to Chefe, Governo Provisório, September 26, 1931, in Interventor, Bahia, 1931–1934, Arquivo Nacional, Rio de Janeiro.

[40] *A Tarde*, October 3, 1931.

[41] Interview with Facó, in *A Tarde*, October 14, 1931; *A Tarde*, October 13, 1931. Also see Prata, *Lampeão*, pp. 169–172.

[42] *A Tarde*, October 12, 1931.

[43] *Diário da Noite*, November 25, 1931.

of action in the backlands. As the bandit's years went, 1931 was a relatively peaceful and uneventful one, except for the loss of Ezekiel in April. The youngest of José Ferreira's sons, he had joined the band in 1927 and was the last survivor of Lampião's brothers except for the one, João, who never became a cangaceiro. Reputedly a fearless and foolhardy young man, Ezekiel was killed in a battle with the Bahia police on April 24 at Umbuzeiro de Touro Ranch, near the falls of Paulo Afonso. Following the death of Ezekiel, Lampião and his men went on a rampage of death and destruction. In one night alone, one of the cangaceiros later estimated, the band killed ten or more persons, choosing as their victims persons whom they encountered along a road they were traveling.[44] Much of Lampião's anger was also directed against Petronilo Reis.

Lampião's reasons for directing his anger against Petro, presumably one of his first friends in Bahia, are not entirely clear, although it is known that their estrangement began not many months after their first meeting. By January, 1929 (Lampião came to Bahia in August, 1928), the Santo Antônio de Glória boss was telling authorities that he wanted to keep the Nazarenos of Pernambuco in his county, in view of their reputation as Lampião's fearless enemies.[45] In March, police reported that Petro's cowboys helped them capture two of Lampião's men.[46] The bandit chieftain, it was said in September, had sworn to exact revenge from Petro by castrating him and reducing him to poverty.[47] It is generally believed that the cause of the falling out between the two men was Petro's failure to keep his early promises of protection and support.[48]

Lampião's actions against Petro were devastating. On May 8, he and a band of over forty attacked Várzea da Ema, one of the rancher's villages, and laid waste to the small settlement. Two of the seven soldiers there died in the battle. On that same day and on the following one, the bandits continued their rampage, burning buildings and fences and killing hundreds of head of cattle on several of Petro's

[44] A description of the battle of Umbuzeiro de Touro and an estimate of the number of people killed is given by Ângelo Roque in Lima, O mundo estranho, pp. 212–215, 217. Also see Prata, Lampeão, pp. 83–88.

[45] SSP to Bonfim, January 29, 1929, telegrams, Bahia.

[46] A Tarde, March 19, 1929.

[47] Diário de Notícias, September 20, 1929.

[48] José Izidro and José Fernandes de Vieira, interviews.

ranches.[49] His losses were enormous, not only in physical destruction but also because people became afraid to work for him or be known as his friends out of fear of what misfortune might befall them. Although he lived for some two decades more, his wealth and influence were permanently impaired.[50]

After their May actions against Petro, the bandits apparently did not have another significant battle until September. It was reported in the middle part of that month that a combined Bahia-Pernambuco force had defeated them near Santo Antônio da Glória. The band had fled, it was said, leaving behind large quantities of arms and ammunition.[51] Claims of victory by the police, of course, were often exaggerated, for, short of suffering a major disaster, they always claimed that they had won. Lampião's habit of fleeing after a short exchange of fire made it easy for them to make such claims.

Several weeks later, in November and December, 1931, Lampião was placed under greater pressure in Bahia by the police campaign, which, by then, was moving beyond the talking stage. In November, Captain João Facó and Colonel João Felix, the secretary and commander, respectively, of the state police, left Salvador to make an inspection tour of the effort. Accompanying them were a force of seventy troops and a Rio reporter. Victor do Espírito Santo was a representative of the *Diário da Noite*, a Rio paper that at the moment was feeding the public desire for news about Lampião. In announcing the reporter's departure, the newspaper declared that Lampião was known beyond Brazilian borders to the extent that his fame equalled Al Capone's.[52] The editors obviously hoped to scoop the celebrated desperado's death.

The Rio newspaperman, however, was able to report only one event of any consequence during the several weeks that he spent in the Northeast. This event occurred on December 7, when one of the volantes was searching for the bandits on the margins of the Raso da Catarina, an unpopulated and difficult area in which it was believed

[49] José Gomes dos Santos, who was present at the attack, told me the story of it in an interview, Jeremoabo, Bahia, August 15, 1975. Also see *Diário da Noite*, May 26 and June 4, 1931.

[50] José Gomes dos Santos, interview.

[51] *Diário de Pernambuco*, September 16, 1931.

[52] *Diário da Noite*, November 18, 1931.

Lampião's most flattering portrait, made during his visit to Padre Cícero in Juàzeiro in 1926. (Courtesy of Museu Histórico, Fortaleza.)

A view from the site of Lampião's birth. The Passagem das Pedras ranch house stood on the place in the lower right of the picture where the tall cactus now grows. (Photograph by the author, 1975.)

José Saturnino (seated on the right), Lampião's major enemy, in front of his home near Serra Vermelha in 1975. To the left of the house lies the pasture where in 1916 he and the Ferreira boys first exchanged gunfire. (Photograph by the author, 1975.)

Agua Branca, Alagoas. Lampião's 1922 raid on this town began his rise to regional prominence. (Photograph by the author, 1974.)

The home of the baroness of Agua Branca. It was for the purpose of looting this house that Lampião came to the town in 1922. (Photograph by the author, 1974.)

A Ferreira family portrait made in Juàzeiro in 1926. Lampião is on the right, his brother Antônio on the left. Standing in the middle is João, the only one of the Ferreira boys who did not enter the cangaço. Ezekiel Ferreira, the youngest of the boys, stands next to João on the right. João's hand is on his wife's shoulder; the other women are the boys' sisters. Others in the group are cousins. (Courtesy of João Ferreira, Propriá, Sergipe.)

Lampião and Antônio in Juàzeiro, 1926. (Courtesy of Miguel Feitosa, Araripina, Pernambuco.)

Lampião (kneeling fifth from the right) and his band in Limoeiro do
Norte on their flight from Rio Grande do Norte in 1927. Their hostages,
Dona Maria and Colonel Gurgel, may be seen in the left of the second
row. (Courtesy of the Museu Histórico, Fortaleza.)

Two young Nazarenos, ca. 1924. The Nazareno clan pursued Lampião
tenaciously. Note their cangaceiro dress; the bandits and their pursuers,
whether police or civilians, often dressed alike. (Courtesy of Cartório,
Floresta, Pernambuco.)

PASSAGEM DE LAMPIÃO NA VILLA DE POMBAL

Lampião (on the far left) and his small band on their visit to Pombal, Bahia, December, 1928. (Courtesy of Miguel Feitosa, Araripina, Pernambuco.)

The Queimadas, Bahia, police station, where in 1929 Lampião and his band murdered seven defenseless soldiers. (Photograph by the author, 1974.)

Jeremoabo, Bahia, and surrounding area, the home of Colonel João Sá, one of Lampião's noted coiteiros. (Photograph by the author, 1975.)

Lampião makes the front cover of a popular Rio de Janeiro weekly magazine, 1932. (Photograph by the author.)

Lampião and Maria Bonita in the *caatinga*, ca. 1936. Lampião poses with a weekly magazine. (Courtesy of Major Alberto Salles Paraiso Borges, Salvador.)

Lampião, Maria Bonita, and their group, with the Syrian film maker Benjamin Abrahão in 1935 or 1936. (Courtesy of João Ferreira, Propría, Sergipe.)

The cangaceira Inacinha in Piranhas, Alagoas, shortly after her capture in 1936. Her right leg was slightly wounded. (Courtesy of Francisco Rodrigues, Piranhas, Alagoas.)

João Bezerra (seated in the prominent position, center, front row) and his Alagoas troop, near the time when they brought an end to Lampião's career in 1938. (Courtesy of the Instituto Histórico, Maceió.)

Sergeant Aniceto Rodrigues (seated) and his Alagoas troop. They also participated in the battle that ended the bandit's life. (Courtesy of Francisco Rodrigues, Piranhas, Alagoas.)

Soldiers and curious civilians view the headless bodies of Lampião and Maria Bonita, barely visible—they had been covered with lime—in the foreground, at Angicos. (Courtesy of the Instituto Histórico, Maceió.)

Some of the trophies taken by the police at Angicos. (Courtesy of Miguel Feitosa, Araripina, Pernambuco.)

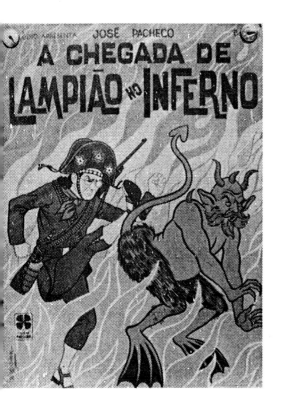

Examples from the 1970s of the popular literature (*literatura de cordel*) written about Lampião. Left: *The Arrival of Lampião in Hell*; right: *Lampião, King of the Cangaço, Loves and Exploits*. (Photographs by the author.)

that Lampião often hid. The Raso ("flatland"), a geographically distinctive region of some three hundred square miles, lies to the northwest of Jeremoabo. It is characterized by its isolation and terrain of loose sand, spiny vegetation, and lack of water. Human passage through it is never easy and in the rainy season becomes extremely difficult because of the almost impenetrable vegetation. For the bandits, to whom isolation was often desirable and discomfort commonplace, it offered ideal camping sites. The troops, while searching the area, saw evidence of recent human passage in a cut branch and a piece of cloth. Picking up a trail, they soon began to hear voices and realized that they had found Lampião's camp. But, before they could adequately position themselves, a shot rang out and the battle was on. After some exchange of fire, the bandits fled in the usual manner, going in all directions. Looking over the scene of the skirmish, they realized that a major hide-out had been discovered. The camp, covering a large area and built to accommodate approximately fifty persons, was dotted with widely dispersed brush shelters. In their flight, the bandits had left behind horses, clothing, food, and a large supply of ammunition. Subsequently, Lampião and his band of thirty-five men and ten women were reported as having gone into Sergipe, probably, it was believed, to secure a new supply of ammunition.[53]

The report of the presence of women within Lampião's band as it fled into Sergipe was not startling. Women had been seen with the cangaceiros since early in the year. But the story that the bandit chief was maintaining a harem of seventeen girls, adorned with jewels and dressed in the finest cloth, in some backlands Baghdad was untrue.[54] In 1930 or early 1931, Lampião, as the chief, apparently had been the first to take a female companion. Maria Bonita ("Pretty Mary"), as she became known in legend, originally was named Maria Déia. In the band, she was called Dona Maria in direct address and, in reference, the "captain's woman." When Lampião met her she was Dona Maria Nenem, the wife of José Nenem. Reared on the small ranch of her father in the Jeremoabo area of Bahia, she lived, after her marriage, in the nearby village of Santa Brígida, where her husband was a cobbler.

[53] Facó, on his return to Salvador, described the battle for *A Tarde*, December 6, 1931.

[54] Women were reported in the band in *A Tarde*, March 31, 1931. A traveling salesman told the harem tale (*Jornal de Alagoas*, August 15, 1931).

Maria and her husband did not get along well, and, as a result, she often visited her parents on the ranch. The ranch lay in the Bahia-Sergipe border area through which Lampião often passed, and he had become acquainted with her parents. They, like most backlanders, probably feared the celebrated bandit, but, at the same time, held him in a mixture of awe and respect, regarding him as a great man. It was Maria's mother, according to one of the cangaceiros in the band at the time, who told Lampião how much her daughter admired him. One day Maria came to the ranch while Lampião was there, and the bandit, it is said, was stricken with love at sight of her. A few days later, when the band departed, Lampião took her with him, with her consent and her mother's blessing.

At the time, Lampião was approximately thirty-three, while Maria was in her early twenties. A fairly typical female backlander in appearance, she was short and well filled out, had good teeth, dark hair and eyes, and light brown skin, and was not unattractive. She remained with him until the end, dying, as he did, at Angicos.[55]

Subsequently, others of the bandits took women also. Most of them, like Maria, regarded the cangaceiros as romantic heroes and willingly joined them; others claimed, at least, that they were practically stolen. Some went into the band as a matter of circumstances when their boyfriends joined. Few, it seems, were motivated by a desire to become professional bandits. In the band, they were, in the main, the bandits' women and not bandits themselves. They were taught how to shoot, as a matter of self-protection, but normally they were kept apart in battle whenever possible. Mostly, the responsibility of the women was to furnish their men with feminine companionship. Since the bandits did not live in settled homes but on the run or in temporary rustic camps in the bush, there were few of the traditional wife's duties to occupy their time. Dona Maria, for one, spent a lot of time sewing. An accomplished seamstress, she often made her own and the bandits' clothes and elaborately decorated such things as the small packsacks (the *bornal*) in which they carried their few personal items

[55] A full account of Maria's romance with Lampião appears in Volta-Sêca's story as told to Gomes, *Diário de Notícias,* April 29, 1959. Also see Goís, *Lampião,* pp. 212–214, and *A Tarde,* August 1, 1938.

and their money, precious stones, gold, and silver. When it could be arranged, a sewing machine was brought to the camp for her use.[56]

The frequent pregnancies that occurred were major problems, but the matter seems to have been resolved in a practical manner. These were backlands girls and women who were accustomed to simple living, hard work, and riding horses or walking long distances. They had seen their mothers give birth to children year after year, fifteen to twenty pregnancies in a lifetime not being rare for a backlands woman. The bandits' women, like their mothers, neither received nor expected the services of a physician. In fact, Lampião usually attended to the births. He had no special knowledge, of course, but, as a cowboy in his youth, he had assisted animals in the birth of their offspring. Given the circumstances in which the band often found itself, the women could be given few extraordinary considerations either before or after birth. When Joanna Gomes, the woman of one of the Engracia brothers, gave birth to her second child, she had to take him in her arms and ride away on a horse within the hour.

Once a baby was born, there was the major problem of what to do with it. Since the cangaço was devoid of almost any conditions propitious to child rearing, little thought was given to keeping offspring with their parents beyond a few days or weeks. At the most, they could remain with them only during a time when the band might be inactive. It thus became the general practice to entrust someone else with responsibility for bringing up the children. Corisco and Dadá gave their young son in 1935 to a cowboy to take to the priest in Santana do Ipanema, Alagoas. The letter they sent along with him asked Padre José Bulhões to accept him and give him a good upbringing. Also accompanying the strange gift was a package of baby clothes that Dadá had made.[57] When Lampião and Dona Maria's daughter, Expedita,

[56] Interviews with two of the bandits' women, Otélia Teixeira Lima and Anna Maria Conceição, are in *Diário de Notícias*, May 18, 1935. Another, with Joanna Gomes, is in *Correio de Aracajú*, April 16, 1937. I interviewed Dadá (Sérgia Maria de Jesus) in Salvador, Bahia, September 1, 1975. In these interviews, the women discussed their reasons for entering the band and their lives in it. Also see Lima, *O mundo estranho*, pp. 53–82; on pp. 64–73, he gives a reason for Dadá's entry into the cangaço which is different from that told me.

[57] Pedro Melo Bulhões, interview, Santana de Ipanema, Alagoas, June 21, 1974; Luciano Carneiro, "O filho de Corisco," *O Cruzeiro*, October 10, 1953. Cor-

was born in 1932, she was left by her parents with a trusted coiteiro in Sergipe. The cowboy and his wife were told to keep her until she reached school age, at which time she should be sent to João, Lampião's one surviving brother. Expedita's birth was kept a highly guarded secret, although her parents passed by the ranch now and then to see her.[58] Other cangaceiros also gave their children to priests and friendly ranchers, and a few even sent them to the police.[59]

The bandits generally lived in free union with their women, although at least one pair, Corisco and Dadá, were formally married. Even without marriage, however, many of the couples remained together for as long as circumstances permitted. When a woman's bandit was killed, she did not always leave the group, for she might become attached to another member. Joanna Gomes, for instance, spent over four years with one of the Engracia brothers and, upon his death, became the woman of Jacaré ("Alligator"). When he, in turn, died shortly thereafter in a battle, the bandits began to suspect that Joanna might be bad luck. Accusing her of possessing occult powers, they expelled her from the band. Fidelity on the part of the women in the band was enforced, quite probably because Lampião knew that squabbles over them could upset the usually harmonious relationships among his men. When Christina, Português' woman, allowed herself to be seduced by another member of the band, the captain personally killed her.[60]

The presence of women among the cangaceiros may have influenced some of their patterns of behavior. There was in the course of the decade, for example, a general reduction in the level of activity among the bandits. They spent more and more time in their hide-outs, living as normal a life as was possible for them, and less time in far-

---

isco and Dadá had a total of seven children, three of whom lived (Lima, *O mundo estranho*, p. 73).

[58] Soon after Lampião and Maria were killed in 1938, a Bahia force, learning of Expedita, seized her and took her to Salvador. João Ferreira went there and, after a legal hassle, succeeded in getting custody of her. He reared her at his home in Propriá, although the couple who had kept her in the interior also wanted her. Expedita now lives with her husband and children in Aracajú. João Ferreira, interview.

[59] *Diário de Notícias*, July 28, 1932, for example, reports such a case.

[60] Interview with Português in *Jornal de Alagoas*, January 10, 1939. Ângelo Roque relates a similar case in Lima, *O mundo estranho*, pp. 59–62.

ranging operations. While this change may be mostly attributable to a higher level of persecution by police, it also may have been an attempt to obtain an approximation of family life. Some of the men, such as Lampião, Luís Pedro, and Virgínio, were realizing perhaps that this was the only kind of life they would ever have the opportunity to lead, and, now, well beyond thirty years of age, they were seeking to settle down a bit.

It is said also that the women moderated the excessive cruelty of their men. Maria reportedly was the only one who could get through to Lampião when he was angry, and she is supposed to have persuaded him at times to refrain from committing cruel acts. An Agua Branca resident attributed the saving of his life to her. Threatened by Lampião with death, he pleaded that he had a young daughter who needed him. Thereupon, Maria, mentioning her own daughter, asked that his life be spared. Later, one of the cangaceiros sent his four-day-old son to the man to be reared.[61] A similar intercession of Dadá with Corisco has been recorded.[62] It would seem to be true that the bandits' women did persuade them in specific instances to act in a more humane manner, but it should be doubted that such entreaties were distinctively feminine, for men in the band also had at times a similar influence on their comrades.

In the absence of firm data, it is difficult to determine whether the presence of women in the band led to a reduction in the incidence of rape by the cangaceiros. The question of rape in Lampião's band is a disputed one, especially as it relates to Lampião himself. Few question the fact that his men committed rape, for such cases were numerous. There have been many assertions, however, that the cangaceiro chieftain was always a respecter of women himself and that the cases of rape by his men were events that he could not control.[63] Such a view seems to fall short of the truth. Discounting newspaper accounts that lack specific data, reliable reports of Lampião's having raped a woman

[61] Rocha, *Bandoleiros*, pp. 104–106.

[62] Manuel Leitão, interview, Mata Grande. Alagoas, June 24, 1974.

[63] This is, indeed, the most prevalent view in the backlands today. It also has been the opinion of several writers on Lampião, as, for instance, Machado, *As táticas de guerra dos cangaceiros*, p. 116. In spite of the title of this book, it is a general treatment of Lampião.

or having attended the rape of a woman by one of his men are not numerous, but the dearth of such reports should not come as a surprise, since neither the women nor the bandits talked much of the matter. As one would expect, ex-cangaceiros almost universally deny that any of their number ever raped anybody.

Such denials notwithstanding, it is clear that rape did occur, and often it was committed against women who were associated with the police—a distinction which the bandits, in their distorted view of society, found valid. One of the most reliable reports of cases personally involving Lampião concerns an event that took place in Paraíba in 1923. There, in Bonito de Santa Fé County, located near the Ceará border, Lampião and his band raped the young wife of a police deputy. Lampião was first and was followed by the twenty-five members of his band. The deputy himself was tied up and made to watch. He lived to tell his story—that was before Lampião began to kill almost all police who fell in his power—to an official who arrived shortly after the event. When the officer arrived the wife was still hysterical.[64] A similar case, involving Lampião's men, took place when the band raided Várzea da Ema in Bahia in 1931. There, a number of them raped the common-law wife of a soldier.[65] That case, within the context of the times, was inconsequential, since, to the bandits, she was the woman of a policeman and, to society in general, she was neither a virgin nor a married woman.

One ex-cangaceiro talked quite freely about the question of rape in Lampião's group. Ângelo Roque, who joined the band shortly after the move to Bahia, related that on one occasion in late 1929 or early 1930 Lampião and his band raped a young woman, apparently on the pretext of being outraged because she had married an old man of eighty years. They beat up the old man. Lampião, Roque added, seemed especially to enjoy taking a woman who was crying. If his assessment is correct, the outlaw chieftain's perversity in this regard was considerably greater than it has usually been pictured. Roque also added that Lampião was not faithful to Maria.[66]

Rape, then, did occur but was not an indiscriminate act. Indeed,

[64] The official, Manoel Arruda d'Assis, told me the story.
[65] José Gomes dos Santos, interview.
[66] Ângelo Roque in Lima, *O mundo estranho*, pp. 58, 227.

the bandits were forbidden explicitly to seduce respectable girls of families with which the band had friendly relations. Punishment for failure to keep this rule was fast and sure. Near Jeremoabo there was a case in which a young cangaceiro was accused by a thirteen-year-old girl of having raped her at a party that the bandits were attending on the ranch of one of their coiteiros. Lampião shot the boy and buried him before leaving.[67] Such an action by the bandit chief, of course, was not indicative of moral values. Rather, it reflected his need to maintain good relations with the rural peoples on whom he depended for so much, a coiteiro who liked him being worth much more than one who served him out of fear.

If the bandits did not often engage in rape, their reasons, other than fear of what the captain might do to them, included the fact that they did not have to in order to indulge their carnal desires. In the backlands every town had a few houses devoted to the oldest profession, and, aside from prohibitions involving faithfully married ladies and young virgins, the moral code as practiced amply recognized the weakness of the flesh. As the backlands' most romantic figures, the cangaceiros were looked upon with considerable desire.

Finally, a bizarre aspect of the bandits' behavior toward the female sex should be noted. Especially during the decade of the thirties, Lampião and at least some of his men attempted to impose on the areas under their influence a prudish view of women's fashions. It was reported as early as 1930 that the cangaceiro leader was whipping women who wore short hair or dressed in short skirts.[68] Soon thereafter, punishment for infractions of the cangaceiros' standards for women's dress was turned over to a bandit called José Bahiano. Bahiano, a tall, strong, black man, joined Lampião along with his cousins, the Engracia brothers, soon after the bandit crossed into Bahia. A man who talked little and seldom smiled (but sang beautifully), Bahiano had a passion for punishing girls who failed to dress in accordance with the bandits' rules. His method of punishment was branding, which leads one to suspect that he sadistically enjoyed inflicting the torture. With his branding iron that bore the initials "JB," he left his mark on the anatomies of

[67] José Gomes dos Santos and Severiano Ramos, interviews; Ângelo Roque in Lima, *O mundo estranho*, pp. 210–211.
[68] *O Povo*, September 24, 1930.

a number of backlands women. He branded some of them on the face, but his imprint was left on others on thighs, buttocks, and above the vagina. Although Lampião did not personally brand women, he approved of José Bahiano's actions.[69]

[69] Volta-Sêca's story as told to Gomes, *Diário de Notícias*, April 30 and May 10, 1959, tells of Bahiano and his actions. Also see: Prata, *Lampeão*, p. 43; Goís, *Lampião*, p. 146; *A Tarde*, March 2, 1931.

9. The Campaign and the Coiteiros

THE reorganized Bahia campaign against banditry, commencing in October, 1931, eventually produced significant results. The optimistic predictions that it would be brought to a successful conclusion within a few months, however, proved to be inaccurate. The first full calendar year of the campaign, 1932, was marked by disruptions from national problems and by defeat on more than one front at home. The year opened with a disaster on the battlefront on January 5.

The meeting on that day, occurring about a month after the bandits had fled from their hide-out in the Raso da Catarina, took place at Maranduba, on the upper limits of the Sergipe-Bahia border. The area, which was being guarded by troops because it was known that the cangaceiros had fled into Sergipe in December, was a popular point of passage and repose for the bandits as they went from the one state to the other. Commanding the troops was Lieutenant Liberato de Carvalho, a native of the border region. Indeed, his brother, José Maria, was known as a leading coiteiro of Lampião, not so much because he liked him as for the fact that he resided in an area in which the bandit's influence was preeminent.[1] Also among the troops were Manuel Neto and his Pernambuco volante. When the battle occurred, the bandits recently had arrived from the Sergipe village of Canindé, where they had burned the police station and branded the soldiers' women.[2] The story of the meeting was an all too common one. Although the soldiers outnumbered the bandits by a three to one margin (approximately 100 to 32), it was they who suffered most. The bandits were well positioned, had ample supplies of ammunition, and were in a favored location when the force approached. In spite of having been told of the bandits'

[1] Severiano Ramos and José Gomes dos Santos, interviews.
[2] Francisco Rodrigues, interview.

whereabouts, the police did not succeed in establishing a good position. Manuel Neto's force was in front, and Liberato's, instead of flanking the bandits, foolishly tried to fire at them over the heads of their Pernambuco comrades. In the two-hour fight, the casualties to the police, made by both the bandits and other police, were numerous. At least five soldiers died at the scene of the battle; several of the dozen or more wounded died later, mostly for lack of medical attention, since there were no doctors short of distant towns, such as Piranhas, Alagoas. The cangaceiros apparently lost four men, two of whom died immediately. Another was so badly wounded that Lampião reportedly shot him to end his suffering. The fourth, Bananeira ("Banana Plant"), sought treatment and was arrested in Alagoas in the following month.[3]

Also in February, the Bahia police received some of their widest publicity yet with the capture of the young cangaceiro known as Volta-Sêca. Lampião frequently had boys in his band, not only because he liked having them around but also because they were useful as spies. A boy sent in to scout a town that the band planned to enter or attack was less likely to be noticed than a man. Volta-Sêca had joined Lampião's band four years previously, in late 1928 or early 1929. A native of Sergipe and at the time a homeless boy in his early teens, he was working on a ranch south of Jeremoabo when Lampião and his band passed. After the boy had done some chores for the bandits, Lampião asked him to accompany them. The boy knew little of what he was getting into, but he was told by the local police chief, who was present, that he would have a good future with the Captain, so he decided to go along. At the least, he said, he knew that Lampião was a brave bandit. After the practice of giving nicknames to those who joined the band, Lampião called him Volta-Sêca, the name of the place where they were at the time. Subsequently, he became one of Lampião's favorites. The cangaceiro chief taught him to shoot, shared his food with him, and nursed him when he was wounded.[4]

Volta-Sêca was captured alone near Santo Antônio da Glória soon

[3] The events of the battle were told to me by Francisco Rodrigues, who was in Piranhas when the wounded soldiers arrived there (interview). Also see: *A Tarde*, January 21, 1932; Ângelo Roque in Lima, *O mundo estranho*, pp. 264–265; Volta-Sêca's story as told to Gomes, *Diário de Notícias*, May 17 and 18, 1959 (Volta-Sêca participated in the battle); *A Tarde*, February 26, 1932.

[4] Volta-Sêca's story as told to Gomes, *Diário de Notícias*, April 25, 1959; *A Tarde*, March 22, 1932; Lima, *O mundo estranho*, pp. 86–105.

after the battle at Maranduba. According to his story, he had left the band because Lampião was angry with him for having acted foolishly in the battle and for refusing to ride double with the wounded Bananeira. In the dispute, he had talked back to Lampião, and several members of the band, fearing what the chief might do, had urged him to flee. Leaving during the night, he went to a ranch where he had a girlfriend. The police, having learned that he frequently came there, had persuaded two brothers on the ranch to act as their agents, under threats that they would be expelled from their land for being Lampião's coiteiros. When Volta-Sêca arrived, they captured him quite easily.[5]

After spending several weeks in Jeremoabo, where he was interrogated, he departed under heavy guard for the capital in mid-March. In Salvador, news of his impending arrival occasioned great interest, for the young cangaceiro had a reputation as one of the most fearsome members of Lampião's band. He had a hand, reports over the years had indicated, in some of the group's worst atrocities, including the Queimadas massacre. When newspaper reporters went to an outlying train station to get an early interview with him, they found a crowd of over 2,000 awaiting his passage. Upon his train's arrival, many in the throng, especially girls and young women, shouted for him to stick his head out the window so that they might get a look at him.[6]

Once in jail, Volta-Sêca talked freely to police officials, revealing, it was said, valuable information about the band's activities and its protectors and suppliers. Reporters who interviewed him marveled that such a seemingly humble and inoffensive young man could have committed the acts of cruelty ascribed to him. He was, they said, friendly to them and to his captors. Moreover, it was reported that the young criminal had said that he would never return to the band, even if he were freed. He would rather be a *macaco*.[7] His popularity with the people continued. The numerous pictures of him that were carried in the newspapers showed him to be a quite ordinary and pleasant-appearing black boy in his late teens. On one day, over 1,000 persons went to the

[5] Volta-Sêca's story as told to Gomes, *Diário de Notícias*, May 17 and 18, 1959; *A Tarde*, March 23, 1932. Also José Izidro and Francisco Motinho Dourado (Salvador, Bahia, November 29, 1973), two officers who helped to arrange Volta-Sêca's capture, told me the story in interviews.

[6] *A Tarde*, March 22, 1932.

[7] *Ibid.*, April 1, 1932.

jail to see him, and on another, when it was reported falsely that he had been killed, hundreds appeared at the Nina Rodrigues Institute to view his body.[8] The medical scholars at the institute, to be sure, were interested in his body. To them, he was a prime specimen to be studied in relation to their theories about the physical typology of criminals. They examined him minutely—*A Tarde* carried a picture of Arthur Ramos, one of the nation's leading intellectual figures, taking measurements of his head—and seemed to be disappointed, according to reports, that his physical makeup was so normal. He possessed, they reported, none of the Lombrosian anomalies.[9]

Although Volta-Sêca seemed to enjoy his first days in the detention house in Salvador and the attention he was receiving, he had little idea, in all likelihood, how long his period of incarceration would last. The judicial proceedings against him were delayed because of uncertainty over whether or not he could be tried as an adult, since no one, it seems, knew his exact age.[10] About a year after his arrest, the trials began, and, before they were over, Volta-Sêca had been condemned to 145 years in prison. A judicial review, however, led to a reduction in the sentence to 30 years, and, after 20 of them had passed, Antônio dos Santos (Volta-Sêca's real name) was pardoned in 1954 by President Getúlio Vargas. He later moved to the south of the country after wandering around the Northeast for a time.[11] Only a few of the other cangaceiros were ever dealt with as harshly by the courts.

Following the battle at Maranduba in January and the capture of Volta-Sêca in the following month, news of Lampião for the remainder of 1932 was neither abundant nor particularly noteworthy. It was becoming apparent, during the year, that the campaign most likely would be a prolonged one, for, while the police did succeed in locating the bandits now and then, the results of the meetings were indecisive. On

---

[8] *Ibid.*, April 15, 1932.

[9] *Ibid.*, March 22, 1932. Cesare Lombroso (1835–1909) was an Italian criminologist who believed that certain individuals were born as criminals and that they could be so identified by their physical characteristics. For an analysis of the physical characteristics of the cangaceiros, see Lima, *O mundo estranho*, pp. 27–52.

[10] See, for example, *A Tarde*, April 15, 1932; Lima, *O mundo estranho*, pp. 93, 94, and passim.

[11] Volta-Sêca's story as told to Gomes, *Diário de Notícias*, May 17, 18, and 20, 1959.

March 13, a volante encountered Lampião and his band on a ranch in Bahia, near Canudos, and engaged them in a battle. It ended when the cangaceiros retreated into the Raso da Catarina, taking their wounded with them. The commander of the volante, a lieutenant, was wounded, as were a sergeant and three soldiers.[12] In May, a force met a small group of bandits, believed to be part of Lampião's band, near Chorrochó, in northern Bahia, and, later in the month, another volante had a brief exchange of fire in Sergipe with Corisco's group. Two persons were reported killed in these battles, one of the bandit's women in the first and the cangaceiro Ventania ("Windstorm") in the second.[13] Then, in June, Captain Facó said that Lampião had crossed over into Sergipe. Corisco, he added, was hidden out in Bahia near the Sergipe border in an area in which water could be found easily—a prime consideration in 1932, since Northeast Brazil was passing through one of its major droughts. Corisco's band recently, the captain said, had sent two babies to the sergeant at Sítio do Quinto, asking that they be cared for.[14]

Through the first half of 1932, the campaign seemed to be operating at a rather low level, a condition resulting not only from chronic lack of money but also from the drought, which greatly limited all activity in the backlands, including, of course, the operations of the bandits. Commencing in July, police efforts were reduced even further by the outbreak of revolt in São Paulo on the ninth of that month. Soldiers were withdrawn from stations all over the backlands to aid in suppressing the Constitutionalist Revolution against President Getúlio Vargas' regime; even though the revolt was over in September, several weeks passed before normal troop strength was restored to the campaign.[15] In the meantime, the officials who were directing the war against banditry tried to compensate partially for the lack of professional troops by hiring more contracted men, the nonprofessionals who had long been used to supplement regular soldiers.[16]

Lampião and his bandits, according to reports, took advantage of the withdrawal of troops to increase their activities. On July 14, Corisco

[12] A Tarde, March 17, 1932.
[13] Ibid., May 16 and 26, 1932.
[14] Ibid., June 14, 1932.
[15] Reports of removal of troops are in A Tarde, August 20 and 24, 1932, and Diário de Notícias, August 17, 1932, among others.
[16] See, for example, SSP to Santa Brígida, July 26, 1932, telegrams, Bahia.

and a band of fourteen men and five women raided properties and robbed stores in the rural areas of Paripiranga County, located in Bahia on the Sergipe border.[17] Lampião and his group were operating one month later just west of there in Cícero Dantas County. In Sergipe, shortly thereafter, they met Lieutenant Manuel Neto's volante in a battle. When the cangaceiros fled, they left a baby on the ground.[18] Just a few days later, the cangaceiro chieftain and his followers were back in Bahia in the Queimadas-Bonfim area, where they attacked ranches and raided the village of Nova Olinda.

For a Salvador physician, the Nova Olinda attack was an event to be long remembered. Dr. Constantino Guimarães was in the village combatting an outbreak of typhoid fever when the bandits arrived. Not content with taking the doctor's watch, medical ring, medicine bag, revolver and gabardine raincoat, Lampião also requested a physical examination. Except for the defect in his right eye, Guimarães later said, the outlaw chieftain appeared to be in excellent health.[19]

While he was in the area, Lampião also made a request, by letter, to a prominent resident of Itiuba, a town that lay on the rail line between Queimadas and Bonfim. His note read:

Distinguished Col. Aristides Simões Freitas—
I send you this letter because I know that you can fill my need and won't ignore it. I ask because I can't work and for this reason I ask. I request 3:000$000 from you. I hope you won't fail me for in my travels I never messed with your ranches nor with the people who belong to you. Therefore I have hope and confidence that you won't fail me. I wait for your answer by the same messenger with all urgency. With nothing more to say, Captain Virgulino Ferreira, known as Lampião.[20]

A force caught up with the bandits two days after the Nova Olinda raid, and a brief battle ensued. When they fled, the band left behind some weapons, thirteen horses and mules, and considerable quantities

[17] *A Tarde*, July 22, 1932.

[18] *Ibid.*, August 18, 1932; *Diário de Notícias*, August 17, 1932.

[19] Guimarães told reporters of his meeting with Lampião several years later, after the bandit was dead (*A Tarde*, August 9, 1938).

[20] *A Tarde*, August 24, 1932. The newspaper did not report whether Colonel Freitas sent the money.

of blood, according to the police.[21] From then until the end of the year, only two additional battles between the bandits and the police were reported. In the first of them, which occurred near Uauá in early October, two cangaceiros were killed. When the desperados fled, the police found large quantities of arms and ammunition at the site. In the other battle, a Bahia force surrounded Lampião and his band in Gararú County, on the lower São Francisco River in Sergipe, on November 14, and reported that their capture was imminent. But, as had happened so many times before, the bandits escaped.[22]

With the end of 1932, the first full calendar year of the reorganized campaign in Bahia had been completed. A few cangaceiros had been killed or wounded during the course of the year, but the majority of casualties had been among the troops. A few other cangaceiros, in addition, had turned themselves in or been arrested while separated from the band.[23] The military effort, hampered in mid-passage by the revolt in São Paulo, had only modest successes to its credit. On another front, however, Bahia was now confronting more directly the problem of the relations between the bandits and the larger society.

The Bahia authorities realized, as had those in Pernambuco earlier, that the support—voluntary or forced—that the bandits received from the civilian population was important. If Lampião could not be eliminated quickly on the battlefield, it was then necessary to weaken him by forcing a withdrawal of his support. Captain Facó had included the "leveling" of the coiteiros as one of the principal aims of the campaign and two months after the opening of it had declared that it would have been successful already were it not for them.[24] The problem of the coiteiro from the police point of view was an immense one, since, to them, almost any resident of the backlands area was an actual or potential friend or protector of the bandits. This being so, the backlanders themselves had serious problems, for they found themselves in the unenviable position of having to try to satisfy both the police and the bandits.

---

[21] A Tarde, August 24, 1932.

[22] Ibid., October 10 and November 21, 1932.

[23] In addition to those previously mentioned, reports of apprehension of cangaceiros appeared in A Tarde, March 17, May 10 and 17, and September 3 and 5, 1932.

[24] Diário de Notícias, October 27 and December 29, 1931.

To the police, there were two differeni types of coiteiros. The first group was made up of the wealthy ranchers, businessmen, and political bosses (usually they were all three at the same time) who served Lampião out of necessity. They sent him the sums of money he demanded or supplied him only to protect their properties, it was said. This was a group that the police could not effectively deal with, since a man like Colonel João Sá of Jeremoabo had political connections that gave him virtual immunity from police action—this was true both before and after the Revolution of 1930. A member of this group might be questioned, as Sá was after Volta-Sêca named him as a coiteiro, but he would neither be beaten nor prosecuted. His problems were "understood" by the authorities. They classed him an involuntary coiteiro. For the police, it was a handy distinction, since they could not touch him anyhow. If there was a change after the 1930 Revolution, it affected not so much the political chief himself as his cowboys and tenants. Because of the increased power of the state and the consequent greater independence of the police, the political chief was no longer as able to protect his dependents from the law as he had been.[25]

The second group of coiteiros consisted of cowboys, tenants, and other persons who had little influence. Among these were small- to medium-size property owners and their cowboys and tenants, as well as village storekeepers and tradesmen. This group received little sympathy or understanding from the police. The police understandably became suspicious of everyone after they learned that they were being given false information by citizens in the areas in which the bandits operated. Whether people in the countryside did this because they liked Lampião or because they feared him made little difference to the police. Either way, the soldiers suffered, as at Mandacarú when a cowboy's lies led them into a disastrous ambush. This class of coiteiros— the poorer among them were often called the "barefoot coiteiros"—suffered more at the hands of the police than they did from the bandits. In actuality, the great majority of them feared the bandits more and, had they been given effective protection, would have cooperated with

[25] On the classification of coiteiros, see: Prata, *Lampeão*, pp. 155–166; Bezerra, *Como dei cabo de Lampeão*, pp. 91–93. Felipe Borges de Castro (interview) also provided information on coiteiros. Bezerra comments (p. 7) on the increased power of the police after the proclamation of Vargas' New State in 1937; it is clear, however, that at least in Bahia, such a trend had been in evidence since 1930.

the police. But adequately policing every village and rural homestead was an impossible task, and, as a result, the ever-present threat of Lampião's arrival and the terrible consequences of his retaliation for disloyalty brought most of the population to deny the police the information they so badly needed to wage their war effectively. An inevitable consequence of this situation was the wave of violence that many a volante left in its wake. Only by brutal methods, it seemed, could they induce the backlanders to inform on the bandits.

The problem of police violence against the general population was an old one, and it was compounded by the war against banditry. It was, as we have noted, a major complaint in Pernambuco, Paraíba, Ceará, and Alagoas. After 1928, it also became a major problem in Bahia and Sergipe. By 1929, only a few months after Lampião crossed into Bahia, reports from the northeastern part of the state were telling of the misuse of police power. "A picture of horror," worse than that painted by Lampião, was the way one newspaper article described it. Along the Bahia-Sergipe border, it was charged, the police were stealing horses and mules, a practice especially galling to backlanders.[26] Moreover, it was a common one, for, in contrast to the bandits, who often returned the animals they took, the police frequently made little effort to do so. Often, in fact, when the animals' usefulness had expired, the police killed them as punishment of their owners, whom they accused of being coiteiros.

Other complaints were also numerous. In April, 1932, for instance, a message from Juàzeiro told of a force having passed through a nearby village, breaking down doors, robbing and implanting terror.[27] A Sergipe rancher, in reference to a Bahia force, asserted: "You can believe that today in the backlands the arrival of Lampião at the door brings less anguish than news of the coming of a police force."[28] Of all the volantes in the backlands, the Nazarenos under Manuel Neto were among the most feared. Pursuing Lampião with fanatical zeal, they were inclined to employ whatever methods were necessary to obtain information. A police captain, in early 1930, indignantly informed his

[26] *Diário de Notícias*, June 16, 1929.
[27] SSP to Barro Vermelho, April 20, 1932; a similar complaint is in SSP to Bonfim, April 23, 1930, both in telegrams, Bahia.
[28] Letter of João Andrade, May 5, 1930, in packet SP' 132, Arquivo Público, Sergipe.

superiors that the group had passed through his jurisdiction, robbing, administering beatings, and invading properties. They were as dangerous, he said, as Lampião himself.[29]

Some of the brutality of the troops was attributable, no doubt, to anger and frustration, but it is clear that violence in many cases was employed as a deliberate policy. One message from the headquarters in Salvador ordered an official in the field to deal severely with those suspected of aiding the bandits, while another, though it did caution against committing injustices, instructed that violence be used when necessary. A captain in the field, in still another communication, reported to his superiors that he had succeeded in getting a confession from a coiteiro after subjecting him to "vigorous punishment." Given official policy and the vexations of the job, it is not surprising that the trails of the volantes were marked by beatings, maimings, and sometimes deaths.[30]

A further contributing cause to the brutality of the campaign lay in the nature of the soldiers themselves. Almost universally, the men were unlettered and uncultured. Brutality to them was commonplace. They were members of a rustic society in which violence was the main avenue for resolving disputes. And in the police, little was done to reorient them. Training for regular forces was brief and there was none at all for the contracted soldiers. Troops who enlisted on contract for supposedly temporary service were used in the campaign against banditry by all of the affected states. In Bahia, as in the other states, contracted soldiers at times made up a significant portion of the forces in the field. Substantial numbers of them passed into regular status before the campaign came to an end; a few of them, for their native intelligence and valor, became officers. But whether the soldiers were regular or contracted probably made little overall difference. If they were not

[29] The comment by the police captain is in SSP to Bonfim, January 22, 1930, telegrams, Bahia. João and David Jurubeba, themselves Nazarenos who fought under Manoel Neto, described life in his troop to me (interviews).

[30] SSP to Santo Antônio da Glória, November 9, 1931, and SSP to Jeremoabo, March 14, 1932, both in telegrams, Bahia; SSP to Chief of Police, Sergipe, October 15, 1932, telegrams, Bahia. Police violence is a major theme in literature on the cangaço. As examples, see accounts by three soldiers: Goís, *Lampião*, pp. 157–159; Gueiros, "*Lampeão*," pp. 168–170; Bezerra, *Como dei cabo de Lampeão*, pp. 25–28. Various former police officials, including Miguel Feitosa and José Izidro, also told me candidly that it was widespread (interviews).

already brutalized on enlistment, they soon became that way because of the conditions of the campaign. Complaints by officers about the quality of their men were chronic. One Pernambuco officer wrote that he commanded genuine wild men, indistinguishable from cangaceiros except for being called police. A Bahia field commander complained to headquarters that his troops included men who were "simply disreputable."[31]

The reasons why men joined the police also influenced the quality of their service. Many enlisted simply to obtain regular employment, since other opportunities were few. Some became soldiers because they found living in the no-man's land between the bandits and the police insupportable. It was necessary to join one side or the other. Others joined the force because the police threatened them. Zé Calú of Agua Branca, Alagoas, for example, was already a criminal when José Lucena made him a proposal. He could join the police and escape punishment, if he would eliminate the males in the Melão family, a group known to be so fierce that Lampião had expelled them from his band. Agreeing, he ambushed them one or two at a time and delivered their ears to Lucena as proof of his accomplishments. Calú subsequently had a long and successful career as a soldier in the fight against Lampião.[32] Octacílio Rodolfo of Rodellas County, Bahia, was a similar case. A coiteiro of cangaceiros, he was offered the choice by the police of turning in a bandit or receiving severe punishment. He chose the former course, but then, knowing that he had become an enemy of Lampião, asked the police for help. They placed him and his relatives and friends (some ten to fifteen in all) among their troops and Octacílio, rising to the rank of lieutenant, became one of Bahia's most noted volante commanders.[33]

Many other persons joined the police because they were enemies of Lampião or of his friends. A goodly number of those who pursued him in Bahia were from Pernambuco, and their enmity toward him was

[31] Gueiros, "Lampeão," p. 170; unsigned and undated document (ca. 1930) from a field commander to SSP, in special packet on Lampião, Arquivo Público, Bahia.

[32] Told me by Zezito Guedes, who recorded the story from Calú (interview, Arapiraca, Alagoas, June 29, 1974). A less detailed version was given me by Calú's brother, Euclides Lunes de Queiroz (interview, Mata Grande, Alagoas, June 23, 1974).

[33] José Izidro, interview.

long established.[34] Among these, the Nazarenos stand out, but there were also many others. In one typical case, Severiano Ramos went into the force because he was an enemy of Lampião's friend, Antônio Engracia. When Lampião came into Bahia, Severiano knew that he was in trouble. He, his brother, two cousins, and a brother-in-law all enlisted in 1928 on the same day.[35] Other men became soldiers in the hope of avenging wrongs done to them or their families by the bandits.

That Lampião was well aware of the motives of the soldiers is illustrated by an incident on the ranch of Manuel Salinas in 1930. The cangaceiro chief, learning that Salinas had informed on him to the police, returned to the ranch, located near Jeremoabo, to retaliate. After Salinas and his four older sons had been barbarously killed, Lampião hesitated before consigning the last one, a boy, to a like fate. Then, ordering the boy's death, too, the bandit chief said that if he spared the boy he would just grow up to become a soldier. The Salinas boy, however, escaped the fate Lampião had set for him. Although having decided already that the boy would die, Lampião ordered him to go upon the roof to break the tiles, an action the bandits often took in order to destroy a house. When the boy went up, one of the other cangaceiros, taking pity on him, told him to jump from the rear and run into the thickets nearby. The boy did as he was told and escaped. As Lampião had predicted, he later became a contracted soldier.[36]

While some backlanders sought to exact revenge or find a measure of safety by joining the police, the vast majority of the people remained in their homes, and many of them helped the bandits when they were asked to do so. Whatever else they may have felt about Lampião, they were afraid of him. They feared the police too, but they feared the bandits more. Mistreatment by the police was as occasional, erratic, and varied as the men and officers who made up the forces. The vengeance of Lampião, on the other hand, possessed in the mind of most backlanders a quality of relentless dependability that commanded respect.

[34] A large number of Pernambucans joined the Bahia force as contracted soldiers beginning with the campaign in 1931; they became regulars in 1934 (Diniz Casemiro do Nascimento, interview, Paulo Afonso, Bahia, August 29, 1975).

[35] Severiano Ramos, interview.

[36] I heard the account from Rosal Marinheiro, who knew Salinas and his family (interview, Piranhas, Alagoas, August 20, 1975). Prata, *Lampeão*, pp. 112–117, also tells the story.

Stories of the fearsome cangaceiro's punishment of disloyal back-landers were well known. It mattered not that some of them may have been exaggerated and a few invented, since people who lived in the areas most frequented by the bandits knew for a fact that such things happened. A part of what made the vengeance so impressive was not that Lampião simply killed informers—though that was impressive enough—but that he also humiliated and tortured them. Examples abound. Near Uauá in 1931, he appeared at São Paulo Ranch, threatening to burn the buildings and fences and kill all inhabitants unless he learned who had told a passing troop of police of his hiding place. To save the others, a man confessed. Lampião killed him by stabbing and then demanded to know who had gone to a nearby village to alert other police. Told that it was a tenant, Lampião found the man, stripped him of his clothes, and paraded him around the ranch before shooting him. The man's wife, similarly stripped naked, was forced to mount a horse and accompany the bandits for a few miles beyond the ranch. Near Bom Conselho, also in Bahia, the bandits in the same year occupied the ranch of a man who had informed on them two years previously. The man was tied up and his wife and six children were brought out into the yard to watch the proceedings. Lampião first extracted the man's eyes with a knife and, next, backing off, shot through the holes with a pistol. In Alagoas on the Pernambuco border in 1934, he ripped out the tongue of a woman he accused of having informed on him.[37]

With stories such as these increasing in number as the years passed, it is no wonder that the back-country people were wont to aid the cangaceiros and conceal knowledge of their whereabouts from the police. It was this that contributed so largely to the difficulties that the police had in the campaign. Conditions virtually dictated that the people in the countryside become the enemies of the police, since to become their collaborators was an invitation to the terrible vengeance of the cangaceiros. For this reason, most endured the injustices of the police and remained at least nominally on the cangaceiros' side.

Of course, there were some backlanders who served Lampião willingly, either because they liked him or because he paid well or for both of these reasons. This was the group on which he most depended. An-

[37] Abreu, *O flagello*, p. 53–54; *Jornal de Alagoas*, February 21, 1931, and December 13, 1934.

tônio Pequeno, a rancher in Pão de Açúcar County on the São Francisco River in Alagoas, was one of these. He did the bidding of the cangaceiros for several years during the 1930s, acting as a coiteiro chiefly of Corisco but also of Lampião. Especially fond of Lampião and Luís Pedro, he spent hours at a time in the bandits' camps, conversing and drinking with them. He brought them supplies, for which he was generously compensated, kept them informed of police movements, and carried letters to other coiteiros. Antônio recalls that Lampião was a real friend. Twice Antônio was beaten by the police and once jailed, accused of being a coiteiro, but he never turned informant.[38]

José Alves, another resident of the same county, also remembers the bandit chief fondly. He was in the corral milking in 1935 when he met Lampião. The bandit, who was camped on the ranch, tapped on the fence with his pistol to get the boy's attention and asked that milk and a goat for roasting be brought to his camp. Although José, who was then fourteen, and his older brother, who was fifteen, were afraid of the outlaws at first, they soon learned to enjoy their company. They spent much time in their camp, several times spending the night with them. At meal time, Dona Maria would prepare the boys' plates before anyone else was served. Lampião was especially taken with the older of the two, calling him his son. José says they both made a considerable sum of money, and his brother earned enough to buy a cow. The boys' father, on the other hand, was much disturbed at having the bandits on his ranch. He fled from the area, not so much for fear of Lampião as for what the police might do to him if they learned that the bandits were camped on his land and served by his sons. He soon also removed the rest of his family from the ranch; they returned only after Lampião's death.[39]

In spite of their problems, those who became Lampião's friends and coiteiros could count on a certain degree of favored status in the community. Their neighbors were not likely to incur consciously the ill will of Lampião's friends, for the bandits were known to do favors for those who served them well. As for other cangaceiros, the only bands of note still operating in the 1930s were those controlled by Lampião.

[38] Antônio Pequeno, interview, Pão de Açúcar, Alagoas, August 25, 1975.
[39] José Alves, interview, Piranhas, Alagoas, August 20, 1975.

He had become, indeed, the "King of the Cangaceiros." His subgroups, however, were equally known for their cruelties, and, since several of them might be operating at the same time, there was the possibility that the friends of one group might be attacked unwittingly by one of the other groups. To reduce such an eventuality—and perhaps also from vanity—Lampião gave his friends a kind of backlands passport. A printed calling card with the bandit's picture on it, it served notice that the bearer was to be given special consideration. On the reverse of one such card, given in 1935 to Colonel Joaquim Resende, the prefect of Pão de Açúcar County, Lampião identified Resende as his friend and stated that he was guaranteed from attack from cangaceiros. It was signed "Captain Lampião."[40] Neighboring Sergipe was so infested with Lampião's bandits, a newspaper in that state complained in 1936, that such a passport was a necessity for traveling and doing business in the interior counties.[41]

Some prominent persons who had amicable relations with Lampião used their friendship with him to attempt to extend protection also to their friends. When Dr. Waldemar Valente was traveling in the back country in the early 1930s as part of a malaria-eradication campaign, he was given a pass by Lampião's old friend, Cornélio Soares, the chief of Vila Bela. The card, requesting that the young physician be given free passage through the area, concluded with "He's one of ours."[42] In actions of a similar nature, Colonel Resende interceded with Lampião to secure the release or humane treatment of various persons who fell into the cangaceiros' hands.[43]

Finally, in spite of the bandit's fearsome reputation, there were some backlanders who tried to take advantage of him. Some of them took the money that he had entrusted to them to purchase supplies and then fled to some distant part of the country, usually to São Paulo in the south. Others, asked by the bandits to serve as messengers in extortion requests, acted in similar fashion. They delivered the note, but, upon receiving the money, decided to relocate, leaving the bandits holding the bag. Still others turned the fear of Lampião to their own gain. Many people paid on extortion requests, it is believed, for which

[40] Rocha, *Bandoleiros*, pp. 123–124.
[41] *A Luta* (Annapolis, now Simão Dias, Sergipe), March 15, 1936.
[42] Waldemar Valente, interview, Recife, Pernambuco, June 14, 1974.
[43] Rocha, *Bandoleiros*, p. 116.

neither Lampião nor his followers were responsible. A good number, no doubt, played the dangerous game successfully, but some did not. Near Pinhão, in Sergipe, a rancher in 1937 received a request from Lampião for money shortly after having paid on a previous one. Rightly suspicious, for the bandit was known to be a reasonable man in such dealings, he went to him, wanting to know why he was being taxed so heavily. Lampião, disavowing knowledge of the second request, ascertained the facts of the case and sent one of his men to deal with the imposter. The cangaceiro, Zé Sereno, stabbed and killed the man and his three teenaged sons. He then sought out the man's brother and killed him. Such harsh retribution kept reasonably limited the number of those who dared to take advantage of Lampião's name, though the problem was not rare in occurrence. On one occasion, the bandit complained, that there were too many "little Lampiãos" around.[44]

In spite of the problems presented by thieves, impostors, and informers, Lampião probably considered his relationship with backlanders generally satisfactory. The relationship certainly contributed largely to his survival as a bandit over so many years. The police, on the other hand, almost always found themselves in a mutually antagonistic connection with the vast majority of the people. Seldom was this fact clearer than in 1932, when Bahia attempted to bring the bandits to submission with an ill-fated reconcentration program.

That year was a bad one for backlanders, even without drastic action by the police. In 1932, the Northeast suffered through one of its most severe droughts in several decades. As the disaster came on, Captain João Miguel, a communications officer who was then commanding the forces in operation against banditry in Bahia, devised his plan to deprive Lampião of support in the countryside. In a meeting at Jeremoabo with other officers and civilian authorities, the captain proposed to group the entire population of the area in the county seats and larger villages. In this way, he asserted, the cangaceiros, deprived of supplies and the help of coiteiros, could be decimated easily or forced to turn themselves in. While the difficulties of such a plan must have been foreseen by some, it was, nonetheless, approved by State Chief of Police

---

[44] Gueiros, *Lampeão*, p. 128; José Melquiades de Oliveira, interview; Severiano Ramos, interview.

Facó and Interventor Magalhães. Sergipe officials, at the same time, rejected Bahia's request that a like policy be instituted there.[45]

The year is remembered in the area as "João Miguel's drought," not only for the natural disaster but for Miguel's as well. The project was implemented to varying degrees, depending on local officials. Few governmental programs in the Brazil of that era were ever effectuated with thoroughness and dispatch, and in this case the shortcomings were probably a blessing. Towns such as Juàzeiro, Bonfim, Uauá, and Jeremoabo became clogged with refugees fleeing from the drought and with those who were forced to leave their homes by the police. In April the number already exceeded a thousand in Juàzeiro, while in excess of 4,000 eventually were congregated in Jeremoabo, Miguel's headquarters.[46] The government, chronically plagued at that time by the inability to meet even ordinary running expenses, extended little aid to the refugees. Those without resources, as most were, had to depend on relatives or friends in the towns for shelter and sustenance or, lacking such recourse, charity. In Jeremoabo, as elsewhere, the only shelter that most found available was under trees or brush arbors in plazas and the churchyard. Persons were allowed to make trips to their homes only with the permission of authorities and accompanied by a guard. To ensure that unauthorized persons did not leave, soldiers patrolled the boundaries of the towns.

Although plenty of people were suffering from hunger, the predictions that the cangaceiros would be starved out were not coming true. Circulars posted in the backlands, guaranteeing the lives of bandits who might turn themselves in, produced only meager results. Three men, reportedly of Lampião's bands, delivered themselves in May, but they seem to have been the only ones.[47]

[45] The story of the plan and the havoc its implementation caused is told partially in Prata, *Lampeão*, pp. 175–202. I obtained additional information from persons who were in the area at the time, especially from José Gomes dos Santos, Severiano Ramos, and José Fernandes de Vieira (interviews).

[46] SSP to Colonel João Costa, April 12, 1932, telegrams, Bahia. The Jeremoabo figure is from Prata, *Lampeão*, p. 201. Prata also states (p. 194) that the total number of persons evacuated from their homes by the police was approximately twelve thousand.

[47] On the circulars and general policy, see *A Tarde*, March 22, 1932, and SSP to all commanders, March 21, 1932, telegrams, Bahia. On the results, see *A Tarde*, May 10 and 17, 1932.

In the meantime, the rural economy was virtually abandoned. Ranchers could get permission to send their cowboys, accompanied by guards, to their properties periodically to see after the cattle, but in a drought that small measure was hardly satisfactory. Oftentimes, the cowboys found the cattle dead or dying because the watering troughs filled on the previous trip were long since dry. Some few very prominent persons were allowed to leave their cowboys on their properties permanently, but humble folks were given no such consideration. Because of complaints and suffering, some modifications were introduced, but the project continued throughout the year. By October, if not before, smaller villages were being added as authorized refugee areas, and cowboys were being concentrated on the larger ranches in order to be nearer their herds.[48] Such a decentralization of the project was deemed necessary, not only because of the appeals from influential persons for relief from the harsh policies and the damage being done to the economy, but also because of epidemics of disease that were sweeping through towns such as Jeremoabo. With the decentralization, however, policing was not abandoned; the additional authorized villages and ranches were also being patrolled.

Although state officials were insisting as late as October that the modified plan be carried out in its entirety in all areas, they were ready by the end of the year to grant more significant relief. The chief of police ordered in December that within the zone of Curaçá and Patamuté the policy be continued only in those places where it might be deemed absolutely essential, in recognition, he said, of the needs of businessmen and ranchers and the necessity of conciliating the campaign with the general interests of the citizenry.[49] In reality, the state was conceding the defeat of the project in all areas, and it was dismantled during the next few weeks. Its author, João Miguel, soon was demoted within the campaign. While Magalhães and other officials tried to maintain the pretense that the program had accomplished satisfactory results, attributing its defects to Sergipe's refusal to follow suit, its intrinsic failure was generally recognized.[50] As one official said,

[48] Indicated in SSP to Jeremoabo, October 12, 1932, telegrams, Bahia.

[49] SSP to Jeremoabo, October 12, 1932, telegrams, Bahia; SSP to Uauá, December 12, 1932, telegrams, Bahia.

[50] For the official view of its success and accusations against Sergipe, see Juracy M. Magalhães, *Exposição feita ao Exmo. Snr. Dr. Getúlio Vargas*, p. 81, and Captain João Facó's interview in *A Noite* (Rio de Janeiro), April 24, 1933.

everybody suffered but Lampião.[51] The bandit seems to have spent most of the year in the better-watered regions of eastern Bahia or nearby in Sergipe. No matter how calamitous the combined drought and reconcentration program made the year for the people of northeastern Bahia, it was a relatively peaceful period for him.

A year such as 1932 afforded the cangaceiros more than ample rest from their labors. The drought made this rest much of an enforced one, but, for that matter, life among the bandits in normal times was well balanced between work and play. As was reported by the few outsiders who had the opportunity to see the cangaço from within, the outlaws in whatever season passed much of their time in peace, either on the property of some trusted coiteiro or in a remote hide-out in an area such as the Raso da Catarina.[52] They rested, hunted, played cards, and often at night made music and danced. While one may assume that in the main they preferred to dance with women, they danced with each other when none were available. Alcoholic beverages were consumed in large quantities, the local *cachaça* being the most common drink among them. Many of the men, such as Corisco, drank heavily, frequently to the point of losing consciousness. Lampião, for his part, preferred more refined drinks such as cognac and was a moderate drinker. Lampião and a few of his men also spent some time reading or listening to others read to them. The bandit leader liked newspapers, especially those which reported his exploits, and the illustrated magazines from Rio de Janeiro and São Paulo.

Even when they were under close pursuit by police, the men did not depart radically from the routine of their lives. As one of their hostages in the flight from Mossoró reported, often they seemed to remain calm and unworried and, even during such a trying time as that, would play cards until the late hours of night.

[51] Felipe Borges de Castro, interview. I could find no news in the press of the reconcentration program while it was in effect. After it ended, I located only one guarded reference (*A Tarde*, March 27, 1933) to its failure. The absence of news was due apparently to press censorship, which was severe under Magalhães.

[52] Some of the best firsthand views by outsiders of the cangaceiros are given by Antônio Gurgel and Maria José Lopez in Nonato, *Lampião em Mossoró*, pp. 192–215 and 184–191, respectively. Also valuable are the accounts in *O Ceará*, December 1, 1926, and *Diário de Notícias*, July 28, 1932, the first by Mineiro Dias, the second by a married couple held hostage for three days in Bahia. Antônio Pequeno and José Alves, both of whom spent considerable time in the bandits' camps in Alagoas, also furnished full descriptions in interviews.

Life in their rustic camps offered few amenities. The bandits slept on the ground, using for cover the blankets that they carried. Food was simple and easily prepared, normally consisting of roasted meat, *rapadura*, and *farinha*. Baths often were few and far between, especially during droughts or the dry seasons when ponds, creeks, and rivers dried up. It is no wonder that one of the luxuries affected by the bandits was perfume. Their heavy use of it—combined with their unwashed bodies and the generous quantities of brilliantine they applied to their hair—gave the cangaceiros the unique smell that became one of their trademarks.

10. In Sergipe with Governor Eronides

WITH the coming of the rains in the early months of 1933, which signaled the end to the drought, the backlands returned to normal. The campaign acquired a new commander in January, when Miguel was replaced by Lieutenant Colonel Liberato de Carvalho, one of the two officers at the Maranduba disaster a year earlier. Lampião continued to operate in a fairly inconspicuous manner for several months, mostly in Sergipe and the immediately adjacent area in Bahia. Occasionally a bandit from one of his groups was killed in a meeting with police, but there were no important battles. One bandit, Esperança ("Hope"), turned himself in, persuaded to do so by his two coiteiro brothers who, in turn, had been subjected to police pressure. Esperança brought with him, as proof of his good faith, the head of one of his bandit comrades.[1] Bahia's chief of police, João Facó, mistook Lampião's relative inaction as a sign of weakness. In an interview in Rio de Janeiro in April, he asserted that the bandits had been reduced to few in number and were low in ammunition, unable, he added, to offer the least resistance to the police. Two months later, Lampião once again showed up Facó's faulty judgment.[2]

In June, the cangaceiro chieftain turned up near Bonfim, accompanied by nineteen men and three women. After failing to locate a Campo Formoso County police deputy, whom he planned to murder, he was reported as heading in the direction of Sento Sé. A few days later, officials at Sento Sé, an isolated town on the São Francisco River to the west of Juàzeiro, sent an urgent appeal for help. With Lampião in the county, they feared a raid on the town itself.[3] The bandits did

[1] A Tarde, March 29, 1933.
[2] A Noite, April 24, 1933.
[3] Campo Formoso to SSP, June 10, 1933, ofícios, Bahia (these documents are

not attack the county seat but did enter the substantial village of Oliveira, lying a few miles up river. Appearing there mounted and well armed at daybreak on July 8, they seized the principal merchants and looted their stores. Their take in money, cloth, jewels, old coins of gold and silver, and other items was estimated at 70:000$000. The village was completely cleaned out, a report said, as a result of the bandits' two-hour visit. The outlaws, seemingly in no hurry, took time to bathe their horses in the river and afterwards poured bottles of stolen perfume over them. Six days passed before the police arrived.[4] After the raid, the bandits camped for some weeks in a nearby area of difficult access that afforded them a bird's-eye view of the surroundings. They left it only to make occasional forays on neighboring ranches. When a police force arrived in early August, they ambushed it, killing two soldiers and gravely wounding another.[5]

The next meeting with the police took place in September in Campo Formoso County to the southeast. The police had been on the bandits' trail for several days when they learned that the outlaws were camped on Pouso Alegre Ranch. Seeking to ensure their victory, the police arranged for coiteiros to take *farinha* laced with strychnine to the bandits' camp. When the soldiers approached the camp, one of their dogs broke and ran toward it, barking. The cangaceiros' dogs responded, and the police learned quickly that the poisoning tactic had failed, for a thirty-minute battle followed. Inspecting the camp afterwards, the police came upon the poisoned *farinha*. It was untouched. The soldiers also found cooking-oil cans filled with gold coins, which, in their haste, the bandits had left. In the battle, one soldier and one bandit perished.[6]

More of Lampião's bandits died in a battle during the next month at Lagoa do Lino Ranch in Monte Alegre County. In early October, the police had sent troops to the Mundo Novo–Monte Alegre area when they learned that Azulão ("Bluebird"), a subchieftain, and five com-

found in the Arquivo Público); referred to in Secretaria de Fazenda e Tesouro to SSP, June 24, 1933, ofícios, Bahia.

4 *A Tarde*, July 24, 1933.

5 SSP to Bonfim, July 20, 1933, and SSP to Sento Sé, August 1, 1933, telegrams, Bahia; *A Tarde*, August 10, 1933.

6 *A Tarde*, September 13, 1933, carries a report of the battle. José Fernandes de Vieira, who was a participant, also described the event to me and told the story of the attempted poisoning (interview).

panions were operating there. Going to the ranch where the outlaws were alleged to be, according to informants, the police found only a woman who denied that they were there. But, questioning a girl who was approaching the house, they learned that the small band was eating in a nearby field. Going there, the police killed or badly wounded four of the six, including a woman, in a fierce fifteen-minute battle. Finishing off the wounded, they beheaded the four bandits and, after displaying the heads in Monte Alegre, sent them to Salvador. A multitude went to the Nina Rodrigues Institute to view the trophies, their interest kindled by the newspapers, which gave out the sensational news with accompanying pictures.[7]

Altogether, the police claimed that they confronted the bandits in battle fifteen times during 1933, killing eight of them. Those eight were to be added to the sixteen previously killed since the beginning of the campaign in October, 1931, according to the police. As for Lampião, he apparently was ready to abandon the far interior of Bahia. The police claimed, and the evidence appears to substantiate them, that he never again led his band into that area. Though his subgroups might penetrate well into Bahia, increasingly his incursions into the state were restricted to the border region.[8]

As Lampião's activities in Bahia declined, so did the campaign. In Bahia, the number of troops dedicated to it during 1934 dropped from a high of nearly 900 in July to approximately 250 by year's end. The number of columns of volantes fell from 22 to 7 during the same period.[9] Most of these were now commanded and manned by Pernambucans, such as Manuel Neto, who either were on loan from their home state or had passed over to the Bahia force. The campaign's decline reflected lessening interest by Bahia officials. At the same time, the other states still most affected by banditry, Sergipe and Alagoas, showed little desire or ability to increase their own efforts. In part, as well, the decline of the campaign was attributable to continuing financial problems. The federal government, which had been aiding the effort since 1931, was falling far behind its promises. The pay of the troops in the

[7] A Tarde, October 9, 18, 20, and 21, 1933.

[8] Liberato de Carvalho, "Forças em operações no nordeste do Estado de Bahia, Jan. 1933 a Fev. 1935," MS, Arquivo Público, Bahia (this is a relatório presented to the SSP); A Tarde, March 17, 1933; José Fernandes de Vieira and Severiano Ramos, interviews.

[9] Carvalho, "Forças," pp. 1–2.

field, Bahia's chief of police wired President Vargas in June, 1934, was eight months behind, a situation that was causing grave inconvenience, demoralization, and lack of discipline.[10]

The Bahia official had a basis for his complaint, as an appeal he received in May from Alagoas shows. The chief of police of that state complained about the activities of an armed group headed by one Odilon Flor, who claimed to be a sergeant in the Bahia police. The band members, claiming that they had not been paid in eight months, were causing numerous disorders. The Alagoas official added, in reference to the sergeant, "If he's one of yours, I ask you to order him to return home." Odilon, one of the Nazarenos, was, like so many of his relatives, a contracted soldier in the Bahia force.[11]

Also indicative of the faltering campaign was the reduced number of combats that the police claimed to have had with the bandits. In contrast to the previous year, when fifteen meetings had been registered, only eight were claimed in 1934, and some of these were scarcely more than sightings.[12] Lampião apparently spent most of the year in Sergipe and Alagoas. He was reported as having attacked a highway construction post in Sergipe in February, and in April he ambushed a volante near the Sergipe border in Paripiranga, Bahia. The Paripiranga battle resulted from another attempt of the police to arrange the poisoning of Lampião. This time, a coiteiro on whose land the bandits were camped was sent to town to purchase supplies for them. There, he was apprehended by the police and forced to return with poisoned food. But, because of his delay, the bandits had eaten before he got back. Lampião said that the food would be saved for the following day. Around midnight, however, a cowboy arrived and told Lampião the story of what had happened. Knowing that the police would be coming out to see if their tactic had been successful, the bandits waited for them and ambushed them. In the ambush, a sergeant was killed.[13]

In July, the police battled Lampião's forces on two successive days in Sergipe and killed one cangaceiro. He was, according to the police, the only bandit killed during 1934.[14] Lampião was in Alagoas for the

10 SSP to President Vargas, June 14, 1934, telegrams, Bahia.

11 Referred to in SSP to Jeremoabo, May 14, 1934, telegrams, Bahia.

12 The number comes from Carvalho, "Forças," p. 15.

13 *O Imparcial* (Salvador), February 26, 1934; SSP to Jeremoabo, April 23, 1934, telegrams, Bahia; José Melquiades de Oliveira, interview.

14 *O Imparcial*, July 18, 1934; Carvalho, "Forças," p. 18.

remainder of the year, and during that time two battles were reported, both in Mata Grande. Meanwhile, his subgroups were roaming over the tri-state area of Alagoas, Sergipe, and Bahia. Of them, the one led by José Bahiano seems to have been the most active. First reported as operating around Patamuté, Bahia, in October, he was by the end of the year robbing sugar mills within thirty miles of the coast in Sergipe. On a Saturday night in December, he entered one where earlier in the day the state's interventor had attended a party.[15] An Aracajú newspaper complained that the bandits were being given free rein in the state's interior. A few days later, the same journal charged that Sergipe's campaign against the bandits had accomplished nothing. Although a campaign was begun there too after the 1930 Revolution, the state's forces had failed to arrest or kill any bandits. They had not even engaged them in battle, the newspaper asserted.[16]

It was clear that Lampião and his bandits enjoyed special privileges in that state. Their relationship with Sergipe was much like the one that had existed between them and Ceará in the 1920s. The state's police left them alone, while they, in turn, confined their worst depredations and atrocities to other areas. Through changing administrations from 1928 forward, and in spite of the 1930 Revolution, the policy held fast. For the bandits, the advantages of the situation were obvious. They had a haven of refuge, strategically located between Bahia and Alagoas. As for Sergipe officials, who almost always denied that the bandits were there, they apparently preferred the shame and criticism that was heaped upon them to turning the interior into a battle ground. Leaving Bahia and, to a lesser degree, Alagoas to wage the campaign, their forces were stationed in towns and villages. Allegedly this was to protect population centers, but perhaps it was also, as critics charged, to avoid Lampião.

One former contracted soldier for Sergipe, commenting on his state's policy of inaction, related that the volante of which he was a part spent over a year in a village in Porto da Folha County without engaging in any action, even though they were aware that Lampião's main headquarters was located on a ranch only ten miles distant. When

[15] SSP to Jeremoabo, August 31, 1934, telegrams, Bahia; *Jornal de Alagoas*, October 13, 1934; SSP to Bonfim, October 23, 1934, telegrams, Bahia; *Correio de Aracajú*, November 28 and December 3 and 10, 1934.

[16] *Correio de Aracajú*, December 12 and 21, 1934.

finally the soldiers were ordered to rout the bandits, they found the camp deserted.[17] The band had been informed of the police movement by a coiteiro, they assumed. No doubt, Lampião possessed an excellent network of coiteiros in that state, where practically all of the interior counties served him on demand. Some portions of the state in particular, such as the Poço Redondo ("Round Well") area, were famous for their links with the cangaceiros. Not only was everyone in that remote village a coiteiro and friend of Lampião, it was said, but they also furnished him with an almost unlimited supply of recruits for his band.

It may have been that Sergipe officials refrained from vigorously persecuting Lampião and harassing his coiteiros not only out of fear of disturbing the peace of the interior, for it is a fact that the renowned bandit had friends in high places in that state. Speculation about his influential friends almost always pointed to two families, the Britos and the Carvalhos. The Britos, who were centered in the then important port city of Propriá on the São Francisco, were among the state's largest landowners. Lampião's contacts with them were excellent; he had known the family, it is said, since he transported hides for them as a boy. His brother, João, who lived much of the time in Propriá, also looked to them for assistance when officials from other states accused him of aiding the bandits.[18]

The Carvalhos also were wealthy and prestigious citizens of Sergipe. Colonel Antônio Caixeiro, as the elder Carvalho was known, was a merchant and landowner whose economic interests stretched over the state. Lampião came to an understanding with him on one of his early trips into Sergipe. Fleeing from a police force, he arrived at Caixeiro's ranch in Canhoba County on the São Francisco and requested permission to camp on it. Complying with his request, the rancher also told him to slaughter sheep and goats whenever he needed meat, asking in

---

[17] Goís, *Lampião*, p. 123–130 and 223–224.

[18] Volta-Sêca named the Britos as protectors and suppliers of Lampião (*Diário de Notícias*, February 25, 1932). Also see the charges in *A Tribuna* (Aracajú), January 23 and 26, 1932. Various police officers in interviews, including José Fernandes de Vieira, named the Britos as coiteiros. João Ferreira, without revealing any substantial details, indicated that they were friends of the family. Some of the most extensive accusations against them are in Trovador Cotinguiba (Augusto Laurindo), *Lampeão: O maior dos bandoleiros*, pp. 34–38, 53–54, 58. Laurindo, a popular poet, traveled in the interior of Sergipe selling literature at the fairs during the time of Lampião.

return only that his property, tenants, and cowboys be respected.[19] That was, of course, what Lampião wanted, in addition to certain other things, such as supplies, which his host was in an excellent position to arrange. Given his many properties in the state, Caixeiro was in no position to refuse to meet the bandit's needs.

In view of Lampião's acquaintance with the elder Carvalho, it seemed likely that not long would pass before the bandit would come to know the rancher's son, Captain Eronides, a physician in the Brazilian army. The opportunity for the two captains to meet came in 1929 when Eronides was spending some time on one of his father's ranches. Eronides himself later told the story of what happened.[20] Following a jocular exchange over who was in command, in which Lampião promoted the doctor to colonel, the bandit was invited in for dinner. Eronides then presented his guest with a thermos bottle and a box of imported cheese, gifts, he said, which he had purchased with Lampião in mind. Following dinner, he photographed the bandit and promised to send him copies of the results. Next, Lampião got down to business, asking that he and Eronides talk in private. According to what Eronides was willing to reveal years later about the substance of their conversation, Lampião wanted cartridges for his parabellum (a pistol of army issue for which ammunition was hard to find). When he was handed a box of cartridges, he divided with Eronides, saying that he should keep some for himself. Subsequently, the army captain said, Lampião frequently sent messages requesting additional ammunition, indicating that his supply had been exhausted. He also sent a messenger a few weeks after his visit to pick up the photographs. Eronides, as his interview was recorded, would have one believe that his acquaintance with the bandit was confined to that one occasion. Evidence, however, indicates otherwise. The chief of police of Sergipe stated in the following year that the army physician was treating Lampião for a medical problem on São Domingos Ranch in Porto da Folha. Although, he added, the Carvalhos denied the charge, trustworthy cowboys in the area told him that the accusation was true.[21]

[19] Caixeiro's son, Eronides, told this story to Nertan Macedo many years later (Macedo, *Capitão Virgulino*, pp. 187–188).

[20] Ibid., pp. 193–197.

[21] Chief of Police of Sergipe to SSP, Bahia, February 1, 1930, Packet SP'7, Arquivo Público, Aracajú, Sergipe.

However many times Lampião may have seen Eronides, his acquaintance with the Carvalhos was, for him, very fortunate, and not only because of the wealth and influence of Antônio Caixeiro. Following the return of constitutional government to Brazil in late 1934, Eronides became the governor of the state, and in 1937 when that government was erased he continued to head the state as interventor. With Eronides as the chief executive, the probability of the state's taking any significant action against Lampião became ever more remote. His use of Sergipe as a place of refuge seemed to be guaranteed.

There were many who suspected that Eronides and his family did not limit themselves to permitting Lampião to camp on their land, or sending him occasional presents of cartridges, or even to using their influence to prevent action against him by the police. Suspicions fell upon them as being among the principal suppliers of his ammunition. The question of the source of Lampião's plentiful supply of ammunition is mentioned often as the major mystery surrounding his activities. In reality, the matter is not as mysterious as it has been pictured, although, given the secretiveness of the transactions, firm data are not easy to obtain. Before 1930, as we have already indicated, the sources were numerous, for the backlands were well armed and ammunition of the common type could be purchased in any county seat. Also, Lampião could count on some assistance from the state police. Subsequently, after the 1930 Revolution effected its disarmament program, ammunition for pistols and high-powered rifles no longer could be found just anywhere. Presumably, only the police forces and the army had access to it through regular channels. However, disarmament was never complete, and arms and ammunition could still be obtained through personal influence and by way of corrupt officials. By 1933, when it had become evident that the campaign against banditry was falling short of original expectations, the ban on arms in the areas terrorized by the cangaceiros began to be eased in order to permit the people to defend themselves. Under this policy, the government distributed arms and ammunition to county prefects and police chiefs and to trusted ranchers as well.[22] While this practice modified the previous ban, it still did not make ammunition easily available on the open market. Nonethe-

---

[22] *A Tarde*, October 11 and 16, 1933 and December 2, 1935; *Jornal de Alagoas*, August 9, 1935.

less, some of it, no doubt, reached Lampião, whether under duress, for profit, or in robberies.

As to specific sources, Lampião guarded carefully his relations with major suppliers. His negotiations with them were conducted in privacy, and the deliveries were effected by means of intermediaries. His men were not supposed to know where the ammunition came from, although evidence suggests that they sometimes did. Once he secured the ammunition, he distributed it to his immediate band and sold it to his subgroups, a practice which led them to expend it with care.[23] He also preserved large quantities for future use, storing it in bottles and hiding them in hollow trees or burying them in the ground in various locations throughout the areas in which he operated. Even many years after his death, such caches of ammunition were discovered.

One specific source of ammunition continued to be the police, although again full information on this matter is difficult to obtain. However, soldiers were seen delivering ammunition to Lampião when he was camped on Belleza Ranch in Pão de Açúcar County, Alagoas, in 1936. Packed in leather trunks and covered over with *rapadura* and *farinha*, it was brought to the camp on the backs of donkeys. It is common knowledge, in addition, that the lieutenant who commanded the detachment of soldiers in that county protected Lampião. When a coiteiro arrived in the bandits' camp one day, a cangaceiro told him that the lieutenant had just left.[24] Suspicion also has fallen on João Bezerra, the Alagoas officer who commanded the force that ultimately eliminated Lampião; a coiteiro has said that Bezerra, too, sold ammunition to the cangaceiro chief.[25] While these bits of evidence are limited to Alagoas, it is likely that individual officers and men of the other states' forces were also corrupted.

The police do not appear to have been the bandits' main source of

[23] Zezito Guedes, interview. Guedes, of Arapiraca, Alagoas, has collected a considerable amount of information on the bandits, most of it from Jose Calú (now deceased) of the Alagoas force. Also see discussions regarding Lampião's handling of ammunition in *A Tarde*, November 7, 1938, and Oliveira, *Lampião*, pp. 112–114.

[24] José Alves (the observer), interview; Antônio Pequeno (the coiteiro), interview; Aldemar de Mendonça, interview, Pão de Açúcar, Alagoas, August 25, 1975.

[25] Joca Bernardes (the coiteiro), interview, Piranhas, Alagoas, August 20, 1975.

ammunition, although they may have furnished some of it. Lampião's use of newer ammunition than that available to the force is much commented on by soldiers who fought him, and a newspaper reported in 1937 that the bandits were using 1935 and 1936 issues of ammunition while the Sergipe police were using 1911 issue.[26] The fact that the bandits frequently possessed newer issues than the police themselves had does not absolve the police of suspicion, but it at least points some of the attention away from them. New ammunition would have been extremely difficult to obtain in northeastern Brazil. Short of the regular army, it was available—and then illegally so—only from supply points in the south of the country. The only way that Lampião could have obtained quantities of new ammunition was from persons who had good connections outside the region. The inevitable conclusion is that he must have purchased it by way of his influential friends. The Britos and the Carvalhos of Sergipe are the most likely candidates. The Britos were named by Volta-Sêca in 1932 as major suppliers, and, since the young cangaceiro's veracity might be doubted, it is worth noting that Sergipe's chief of police confirmed the charge. Also, earlier in that year, when Sergipe police in a rare action raided the Britos' homes and ranches in the Propriá area, eight rifles and large amounts of ammunition were uncovered. Volta-Sêca also named João Sá of Jeremoabo as a supplier of ammunition.[27]

As for the Carvalhos, Eronides, it will be remembered, admitted that he kept Lampião supplied with cartridges for his pistol. Quite likely, he and his family did much more than that. Even more so than the Britos, they had broadly based commercial connections outside the state, as well as within. Under the cover of their commercial activities, they could secure the ammunition and get it to the bandits without arousing suspicion. With Eronides as governor, the Sergipe end of the enterprise was without problems. If evidence to substantiate the charges against Eronides and his father as major suppliers of ammunition is weak, one incident at least lays the basis for strong suspicion. A rancher in Sergipe's interior, who was an unusually reliable informant, related that he knew personally of the delivery of two new army rifles

[26] *Correio de Aracajú*, June 25, 1937.

[27] SSP to Rio de Janeiro, March 1, 1932, telegrams, Bahia; *A Tribuna* (Aracajú), January 30, 1932; SSP to Rio de Janeiro, March 1, 1932, telegrams, Bahia.

that were sent by Eronides to the cangaceiro chieftain and his lieutenant, Luís Pedro.[28]

The question of the bandits' source of arms is not as complex as the matter of ammunition. They were given new rifles in Juàzeiro in 1926, and obtaining additional ones was not particularly difficult. Rifles could be taken occasionally in raids on important ranches, they could be picked up from dead or wounded soldiers, or they could be supplied by friends such as Eronides. Corisco once showed a new pistol to one of his coiteiros in Alagoas, telling him that it had been given to him by an officer.[29]

In sum, the so-called mystery of the source of Lampião's ammunition may not be such a mystery at all. As contemporaries suspected, his sources appear to have been numerous. As always, he had the ability to pay his suppliers handsomely, and he had a well-known history of effective reprisals against those who would not cooperate with him, a combination that made refusing him difficult. If the details of the matter are scarce, the cause does not lie in any probability that such dealings did not exist. Rather, it lies in the nature of the transactions, which lent themselves to bequeathing to posterity neither documents nor impressive collections of confessions of wrongdoing. Barring belated revelations by minor participants—for probably the major ones are all dead—reasonably complete details of how the celebrated bandit obtained his ammunition may never be known.

If Sergipe was Lampião's most reliable place of refuge during the last few years of his life, Alagoas also began to see more of him. He had operated there frequently in earlier years, but, after passing to Bahia in 1928, his visits were few. By early 1935, however, it was evident that he was paying an extended visit to that state, having been there since the previous July. Through the first months of 1935, he remained in the area and was spending much of his time in Mata Grande County. According to reports from the county, the damage that he was doing in attacking ranches and extorting money was considerable.[30] It was near

[28] José Melquiades de Oliveira, interview. Also on the Carvalhos, see Góis, *Lampião*, p. 156.

[29] Joca Bernardes, interview.

[30] Carvalho, "Forças," p. 19; *Correio do Sertão* (Jatobá, Pernambuco), March 10, 1935.

the middle part of the year before he left the area. Meanwhile, his other bands were operating in various locations. In February, the groups headed by Ângelo Roque, Mariano, and Corisco were in eastern Bahia along the Sergipe border, while Cyrilo de Engracia's and Jurema's groups were further west in the state's interior. Each of the bands, the police believed, comprised four men. In March, José Bahiano and his followers were robbing prosperous ranches in Sergipe. Corisco, in late April, sacked a ranch in Mata Grande, killing its owner.[31]

A group in which Virgínio ("Moderno"), Lampião's brother-in-law, was a part castrated a young man in Pão de Açúcar on June 24. The cangaceiros arrived at the ranch to punish the man's father for having informed on them to the police. They killed the father and emasculated his son. It was the cangaceiro known as Fortaleza who performed the operation. Although the young man suffered much, losing large quantities of blood, he survived and is still living in Pão de Açúcar.[32] The castration of Beijo ("Kiss"), as the young man was known, was not the only such incident in the cangaceiros' history. They similarly operated on at least three other men. On one occasion at a dance on a ranch in Porto da Folha, Sergipe, Lampião, apparently acting on a whim, castrated a mulatto. The cangaceiro said it was for the purpose of fattening him up. Lampião's woman, Maria, strongly objected to the act, it is reported. Another case, at least as it is told, was related to the bandit's pretensions to protecting womanhood. In that instance, a rancher in Sergipe told Lampião of his daughter's problems with her rakish husband. Married to the one daughter, he had seduced one of her sisters. Although the rancher did not want him killed, he indicated that he should be punished. Lampião met the young man a few months later and personally castrated him. He also cut off a part of one of his ears. Finally, a twenty-two-year-old man was castrated by Virgínio near Buique, Pernambuco, in 1936.[33]

Following his long stay in Alagoas, Lampião moved up into the Bom Conselho–Garanhuns–Aguas Belas area of Pernambuco in mid-

---

[31] Ibid.; *Correio de Aracajú*, March 19, 1935; *Jornal de Alagoas*, April 28, 1935.

[32] Antônio Pequeno, interview; *Diário de Pernambuco*, July 21, 1935, carried the victim's story.

[33] Goís, *Lampião*, p. 227; Volta-Sêca's story as told to Gomes, *Diário de Notícias*, May 1, 1959; *Diário de Pernambuco*, May 26, 1936. Ângelo Roque in Lima, *O mundo estranho*, pp. 199–200, tells the story of still another castration.

year. In late May in that area, he met the police in a battle along the Pernambuco-Alagoas border.[34] In the middle part of July, near Bom Conselho, he engaged the police again and then moved toward the village of Serrinha, in the same county. Just after midnight on July 20, the people of Serrinha learned that the cangaceiros were headed in their direction. All left the town except for a small party of men who remained to defend it. Upon the bandits' arrival on horseback just before daybreak, several minutes of firing took place. One of the band's dogs was killed, and two of their women were wounded. One was Maria, Lampião's woman. The bandits left with her and arranged at a ranch for four men to transport her in a hammock to a hiding place on a nearby mountain. The men later said that they and the bandits wore their sandals backwards to confound the police. Lampião sent Serrinha a letter, threatening to reduce it to a "pile of dirt." His vengeance, he said, would be "without limits."[35] Meanwhile, several police forces, including Manuel Neto's volante, gathered in the area to mount an attack on the bandits' hide-out. The police thought that they had the bandits sealed in, and, with all exits under guard, Lampião's liquidation was expected at any moment. Once more, however, he and his small band proved equal to the challenge. Apparently scaling an escarpment of extremely difficult access, carrying their wounded, they escaped down the other side of the mountain. The police attributed their own failure to the difficulty of the terrain.[36]

During the same month, the various states affected by banditry sent representatives to a meeting in Recife to discuss the faltering campaign, apparently believing that still another reorganization would help. Several state chiefs of police, including Abelardo Cardoso of Sergipe, granted interviews to the press. While not denying on this occasion that his state had cangaceiros, he stated that they were isolated and ephemeral groups. Colonel Liberato de Carvalho, who represented Bahia, also claimed that bandits were no longer a problem in his state. The major provision in the reorganization effected by the meeting established a unified command under Bahia's general direction, with Colonel Liberato as its head. In addition, a more liberal exchange of information was

[34] *Jornal de Alagoas*, May 31, 1935.
[35] *A Tarde*, July 19 and 31, 1935; *Diário de Pernambuco*, July 25, 1935.
[36] *Diário de Pernambuco*, July 28 and August 1 and 4, 1935; *A Tarde*, July 29, 1935.

promised, as was better support of troops. Subsidies for daily living expenses were to be paid in advance, so that troops would not have to requisition supplies in the field. No substantial changes in practice appear to have followed the agreement. To be sure, the chief of police of Alagoas claimed that his forces were being strengthened. He had ten volantes in the field, he said, each one with fifteen men. But such an action probably was not a result of the meeting. More likely, it was a reaction to the fact that Lampião was spending so much more time in the state than he had for several years. Money for all the states remained tight. On the day after Lampião attacked Serrinha, the federal senate rejected a bill to appropriate 200:000$000 to the campaign.[37]

The police did not seem to know where Lampião was during the weeks immediately following his daring escape. While there were reports of his having been sighted in Alagoas, others said that he was holed up on the ranch of a prominent citizen near Buique, Pernambuco.[38] With his followers divided into so many small bands, it is no wonder that the police were confused. Wherever he was, he lost some of his men during August and September. The killings were accomplishments for which the police could claim no credit, for the five all fell to civilians. The first to die was Cyrilo de Engracia, one of the Engracia brothers who had joined the band soon after Lampião came to Bahia. His death came in early August in Mata Grande, when the occupants of a truck he assaulted put up unexpected resistance. He was known as Ponto Fino, the same nickname that Lampião's brother, Ezekiel, had worn. Lampião usually passed on to others the names of his dead comrades in an attempt to conceal his losses. Four other bandits died in September, also in Mata Grande. In a gunfight, six civilians killed Suspeita ("Suspicion"), Medalha ("Medal"), Limoeiro ("Lemon Tree"), and Fortaleza, the cangaceiro who had castrated the man in nearby Pão de Açúcar. Felix Alves, the owner of the ranch where the battle occurred, died at the same time.[39]

Lampião, who was back operating in Mata Grande by October, threatened in revenge for the bandits' deaths to kill two hundred people in the county, the majority, he said, to come from the Alves family.

[37] *Diário de Pernambuco*, July 11 and 13, 1935; *Jornal de Alagoas*, August 28, 1935; *A Tarde*, July 21, 1935.
[38] *Diário de Pernambuco*, August 4, 1935; *A Tarde*, August 2 and 3, 1935.
[39] *Jornal de Alagoas*, August 28 and September 20, 1935.

When Lampião killed two people, a young girl and an old man, in an attack on a ranch in Mata Grande, *A Tarde* of Bahia on November 1 opined that the recent agreement in Recife seemed to be having no effect. The *Correio de Aracajú*, on November 21, reported the extortion of money from a ranch in Sergipe's interior and complained that the state's backlands counties had been turned over to the bands of José Bahiano, Ângelo Roque, and Mariano. By February of the next year, Bahia also was suffering again from the bandits' incursions. Mariano's and Corisco's bands were operating in the Jeremoabo area, and a brief battle with them had taken place, the police reported.[40]

Also in February of 1936, the many people who avidly followed Lampião from afar were treated to a rare story. In an interview in Rio de Janeiro, André Zambrano, a Venezuelan Boy Scout, told the press of a meeting with the great bandit a few months previously. Zambrano was traveling through the South American continent on foot—such international jaunts or "raids," as they were called in Brazil, were popular in the 1930s—when in central Alagoas he and his small party were taken captives by Lampião's band. When he was taken to meet the chief, he found him sitting in a hammock in his rustic camp, taking money from a large leather bag and counting it. In the interrogation that followed, Lampião became angry with Zambrano because of the peculiarities of his speech and accused him of being a policeman from São Paulo, the city which to most backlanders not only lay in the most remote part of the world but was also where all strange people came from. When the Boy Scout—actually he was twenty-two, he said—told him that he was from Venezuela, the cangaceiro wanted to know where that was and ordered him to "talk right, you shameless monkey." Probably not knowing just what to make of the youthful adventurers, Lampião ordered them stripped naked and tied to trees. They were given coffee with salt in it and water containing hot pepper, presumably as their last meal. Zambrano credited his salvation to Maria Bonita, who arrived in the camp somewhat later. Walking over to him where he was tied to the tree, still naked, she wanted to know how old he was. On his reply, she playfully hit him on the shoulder and told him, "Boy, you sure are cute." The next day, the scouts were released, although without their clothes, and, after getting assistance at a ranch, continued

[40] *Diário de Pernambuco*, February 14, 1936.

their "raid." At first opportunity, Zambrano added, his companions returned to Venezuela.[41]

For the next few months of 1936, Lampião and his closest companions operated mostly in Pernambuco, in an area less than 150 miles
from Recife. Either Virgínio or Luís Pedro frequently was reported as
heading groups. Lampião, news from the backlands indicated, was suffering from rheumatism. In March and early April, the bands were ter-
rorizing an area stretching across the state from Alagoas to Paraíba. In
one village near Buique, they forced a man to go to town to purchase
cloth for them and held his twelve-year-old son as hostage. This tactic,
often used by the bandits, was a reasonable guarantee that the man
would not inform on them to the police. Serrinha, the village that Lampião had earlier threatened with destruction, was heavily armed, waiting for an attack. But the attack never came, although it was believed
that four bands, totaling forty-two cangaceiros, were assaulting the
zone. Troops, including Manuel Neto's volante, were pursuing the bandits; the police, however, reported no contact with them. In late May,
the bandits' activities increased in Pernambuco and also reached up
into the Monteiro area of Paraíba, a state which had not been afflicted
with the presence of Lampião's cangaceiros for many years. There, cut-
ting telegraph lines to impede communications, the bandits continued
their spree of extorting money, assaulting ranches and villages, and
seizing persons for ransom. In all, they killed at least nine persons in
late May. Pernambuco authorities, reacting to the upsurge of violence,
announced in early June that they would intensify their efforts against
the bandits. The joint-action plan devised during the previous year,
they said, had been ineffective.[42]

In early June, one of Lampião's subordinate groups was wiped out,
and among those killed was the infamous José Bahiano. Again, the
work was done by civilians, which surely indicated that a widespread
distribution of arms to the backlanders would have been more effica-
cious than police action. Antônio de Chiquinha of Frei Paulo County,

[41] A report of Zambrano's interview was carried in the *Diário de Pernambuco*, February 22, 1936. *A Tarde*, February 4, 1936, reported an earlier interview
from Belo Horizonte.

[42] For accounts of the bandits' activities in March–June, 1936, see: *A Tarde*,
March 12, May 22, 23, 25, 29, and June 6, 1936; *Diário de Pernambuco*, April 8
and May 26, 1936. *O Norte* (João Pessoa), December 16, 1973, has an article that
contains interviews with some of the victims of Virgínio's raid into Paraíba.

Sergipe, and five companions did the deed. The occasion of the feat was a meeting that Bahiano had requested with Chiquinha in an isolated spot in the county. At the meeting, Chiquinha and his men in a surprise attack fired simultaneously and killed the four cangaceiros. They found a large sum of money on Bahiano and, in addition, took as trophies a handsome knife and his JB branding iron. The knife, said to be a gift from Lampião, was a work of art, wrought with gold and silver, and its value was considerable. Chiquinha was taken on by the Sergipe police as a contracted soldier to lead a volante, probably as much for his protection as anything else.[43]

Lampião by September was again heading his band. He, together with thirty-three men and women, entered Paripiranga County, Bahia, in the early part of the month, operating as usual. Residents of the area complained that the state had recently withdrawn numerous police contingents from northeastern Bahia, leaving the population defenseless.[44]

Later in the same month, one of Lampião's subgroups attempted a major attack on Piranhas, Alagoas. Piranhas, a picturesque little town that clings to the steep hills rising from the São Francisco River, was in those years an important port. It was the eastern terminus of the railroad that, coming from Jatobá (now Petrolándia), Pernambuco, carried cargo overland for some sixty miles in order to form a link where the river traffic was broken by the Paulo Afonso Falls. It lay in the heart of the Sergipe-Alagoas border area in which Lampião and his bands spent so much time during the middle 1930s. The cause of the attack was anger and the desire for revenge. Lieutenant João Bezerra, the commander of the force at Piranhas, had gone out to rout a den of bandits on Picos Ranch and in his attack wounded and captured Inacinha, the woman of Gato ("Cat"). The troops then headed with their prisoner, who was wounded only in the foot, toward a nearby station on the railroad. Gato and his companions, chased from the ranch, united with Corisco and others of their comrades to attack Piranhas and to take Bezerra's wife. The band of about twenty-five arrived at

[43] *Correio de Aracajú*, June 25, 27, and 30, 1936. About a year later, Chiquinha was dismissed; often drunk and disorderly, it was charged, his volante had accomplished nothing (*O Estado de Sergipe* [Aracajú], August 5, 1937). The *Correio de Aracajú*, however, defended Chiquinha, asserting his dismissal would aid the coiteiros.

[44] *A Tarde*, September 5 and 12, 1936.

the edge of the plain above the town just before noon on Monday, September 28. Having been told by a man on the road that there were no troops in the town, the bandits expected to take it by surprise.

Unbeknownst to the cangaceiros, the town had been warned, and a brave handful of citizens prepared to receive the bandits with fire. In the town, terror reigned among most of the population, for news had arrived that the outlaws already had killed six people on a ranch two miles away. When the bandits began to descend the steep street leading down into the town's small commercial district, shots rang out from below and the fight was on. During the hour in which the battle raged, a mere half-dozen stalwart civilians, firing from the second-story windows of some of the town's impressive buildings, held off the attackers. They also succeeded in killing Gato and badly wounding another bandit, who soon died. Two of the townspeople also were killed. One of them was the man who had told the bandits there were no soldiers in town. He told the truth, of course, but the desperados killed him anyhow, because they met such determined resistance. After the firing had ended, the bandits remained in the town's upper parts for a few minutes, dancing and singing and shouting curses to the people below. Thwarted in their thirst for revenge, they then left the town.[45]

Little of special note seems to have happened to Lampião for the remainder of 1936, excepting the loss of three of his men in October and a major disappointment for him at year's end. In late October, the Bahia volante of José Rufino battled Mariano and his group in Sergipe near Porto da Folha and killed three of them, including Mariano. The soldiers cut off the bandits' heads and brought them in, a practice that had become almost standard procedure.[46] Lampião for long had regarded Rufino, a Pernambucan who was a contracted soldier for Bahia, with respect because he was known to be one of those few who pursued the bandits with resolve and fearlessness. Lampião plotted to eliminate him after the death of Mariano and believed that he had found his chance in mid-December. Rufino was passing through Sergipe on his way to Serra Negra, Bahia. When he arrived in Poço Redondo, he found the village in a festive mood, celebrating the mar-

---

[45] Ibid., October 1 and 6, 1936, has stories of the attack. Francisco Rodrigues, one of the defenders, also told me the story in an interview.

[46] *Correio de Aracajú*, October 27 and 30, 1936.

riage of a local police sergeant. Using strong-armed methods to force information out of a coiteiro, Rufino learned that the bandits, camped not far from the village, were planning to ambush him and his force. He also learned that the revelers had been sending drinks out to the cangaceiros' camp. There was no way, Rufino later informed his superiors, that the Sergipe volante stationed there could not have known about Lampião's presence so near the village. To escape the noose that had been made for them, Rufino and his men left town in regular fashion but once outside, took another route. They arrived in Serra Negra safely. Lampião, with thirty-six men, had been waiting for them on the main route.[47] Rufino outlived his wily adversary by many years.

The last full calendar year left for Lampião was 1937, and for him and his men it was a fairly busy though unspectacular period. The police claimed that they met the bandits in battle sixteen times during the year, killing eight of them.[48] Three of the deaths were registered in Bahia in March when the volante of Octacílio Rodolfo battled a small band between Uauá and Barro Vermelho. Beija-Flor ("Hummingbird") was the only one of the group to escape with his life.[49] Most of the battles, however, were fought in Sergipe, although, as usual, the forces were from out of state and were led by such men as José Rufino and Odilon Flor. An Aracajú newspaper in June questioned Governor Eronides' contention that the recent deaths of three bandits in his state were demonstrations of the determination of Sergipe's forces. The outlaws had been killed, the paper said, by Odilon Flor's Bahia volante. The Sergipe forces were not to be blamed, another issue of the paper said, since the problem lay in the state administration. The police, the journal charged, had orders not to attack the bandits.[50]

Most of the bandits' operations during the year were in Sergipe and immediately adjacent areas in Alagoas and Bahia. Making no major raids, the cangaceiros limited themselves chiefly to extorting money. They probably did not feel the necessity to raid, since, as was reported from Sergipe, leading citizens from the interior towns regular-

[47] Rufino's report on the event is in SSP to Chief of Police, Sergipe, December 17, 1936, telegrams, Bahia. A participant, Severiano Ramos, also told me the story in an interview.
[48] "Destacamento do nordeste, Relatório . . . de 1937," MS, Arquivo, Polícia Militar, Bahia.
[49] A Tarde, March 13, 1937.
[50] Correio de Aracajú, June 25 and 26, 1937.

ly remitted money to the bandits.[51] Major José Lucena of Alagoas, answering criticism that his forces were not doing enough against Lampião, argued that the cangaceiros' pattern of activities was changing. While in the past they had sacked, burned, and killed, they now lived safely in hide-outs and were well supplied with money sent to them on request, he said. The major intimated that, living in such a manner, they were less susceptible to police action.[52] Lucena may have been correct about the changing pattern of the bandits' activities, but, nonetheless, they still were causing a considerable amount of suffering and widespread disruption in the backlands. In April, among other deaths that they were responsible for during the year, they killed a man in Mata Grande because he was a brother of a coiteiro who had turned against them.[53] Also, Lampião's war against highway construction was still in progress. In December, the bandits were hampering seriously the federal government's construction of a road in the interior of Sergipe. In Salvador, the construction supervisor announced the receival of a shipment of Thompson submachine guns that were to be used in protecting road workers.[54]

When the end of 1937 arrived, Lampião had not quite seven months to live.

[51] *A Tarde*, April 5, 1937.

[52] Letter from Lucena, published in *Gazeta de Alagoas*, August 21, 1937.

[53] *Jornal de Alagoas*, April 11, 1937. Four other killings in Alagoas by the bandits were reported in *A Tarde*, November 16, 1937.

[54] *A Tarde*, December 10, 1937.

11. The Measure of a Man

THE police attack at Angicos in late July of 1938 would bring the end
to a career remarkable not only for its feats and its durability but also
for the character of its architect. For an outlaw, Lampião led an unusually public life, and, consequently, more is known of him than might
be expected in the case of a rural bandit in an essentially premodern
society. He was interviewed, frequently photographed, and even appeared in a movie. He also became, early in his career, the subject of a
growing body of literature. Lampião's first appearance on the printed
page, apart from newspaper stories, may have been in 1923. In that
year, a booklet of popular verse about him, *História do bandoleiro
Lampeão* (History of the bandit Lampião) was published in Rio de
Janeiro. In it, the anonymous author, writing as if he were Lampião,
gives an unflattering portrayal of the bandit's life to that point.[1] Two
years later, another booklet, entitled *Lampeão foi cercado* (Lampião
was surrounded), appeared. It told the story, again in verse, of an escape by the bandit. The author of it was João Martins de Ataide, one
of the best-known creators of the *literatura de cordel* (literally, "literature of the string").[2]

Cordel literature tells popular stories in verse. Although characteristically based on contemporary events, the stories show ample evidence of the use of the author's imagination in both style and content.
Printed on cheap paper and usually having either eight or sixteen

[1] Referred to in Barroso, *Almas de Lama*, p. 98.
[2] On the *cordel* literature, see: Waldemar Valente, *O trovador nordestino:
Poesias de João Martins de Ataide*; Mário de Andrade, *O baile das quatro artes*,
especially pp. 73–103; Mark J. Curran, *Selected Bibliography of History and Politics in Brazilian Popular Poetry*; Mario Souto Maior, "Literatura popular em verso,
literatura popular nordestino, literatura de cordel: Uma introdução," in *Literatura
de cordel: Antologia*, 1: 5–30.

pages, the booklets have long been sold in villages and towns, especially on market day by wandering peddlers. It was the peddlers' custom of draping the booklets across a string (or *cordel*) for display that gave the literature its distinctive name. As a form of literature, it came to Brazil from Portugal during the colonial period and, being popular in origin, readily adapted itself to Brazilian themes. Lampião, like Antônio Silvino before him, quickly became one of the most exploited subjects for the stories. Stories based on him run the gamut from his boyhood in Pernambuco to his supposed encounter with Lucifer in hell —an encounter, incidentally, that resulted in something of a draw. As the only kind of literature with which most backlanders were acquainted, the booklets played a role in the formation of an image of Lampião that magnified his feats and contributed to the legend that he was becoming even years before his death.

In addition to the *cordel* literature, there were several other books published about Lampião during his lifetime, all of these purporting to contain factual accounts. The first, published by the official state press in Paraíba in 1926, was entitled *Lampeão, sua história*, and credited authorship to Erico de Almeida. It has been argued, however, that the book was written by the then Paraíba governor, João Suassuna. Containing a chapter praising Suassuna, its account of Lampião is marred by many inaccuracies. By far the best of the early books was Ranulfo Prata's *Lampeão*, published in 1934. Centering on the bandit's depredations in Bahia, it was a strong appeal for more vigorous police action but also contained a large amount of reliable data. These books, together with others published during the period and the intense coverage in newspapers and popular magazines, made their contribution to the formation of an image of Lampião as a wily, cruel, daring, and virtually invincible bandit leader.[3] News of his feats also spread beyond Brazil's borders well before his death. The *New York Times*, which in 1930 carried its first news about him, in 1931 declared him

---

[3] On the Almeida book, see Andrade, *O baile das quatro artes*, pp. 102–103. *O Ceará*, October 5, 1929, reprinted a portion of it. I have not seen the complete work. Also among the books that appeared during Lampião's lifetime are: Moysés de Figueiredo, *Lampeão no Ceará: A verdade em torno dos factos (Campanha de 1927)*, published in 1927 or soon thereafter; Leonardo Motta, *No tempo de Lampeão* (1930); Gustavo Barroso, *Almas de lama e de aço (Lampeão e outros cangaceiros)* (1930); *Os dramas dolorosos do nordeste* (1930) and *O flagello de "Lampeão"* (1931), both by Pedro Vergne de Abreu.

(calling him the "Lamppost") to be among South America's most notorious outlaws.[4]

In Brazil, his fame led to the exploitation of his name for commercial purposes. For a time, Lampião hats were a fad. A Fortaleza newspaper in 1926 complained that the fashionableness of the cangaceiro-type headdress was obscuring the view in busses, movies, and other public places.[5] In 1933, a Salvador musical group adopted the name "Lampião and His Band." Their picture in the newspaper showed eight male musicians dressed in typical cangaceiro clothing. Unfavorable comment on the name caused the group to adopt the much less colorful, but probably more appropriate, "Singers of the Northeast."[6]

A portrayal of Lampião in film also came at an early date, with the release in 1930 of *Lampeão, Fera do Nordeste* (Lampião, beast of the Northeast).[7] That he would be the subject of a film came, of course, as no surprise to Brazilians. In view of the popularity among them of western movies from the United States, their own famed desperado was a natural subject. But what may have been surprising was the announcement in Fortaleza in early 1937 that the bandit had played himself in a documentary film that would soon be released. The producer of the film was Benjamin Abrahão, a young man of Syrian origin, who had once worked for Padre Cícero in Juàzeiro. In 1935, with backing from Aba Filme, a photographic firm in Fortaleza, he went into the bush to seek out Lampião and film the way of life of the cangaceiros.[8]

According to Abrahão, he found Lampião in Bahia after a search of several months. The astute cangaceiro already knew about the Syrian, for spies had told him that a strange man was looking for him. Wary as always, Lampião suspected that he had been sent by the police. Before he would consent to being filmed, he insisted that Abrahão first sit before the camera while it was in operation. Afterwards, it having been established that the machine did not conceal a gun, Lampião enthusiastically cooperated. He had seen at least two movies (in

[4] November 29, 1930; February 28 and March 22, 1931.
[5] *Correio do Ceará*, January 5, 1926.
[6] *A Tarde*, June 26 and 29, 1933.
[7] Alberto Silva, "O filme de cangaço," *Filme e Cultura* (November/December, 1970), p. 45.
[8] Interviews with Abrahão were carried in *Correio de Aracajú*, October 21, 1936, and *O Povo*, January 12, 1937. Also see *O Povo*, December 29, 1936.

Capela and Queimadas) and, no doubt, looked forward to starring in one himself. His fondness for having his likeness preserved on film was well established. On the first trip, the cameraman spent only five days with the band, but, after finding the results unsatisfactory, he went back for a second visit. His major regret was not having been able to film a battle with the police. He was, he said, in Piranhas one day when Corisco met a volante just on the other side of the river in Sergipe, but he could not find anyone fearless enough to row him across to the scene of the battle. In spite of the promise of Abrahão's enterprising venture, things did not turn out well. The Ceará police, objecting to the Syrian's efforts, confiscated the film. Abrahão unfortunately did not outlive Lampião. A bachelor, he was shot and killed, allegedly by a jealous husband, in Vila Bela in May, 1938, two months before the cangaceiro died.[9] The film lay forgotten and unattended to for many years, and when it finally was rediscovered in 1957 all but a few scenes were no longer usable.[10]

The portrayals of Lampião in verse, book, newspaper, and movie reveal a good deal of what the larger public thought of the bandit as well as approximations of what he was in reality. His intelligence, cruelty, foxiness, and daring, but also his penchant for caution and thorough planning, came through in clear relief. Such traits were the epitome of the bandit's public career, and there is ample evidence of their existence. There were other traits in his personality and other aspects of his life that also merit examination.

Two traits that impressed backlanders were his reputed reliability and loyalty. In the first place, Lampião was a man of his word. If he borrowed something from you—which meant that he did not consider you an enemy, for then he would have just taken it—you could count on its return. Many stories attesting to this quality are told. He sent back to its owner, for example, a prize mule that he borrowed when he left Queimadas, and in Mata Grande he returned an accordion with thanks to a rancher from whom he had borrowed it six months earlier.[11] While some of his actions in this respect were designed, no doubt, to

[9] *Correio de Aracajú,* May 11, 1938.

[10] The scenes that could be used are found in the film, "Memórias do cangaço," made in 1965. On the history of the Abrahão film, see Nonnato Masson, "A aventura sangrenta do cangaço," *Fatos e Fotos,* December 1, 1962.

[11] Umbelino Santanna, interview; Silva, *Lampião,* pp. 141–143.

set the stage for continued favors, others seem to have been motivated by his desire to be known as an honest man. He was, if you please, a bandit of class and not a "goat thief" (*ladrão de bode*), a kind of petty criminal who in northeastern Brazil was looked upon as among the lowest forms of human scum.

Lampião's loyalty to those to whom he owed some debt of friendship or gratitude was equally extolled. One well-known incident occurred when he returned to Serra Vermelha to kill José Saturnino, his old enemy. When he attacked the house, fire was returned from the inside, but he ceased his assault when Saturnino's mother appeared at the door. A woman whom the bandit respected from the days when the two families were friends, she told him that her son was not present and asked him not to kill the two men who were inside the house. The favor she requested was not an easy one for Lampião to grant, for the men were among his capital enemies. But he went into the house to talk with them and, on their avowal never to pursue him again, spared their lives.[12] On another occasion, he freed Sergeant Maurício Vieira de Barros, a volante commander whom he had captured, because he owed him a debt of gratitude. When the force from Agua Branca had killed Lampião's father, it was Maurício, then the police chief of Mata Grande, who went to the site and buried the body. On freeing him, Lampião informed him that the debt was paid and told him that he could expect no more favors.[13] Lampião in 1934 also spared another soldier when he learned that the man was from a family that lived on the land of Colonel José Abílio of Bom Conselho. Saying that he was thankful for the protection given his younger brothers and sisters by the colonel after their father's death, he let the soldier go.[14]

Lampião was also capable of other acts of mercy when he believed the situation warranted them, as is shown by an incident involving Zé Pacotia of Bahia. Pacotia decided to enlist in the police force simply because he needed a job. A coiteiro told Lampião of Pacotia's intentions, and the bandit went to the man's ranch to kill him. When he arrived at Pacotia's house, Lampião asked him if it was true that he intended to become a soldier. Upon hearing the affirmative answer, the bandit told him that he was going to die, but then acceded to the

---

[12] Genésio Ferreira and José Saturnino, interviews.
[13] Miguel Feitosa, interview; Luna, *Lampião*, pp. 46–47.
[14] *Jornal de Alagoas*, January 15, 1934.

man's request that he be permitted to tell why he was becoming a soldier. The condemned man explained that he had no enmity toward Lampião, that he was motivated solely by the need to provide for his children, whose limbs were thin and stomachs swollen for lack of food. Lampião, considering the matter, decided that Pacotia could live, although he did not permit him to escape punishment. José Bahiano branded him on the cheeks, and, as the band left, each man gave him a blow with his lash. Pacotia then enlisted and became one of the Bahia force's best trackers.[15]

Lampião, then, was capable of an occasional act of mercy, but such actions were not broadly representative of the pattern of his behavior. Many another man died at his hands, also begging that he be spared to rear his children. The reasons for his killing them lie chiefly in the nature of his quest for survival and his systematic use of terror to achieve that end. He told one man who was pleading for his life that if he consented to all such entreaties he would kill no one. He once said that if he did not kill those who failed to obey him, he would lose the respect of the people, and that, he added, would be his undoing.[16] Lampião may also have killed, at times, solely out of blind anger, choosing his victims at random, but such cases seem to fall outside the general pattern of his behavior. Nonetheless, he did kill many persons, not because they had done him some disfavor, but because they were related or linked in some way to someone who had displeased him. His anger or his terror, as the case might be, often cut a wide swath.

That Lampião left an immense number of deaths along his path in the course of his career is impressive enough, but what often shocked his contemporaries was the coldness with which he could kill. According to Volta-Sêca, Lampião often said: "If you have to kill, kill quickly. But, for me, killing a thousand is just like killing one. It's the same thing."[17] One incident illustrates well the apparent casualness with which the bandit regarded the taking of a life. It was a classic case in-

[15] Severiano Ramos, interview.

[16] José Melquiades de Oliveira, interview; *A Tarde*, November 10, 1937.

[17] Volta-Seca's story as told to Gomes, *Diário de Notícias*, April 30, 1959. One of Lampião's men, Cobra Verde (Green Snake), told the press in a jailhouse interview in 1938: "I was accustomed to seeing so many people killed that for me it was no different from eating a good meal" (*Jornal de Alagoas*, November 9, 1938).

volving a man who had informed on him to the police. Manuel Silvestre lived in Bebedouro, Bahia, a village near the Sergipe border. Lampião arrived at his ranch one day in 1931 and, after accepting the offer of a cup of coffee, asked his host to show him a safe place to hide from his pursuers. When the band had gone to the place he had indicated, a volante arrived and, under pressure, Manuel told the soldiers of the hide-out. The volante attacked, and the outlaws were forced to flee. Fully aware that he was in trouble, Manuel moved to Sergipe. But, in the next year, Lampião found him, accompanied by one of his cowboys, and told him that he was going to die. The cowboy was sent to secure a shovel, and, on his return, Manuel was instructed to dig his own grave. Meanwhile, the bandit chief ordered a goat slaughtered and roasted, as the hour of the midday meal was approaching. When the burial place was prepared, Lampião asked his men if any one of them wished to kill the man, but no one volunteered. He asked the cowboy if he had ever seen a man shot to death, and when the cowboy gave a negative answer he told him to watch closely. He then performed the service himself. With Manuel pleading for his life, Lampião shot him twice with precision, first into the mouth and then through the ear. Manuel fell to the ground, and, after the body had ceased movement, Lampião ordered him buried. By the time this was accomplished, dinner was ready. The desperado sat down on the mound of dirt that marked the final resting place of Manuel Silvestre and ate the roast goat, cooked to a rare state and oozing blood.[18]

For Lampião and his cangaceiros, killing was not only a casual occurrence but something of an art. They were excellent shots with pistol and rifle—Lampião excelled in aim, even though he was blind in one eye—and they also took pride in their skills with the knife. They specialized in dispatching a man quickly and cleanly by plunging their long knives down into the flesh behind the collarbone directly into the body's vital organs. The most impressive thing about Lampião, according to a Sergipe rancher who as a boy visited his camp, was his long knife. His commanding presence, cangaceiro dress, pistol, and rifle, while impressive enough, paled beside the sight of that elaborately decorated twenty-inch-long knife stuck under his belt. It was particu-

[18] José Melquiades de Oliveira, interview. The cowboy who witnessed the event told the story to Oliveira.

larly fearsome when you knew people, as the boy did, who had been victims of it.[19]

It was no wonder that people all over the backlands trembled at the news that Lampião had arrived in their vicinity. A reader today of those yellowing newspapers telling of people deserting their homes in some backlands village to flee into the *caatinga* in advance of Lampião's coming is inclined, after so many such notices, to believe that many reports were exaggerated. Even today, however, anyone going into the backlands and talking to people who lived in that era in those isolated and forgotten spots realizes that the terror was real. On news that the bandit was in the area, normal life came to a standstill. Work was dropped, dances were ended, and funerals were abandoned. A normally prosperous ranch, village, or town, by its appearance, might as well have been inhabited solely by ghosts. A story told of a priest in Bahia illustrates the panic that could be occasioned by news that the bandit was near. That priest, when he saw the cloud of dust raised by a band of approaching horsemen, thought it was the bandits and fled from his church. Once in the *caatinga*, he remembered that he had left his money in the parish house and, with temerity, returned to get it. On approaching the church, he saw that the horsemen had been the wedding party of a couple whom he had earlier consented to marry at that hour.[20]

There were, of course, exceptions to this general pattern of fear, especially among the bandits' coiteiros and friends and among the residents of some villages and small towns that he frequently visited in a peaceful manner. It is true also that in instances where his pacific purpose was established, people, in their curiosity, flocked around him and his men. Apart from these specific occasions, it is clear that fear of him was widespread and deeply felt.

In contrast, there is a tradition, current even when the bandit was living, that he was something of a Robin Hood-like brigand who stole from the rich to give to the poor. From far away, the *New York Times* gave him such an identification in 1931. Earlier, in 1927, an article of similar import was published in Rio de Janeiro, but it was received very coldly in Mossoró, the Rio Grande do Norte city that Lampião had

---

[19] José Melquiades de Oliveira, interview.
[20] *A Tarde*, October 16, 1933.

recently raided. After Lampião's death, the tradition continued to evolve, and, in recent years, such characterizations of him have become more common. But the fundamental question of whether or not there was any substance to the tradition has remained unanswered.[21]

In an objective analysis of the tradition, it should be said that Lampião was capable of generous acts. In Ceará in 1926, it was reported that he had given a sizable amount of money to help repair a chapel and another sum to an old lady. He also had made one of his men return money taken from a poor farmer. Volta-Sêca has said that the bandit would reach into his money bag and pull out a handful of bills to give to a poor person to whom he had taken a liking. He did this with a good deal of ostentation, Volta-Sêca added. The bandit would also throw coins into the street for boys to scramble after, as he did in Juàzeiro or Limoeiro do Norte. A poor woman, fleeing from the drought, told the press in Bahia in 1933 that "Mr. Lampião is not as bad as he is said to be." The last time that she had seen him, the woman said, he had given money to her small sons. There was also a report two years before then, when the area was undergoing a partial drought, that he had given alms to persons fleeing from hunger whom he had met on the road.[22]

There were also other kinds of generosity that Lampião practiced. He was known to be generous to his coiteiros. When he first crossed over into Bahia, he gave favors to people whom he liked, buying them drinks, making presents to them at weddings, or, in other ways, demonstrating that he was a good fellow. Occasionally he distributed freely the merchandise of a store that he had looted. In one such instance, in Traipú County, Alagoas, he threatened to punish anybody who would not accept the bolts of cloth he was handing out.[23]

The pattern that emerges from Lampião's acts of charity is one of limited and personal acts conforming to common conceptions of human

[21] *New York Times*, February 28, 1931; *O Ceará*, July 15, 1927; as examples of recent opinion, see, Oliveira, *Lampião*, p. 213; editorial comment in *Verdade* (Novo Friburgo, Rio de Janeiro), March 8, 1974. Eduardo Barbosa, *Lampião: Rei do cangaço*, a popular history with no scholarly pretensions, also supports the view.

[22] Interview with Francisco Xavier in *Correio do Ceará*, February 13, 1926; Volta-Seca's story as told to Gomes, *Diário de Notícias*, May 3, 1959; *A Tarde*, April 11, 1933; *A Noite*, June 3, 1931.

[23] *Jornal de Alagoas*, April 28, 1938.

nature. There were, in short, some spontaneous acts of charity, motivated by sympathy for the plight of the recipients. There were other acts of generosity that seem to have been designed to secure and keep the friendship and loyalty of people whom the bandit needed. It may not be at all coincidental that much of his generosity occurred in his first few years in Bahia, for that was a period in which he was establishing a network of support without which he could not survive. Finally, he was generous with some people simply because he liked them. In considering his acts of charity, it should be remembered that Lampião was in a position to be generous, since money was something that he seldom lacked.

There is a tendency for history to largely absolve men and women of their crimes if their good deeds outweighed their evil ones. Therefore, the wrongs committed by a bandit who stole from the rich to give to the poor might not be forgiven, but they probably would be overshadowed. Lampião's behavior does not fit this pattern in any suitable fashion, for, while he was capable of kindly acts, they do not constitute overriding factors in his career. Nonetheless, if the celebrated outlaw was not a Robin Hood, he was at least a man in whom the stream of human kindness never ran completely dry. In spite of the brutalizing influences of his profession, he remained much of an ordinary man with ordinary human impulses.

In any discussion of Lampião by backlanders, the bandit's religiosity projects a larger image than does his generosity. That it would be so is natural, for, to them, his strong religious faith was an integral part of the aura of invincibility that surrounded him. The bandit's religious beliefs were primitive, but they were a near-perfect reflection of backlands Catholicism. Its major premise was the appeasement or manipulation of supernatural forces (and virtually everything fell into that category) for one's protection and enhancement. While backlands religion was perhaps not totally devoid of moral content, the morality of the Sermon on the Mount was not a prominent part of it. Within it, Lampião, whose sins were heinous, could be regarded as one of its most successful practitioners.[24]

24 Much of the content of the type of folk Catholicism that Lampião believed in is discussed in Wilson Lins, *O médio São Francisco: Uma sociedade de pastôres e guerreiros*, pp. 165–176. Specifically on the religious beliefs of the cangaceiros, see Lima, *O mundo estranho*, pp. 107–134.

The bandit's religious practices were well known.[25] He often prayed several times daily and always at midday. He revered priests profoundly and sought them out whenever the opportunity arose. He reputedly had a friendship with Padre José Kehrle that lasted for many years. To him, as to most backlanders, Padre Cícero was a saint. According to a story, the life of a policeman's wife in Jatobá, Pernambuco, was saved when an old man grabbed a picture of the Juàzeiro priest and placed it between Lampião's raised dagger and the woman's breast.[26] The bandit carried little books of prayers, kept the images of saints in his billfold, and pinned pictures of Padre Cícero to his clothing. He also wore scapulars on his chest and back as indications of his religious devotion. He tried to keep Fridays holy, fasting and staying apart from others. During Holy Week, he ate no meat, ceased his operations, and avoided the police, preferring to rest on the ranch of a coiteiro. As the years passed, signs of his religious devotion grew. It was not surprising that he should become so religious, since, in view of the dangerous life he led, he needed all the protection he could muster.

Quite possibly, the central element in the bandit's religion was his belief in the *corpo fechado* ("sealed body"). It was this, among his beliefs, that offered the greatest measure of protection. According to the backlanders, a person's body could be protected from harm through prayers. These special prayers were often passed handwritten from person to person, but they could also be bought in little booklets like the *cordel* literature. Lampião had several such supplications with him when he died at Angicos. One was the "Prayer of the Crystal Rock."

"My crystal rock that was found in the ocean between the chalice and the sacred host. The earth trembles but not our Father Jesus Christ. At the altar also tremble the hearts of my enemies when they see me. . . . With the love of the Virgin Mary I am covered and with the blood of my Father Jesus Christ I am bound. Whosoever should want to shoot me cannot do so. If they shoot at me water will run from the barrels of

[25] Among many other references, see Volta-Sêca's story as told to Gomes, *Diário de Notícias*, April 30, 1959; "Memórias de Balão, um velho cangaceiro," *Realidade* (November, 1973), pp. 45–47; interview with Gato Bravo ("Wildcat") in *Diário de Pernambuco*, August 6, 1938; Victor Santos in *Diário da Noite*, December 24, 1931; the journal of Gurgel in Nonato, *Lampião em Mossoró*, p. 213.

[26] *Diário da Bahia* (Salvador), August 11, 1932.

their guns. If they try to stab me the knives will fall from their hands
. . . and if they lock me up the doors will open. Delivered I was, delivered I am, and delivered I shall be with the key to the tabernacle. I seal myself."[27]

In addition to saying the prayers, there were certain rules to be followed if the spell was to hold. Among them was abstinence from sex. It was believed by many that Lampião's failure to observe this requirement doomed him at Angicos.[28]

Within the context of a society in which such beliefs as the *corpo fechado* were common, Lampião became almost a *beato*, a kind of holy person common to northeastern Brazil. His magic was obviously potent, else he could not survive for so long a time against such great odds. And as the years passed and his feats grew, backlanders came to look upon him as invincible, at least when compared to the police, who were accorded little respect. The awe in which backlanders held him helps to explain their submission to him. It equally explains the reluctance and fear with which most soldiers approached a battle with him, for they came from the same society and shared the same beliefs. Time after time over the years he accomplished such feats as avoiding an ambush that he seemingly could not have known about, or scaling a seemingly impassable cliff to escape them, or breaking out of an encirclement that appeared fast, and the backlanders came to believe that his influence with the powers that govern life were obviously superior to theirs. And only the belief that he was invincible adequately explains why so many backlanders affirm almost forty years after his death, that he still lives.

Another matter often comes up in conversations about Lampião, particularly among people who knew him well, that has never been dealt with in any satisfactory manner by those who have written about him. It is the question of what the man himself thought about the life

[27] Lampião's copy of the prayer, handwritten, is held by the Instituto Histórico e Geográfico de Alagoas, Maceió, along with other items found in his possession at the time of his death.

[28] The cangaceiro Ângelo Roque ("Labareda") gave this as the reason for Lampião's death to José Calazans, the Bahia historian (José Calazans, interview, Salvador, November 25, 1973). Also see "Memórias de Balão."

that he was leading. Fortunately, Lampião left a number of statements that reflect on some of his more personal thoughts about his life.

It is evident that he wanted to be seen as a victim of circumstances. He entered the life of banditry, he said time and again, because it was left to him to avenge the death of his father. The assassins, he once said, had the law on their side; only by his own hands could justice be done. This contention provided justification for his life as a bandit, and many of his fellow Brazilians, then and now, have accepted it as valid. He also wanted to be known as an honorable man. Asked in one Juàzeiro interview if it did not bother him to have to extort money for a livelihood, he answered that he never did that; he lived, he retorted, by requesting money from his friends. In another Juàzeiro interview, he admitted that he sometimes did take by force, but only from the rich, and he added that he also gave alms to the poor. In answer to a question on the same occasion about his violence, he responded that it was for the purpose of exacting revenge from his enemies and punishing those who pursued him. At a later time, he gave the answer that his violence arose from the need to enforce obedience to his will. When a woman in Pernambuco wanted to know why he and his band violated women, Lampião showed hot indignation. They never did that, he said, and, if he should find someone saying that he did, he would split his tongue![29]

As to whether or not Lampião liked life in the cangaço, his expressions of opinion over the years were not always consistent. On occasion, he wanted his listeners to believe that he was enjoying the life that he was following. In Juàzeiro in 1926, at the same time that he was telling Padre Cícero that he wanted to be regenerated, he told a reporter that the cangaço was a good business and he had never thought of giving it up. But specifically asked if he planned to ply the trade for the remainder of his life, he indicated that he might like to try something else. Three years after the Juàzeiro visit, in Capela in 1929, Lampião again said that he found the cangaço to be an enjoyable life.[30] Not long before his Capela statement, however, he had given a more judi-

[29] Juàzeiro interview of March, 1926, reprinted in *Correio do Ceará*, April 4, 1970; *O Ceará*, March 17, 1926; *A Tarde*, November 10, 1937; *Diário de Pernambuco*, June 9, 1936.

[30] *O Ceará*, March 17, 1926; *Correio de Aracajú*, November 29, 1929.

cious view to an interviewer in Tucano, Bahia. "I know," he said, "that this life is not very good, but, if I have suffered, I have also enjoyed myself a lot, in compensation."[31]

Lampião's expressions of fondness for the life of the bandit may have been uttered mostly for public consumption or in conformance to a temporary mood. On balance, they appear not to have been the main thrust of his opinions over the course of his life. There is an ample amount of evidence to support this view. In 1921, when his career as a professional bandit was beginning, he counseled a group of young men not to follow his example. Several brothers from Floresta County who were involved in a quarrel with a rival family had sought him out and asked to join his band. He questioned them at length about the nature of the dispute and how far it had gone; then, indicating that he thought there was still hope for reconciliation, he advised them to go back home and work out an accord with their enemies. Patting his rifle, he told them that it was no good life that he was leading. He said that he had experienced already the life of a farmer, cowboy, mule driver, and bandit. Of the four ways of making a living, he said, banditry was the worst. The brothers took the young outlaw's advice and in their later years have remembered Lampião and his wisdom fondly.[32] Later, around 1925, Lampião told other persons that he considered his entry into banditry a misfortune and that he was made to be a rancher, not a cangaceiro.[33]

Adding to the view that Lampião did not find the cangaço to be a satisfactory mode of life is the considerable evidence that he sought a way out of it. When the circumstances of his visit to Padre Cícero in Juàzeiro in 1926 offered him his best opportunity to accomplish this, he seemed interested in taking advantage of it. Unfortunately, the enmity of the Pernambuco police for him and the Juàzeiro patriarch's refusal to see him again ended whatever chances for success that opportunity may have held. The Juàzeiro episode aside, there is evidence that on other occasions Lampião also sought to reverse the course of his life. When he was recuperating from his wounds on Marcolino's ranch in

---

[31] *O Ceará*, February 2, 1929.

[32] João Ignácio de Souza, one of the brothers, told me of the incident in an interview, Floresta, Pernambuco, August 2, 1975.

[33] Luiz Andrelino Nogueira, interview, Serra Talhada, Pernambuco, July 30, 1975.

Princeza in 1924, he entered into contact with Padre José Kehrle, asking him to convey a message to the commander of the forces in interior Pernambuco, Teófanes Torres. According to the priest, Lampião offered to deliver himself to the police in exchange for a guarantee of his own life and the lives of his men. Teófanes agreed to guarantee Lampião's life, but he would not make the same promise to the men. Lampião turned down the offer. Padre Kehrle also said that somewhat later he succeeded in persuading Lampião to agree to turn himself in to the state chief of police but that the bandit backed out when Antônio would not accompany him. Sebastião Pereira, Lampião's old comrade, has related that in the mid-1920s he sent the bandit a letter inviting him to abandon the cangaço and come to Minas Gerais (where Sebastião was then residing) to live under the protection of the governor's brother. Lampião, he said, never answered his letter.[34]

No doubt, it would have been easier for Lampião to arrange a departure from the cangaço during his first years of banditry. Until Pernambuco initiated its major campaign against the bandits, there seems to have been quite a tolerant attitude toward him. An exit similar to that made by Sebastião Pereira was a possibility, and had someone like Padre Cícero put his full weight behind the effort, it probably would have been tolerated by officials. But, after the beginning of the Pernambuco campaign and similar ones in other states in later years—strengthened by the commitment of the federal government after 1930—such a possibility became ever more remote. And it is clear that Lampião knew it. Late in 1928, he said in Tucano that he would be willing to leave the cangaço only if he could find someone to protect him, and he added that he knew of no such persons. In Capela in the next year, he expressed the opinion that it was too late for him to cease being a bandit. As an indication of his increasingly fatalistic attitude, in his later years he carried a vial of poison that he intended to take if he should ever be faced with capture. He had it with him at Angicos. He also told his brother the year before Angicos that he would be fighting until he died.[35]

[34] Noblat, "Lampião morreu envenenado," an article that is mostly an interview with Padre Kehrle; Macedo, *Sinhô Pereira*, p. 21.

[35] *O Ceará*, February 2, 1929; *Correio de Aracajú*, November 29, 1929; Rocha, *Bandoleiros*, pp. 48–49. Rocha states that he sent the vial found at Angicos to Rio de Janeiro for analysis.

João Ferreira saw his brother in mid-1937 for the last time. João had just returned to Propriá, Sergipe, after having spent several years living in Piauí, when Lampião sent word that he wanted to see him. The two brothers met on the ranch of a coiteiro not far from the city. The bandit looked old and tired, and João counseled him to try to seek a way out of the cangaço. Maybe with the help of his influential friends he could go away to some distant place where he would not be known. Lampião replied that he was too well known to hide and that he did not trust any of his acquaintances enough to entrust his life to them. He did not want to die of treason, he said, and added that the only thing that he could do was to be a bandit until he died. Nonetheless, it seems that the outlaw continued to harbor the thought of a return to normal life. Dadá, Corisco's woman, heard him say that he could leave the cangaço if Sergipe's Governor Eronides were president.[36]

It is an intriguing and not entirely fruitless exercise to speculate on what Lampião might have done had he been able to extricate himself from the cangaço, for a man is to be measured by what he wanted to do as well as by what he did. Lampião saw himself as being capable of becoming something other than a mere roving bandit. In speaking once of raising an army of 1,000 men to wage war against the Pernambuco and Paraíba police—for the purpose, he said, of winning amnesty for himself and his men—he envisioned gaining not only respectability but, possibly, power and influence as well. He once stated that he would like to be governor of a new backlands state to be composed of portions of Bahia, Sergipe, Alagoas, and Pernambuco.[37] Reportedly, he even said that he would leave the cangaço only if he could become the president of the republic—a statement that was followed by the inevitable comment of a back-country editor that Lampião in the chief executive's chair might not be any more calamitous than some others who had sat there.[38]

Such statements by Lampião might be dismissed as the jestings of an ignorant bandit, and perhaps they were, but it should be remem-

---

[36] João Ferreira, interview; Dadá, interview.

[37] Interview with Francisco Xavier, who had recently spoken with Lampião, *Correio do Ceará*, February 13, 1926; *Correio de Aracajú*, April 16, 1937. Also, for reports of similar statements, see *Diário de Notícias*, July 22, 1929, and Volta-Sêca's story as told to Gomes, *Diário de Notícias*, May 1, 1959.

[38] *O Ceará*, April 19, 1929.

bered that Lampião in the course of his career became a man of considerable breadth of experience. He in effect ruled sections of the backlands, administering justice (of a sort) and levying taxes. He met political bosses as their equal and humbled most of them with his power. He developed amicable relations with a state governor. He deployed his own forces with uncommon effectiveness, showing an almost uncanny sense of timing and a remarkable ability to develop and utilize the tactics of guerrilla warfare. He read newspapers and magazines when they were available. His bearing as a man was impressive, by almost all accounts. He was on the verge, at one point, of becoming a legally recognized military commander—called by an official acting under presidential authority and commissioned by one of the region's most powerful figures. Lampião, indeed, was no paltry figure in terms of his qualities and experiences. Had the nation in his time been undergoing a period in which established power and institutions were crumbling and in which natural ability could win out over position and privilege— comparable, say, to Mexico during its revolutionary era—it is entirely conceivable that he could have bridged the gap separating him from acceptability and carved for himself quite a different niche in his nation's history.

But Brazil was not experiencing such an upheaval and Lampião remained a bandit. For that matter, even had he been able to make the leap into respectability and a position of influence—within the fabric of the Brazil of the time—there is little reason to believe that he would have been anything other than a backlands boss (*caudilho*) of the common variety. Lampião did not object to the patterns of authority and privilege in his day; rather, he was angry because he had been denied his rightful place in them. He was, in terms of his ideas and prejudices, quite a conventional backlander. Asked in Juàzeiro what he would like to do if he should ever abandon the cangaço, he replied that he thought he would be happy as a businessman. At other times, he said he wanted to be a rancher. It was the conservative classes, he said, that he admired most. He told a reporter that he liked farming, ranching, and business, the enterprises of industrious men.[39]

The bandit's ideas of race were also conventional. Backlanders

[39] Reprint of Juàzeiro interview of March, 1926, *Correio do Ceará*, April 4, 1970; *O Ceará*, March 17, 1926.

have long prided themselves on their relative whiteness in comparison to the blacker population of the coastal region, and, while anti-Negro feelings have not generally been institutionalized, they have been present. Lampião frequently had Negroes in his band, as he would have had them on his land had he been a rancher, but he showed contempt for the race in general. According to Volta-Sêca, he said, in reference to one of the soldiers, a black, killed in Queimadas: "The Negro was never a human being . . . the Negro is an image of the Devil." He once sent a note to a black sergeant in Pinhão, Sergipe, taunting him for his color. "I don't like Negroes," the bandit wrote, "and even less when they're soldiers."[40]

If Lampião was typical of backlanders in many ways, so were the men who accompanied him. The vast majority of them have remained relatively unknown, impressively overshadowed by their leader. Without him, some of them might never have become criminals; others, no doubt, would have been petty thieves and murderers of little distinction. It was Lampião who brought them together and, molding them into a band that commanded fear and respect, gave them a measure of fame. He also led many of them to an early death.

Lampião's men were drawn in general from the submerged classes that made up the vast majority of backlanders. While the band might attract a type such as a cowboy or hired gun from time to time, most of its members came from the tenant or small-property-owning classes. Geographically, they came from the several northeastern states, although some villages and counties gained the reputations of being major suppliers of bandits. The northwest of Sergipe—especially Poço Redondo—and the Bahian village of Bebedouro, located near the Sergipe border, were well known for the large numbers of bandits they furnished. Juàzeiro in Ceará was also a likely source during the years in which Lampião operated in that area, simply because it attracted so many rootless and adventuresome men. The ages of the men who followed the bandit varied greatly, ranging from boys not yet into puberty to men of seventy years or more; most, however, were from eighteen to thirty-five. Some of the men, like Luís Pedro, remained with Lampião for many years. Others stayed only for a few weeks or a few months.

[40] Volta-Sêca's story as told to Gomes, *Diário de Notícias*, May 3, 1959; José Melquiades de Oliveira, interview.

All, it seems, were rechristened on their entry into the band, receiving from Lampião colorful names drawn from places, birds and animals, natural forces, or some purely whimsical source.[41]

Why the men became cangaceiros is not always easy to determine. Most of the information on their motives comes from the men themselves, and the truthfulness of it must, of necessity, be suspect. They had a strong and quite understandable tendency to attempt to justify their entry into a criminal career in terms of wrongs or injustices done to them or their families. Such explanations would be expected not only because the accused normally wished to have themselves seen in the most favorable light, hopefully making their crimes appear less heinous, but also because the men were aware that, within the traditions of the cangaço, they were expected to have been motivated by a zeal to avenge wrongs. Listening to them would be much like listening to Lampião himself; the reasoning would include little or nothing to illuminate the complexities of the case or the culpability of the person himself.

Something of the difficulties of finding reliable explanations is illustrated by the various stories told by Volta-Sêca. When still a boy, Volta-Sêca was caught by the police and told a straightforward story to the effect that he joined the band because he did not have much else to do and had been told that he would have a good life in it. Many years later, when he was asked to explain his reasons for publication in a popular magazine, he talked about having gone into the group because he killed a soldier. His sister, Volta-Sêca said, had been raped by the soldier.[42]

It is true, of course, that a number of Lampião's men were drawn into the band because of injustices done to them or their families. It has long been asserted in the backlands that the police, with their harsh methods against alleged coiteiros, created far more cangaceiros than they ever killed or captured. Some backlanders, finding themselves in that hazardous no-man's land between the police and cangaceiros, enlisted in the police, and others, fearing the police or having suffered at their hands, joined the bandits. Other men sought out Lampião's band in the hope that they could avenge a crime committed against them or

[41] My characterization of Lampião's men is based primarily on data I have collected on approximately fifty of them.

[42] A Tarde, March 22, 1932; interview with Volta-Sêca in Jorge Audi, "Eu sou o Labareda de Lampião," O Cruzeiro, October 19, 1968, p. 13.

their family by a personal enemy or a rival family. For instance, Oliveira, a sixteen-year-old boy from Floresta County, accompanied the bandits in order to seek revenge against a member of the Ferraz family who was alleged to have murdered Oliveira's father. The young cangaceiro apparently gained some measure of satisfaction when Lampião killed 360 head of the man's cattle.[43]

The motives, however, of quite a large number of cangaceiros were unrelated to vengeance or mistreatment by the authorities. Some of them sought out Lampião because they were in trouble with their families. Azulão ("Bluebird") fled from his family to save his life. He had seduced one of his sisters, and he feared that his father would kill him. Boa Vista ("Good View") left home for a similar reason, although, in his case, the dispute was over his father's lover. Others became bandits for a wide variety of reasons. A few joined the band after having deserted the police forces. One boy, aged thirteen, went with Lampião after the bandit had asked the boy's father if he could take him along. Lampião, the boy said, treated him much better than his own father did.[44] A number of boys and men joined the band because they already had brothers or other relatives in it. A sizable group, no doubt, threw in their lot with Lampião because they did not have much else to do. The back country offered boys and young men few opportunities beyond working in the fields with an axe and hoe as their fathers did. Widespread migration from the backlands to cities like Rio and São Paulo had scarcely begun in this era. Thus, the lack of other alternatives may have produced as many cangaceiros as anything else.

Besides, if staying at home was a bleak prospect for the backlands boy, it was equally true that the cangaço had a strong attracting force of its own. Celebrated in song and verse and a never-ending string of tales, life as a cangaceiro was looked upon by many a boy and young man as an exciting and romantic career in spite of its dangers—and maybe because of them. The bandits' independence, moreover, represented freedom from the hardships of life: the physical toil, the droughts, and the lack of justice. Velocidade ("Speed") joined the band, he said, because he found the cangaceiros "thrilling" and envied the lives they led, while Peitica ("Trouble") did so because he thought

[43] *A República*, June 21, 1927.

[44] Volta-Sêca's story as told to Gomes, *Diário de Notícias*, May 13, 1959; *A Tarde*, December 7, 1938; *Jornal de Alagoas*, February 20, 1937.

that such a life would be "beautiful."[45] Gitirana believed his invitation to join the cangaço, tendered in 1936 by one of Corisco's coiteiros, to be an honor; to him, at age twenty-two, it offered the promise of money, women, and freedom.[46] In short, within the limited geographical and cultural confines of a place like Bebedouro or Poço Redondo in the 1920s and 1930s, becoming a cangaceiro was almost as natural and fully as attractive for the son of a tenant or penniless small farmer as going to law or medical school was for the sons of the Recife or Salvador elite.

Whatever their motives, once they were in the band the men seemed to develop an affectionate respect for their chief. Lampião was, they said, good to them.[47] But he was also a stern disciplinarian. He was quite capable of ordering the execution of a young bandit who seduced the daughter of a trusted coiteiro or of giving a severe beating to a band member who threatened to desert. He also arranged the killing of Antônio Rosa around 1924 when he believed that Rosa, a member of his first band, was trying to undercut his influence.[48] Yet, the outlaw chief did not often have to take such harsh measures, and generally the atmosphere in his band was relaxed and easy. Undoubtedly, it was the quality of his command that fostered such a loyal and cohesive group. Indeed, a large part of the success of the cangaço can be comprehended only within the context of the story of that illustrious figure.

[45] *Jornal de Alagoas*, January 10, 1939; José Romão de Castro, *Figuras legendárias*, p. 29. The latter, written by a former director of the Alagoas penetentiary, contains valuable data on ten cangaceiros.

[46] Gitirana was interviewed in *A Tarde*, August 7, 1940.

[47] Many such references by his men exist, among them comments by Gengibre in *O Ceará*, October 3, 1929, and Gato Bravo in *Jornal de Alagoas*, August 4, 1938.

[48] Report by a witness in *O Ceará*, April 18, 1926; Genésio Ferreira and Miguel Feitosa, interviews; Antônio Neco, interview, Serra Talhada, Pernambuco, July 25 and 26, 1975.

12. Angicos

THE year 1938 opened with a report that the celebrated bandit had died on a ranch in the interior of Sergipe. The cause of death was said to be tuberculosis. The place of death, the newspapers indicated, was Canhoba Ranch, the property of Antônio Caixeiro, the father of the state's interventor.[1] The report brought forth an angry reaction from Interventor Eronides' government, which declared that the news was false. Moreover, the government claimed, the bandit had not been in the state during the three years in which Eronides had been its chief executive.[2] However shameless the lie was concerning Lampião's whereabouts during the preceding years, it was nonetheless true that the bandit was not dead. Not yet, anyhow.

As to where Lampião was, he may well have been in Sergipe on one of Caixeiro's ranches. At least that was the opinion of officials in Alagoas, who, it should be added, never denied that the bandits spent a lot of time in their state.[3] As to his health, it was apparently undisturbed. There is no reliable evidence that he suffered from lung disease. João Ferreira, who saw his brother in mid-1937 for the first time in eleven years, has said that he looked old for his years (he was then forty) but that his health seemed to be good. And a coiteiro who saw him the week before he died has given a similar report.[4] In view of the hardships of the life he led, it is no wonder that he looked old beyond his years.

[1] *Diário de Notícias* of Salvador broke the news on January 11, 1938.

[2] *Jornal de Alagoas*, January 13, 1938; *Correio de Aracajú*, January 13, 1938. *The New York Times* ran the notice on January 13 under the heading, "No. 1 Bad Man Dies in His Bed in Brazil."

[3] *Jornal de Alagoas*, April 1, 1938.

[4] João Ferreira and Antônio Pequeno, interviews.

Even though he was, by all reliable reports, in good health, he was not particularly active during the last few months of his life. Little was heard of him, although various of his bands continued their normal operations in Bahia, Sergipe, and Alagoas. They were, it would appear, under fairly severe police pursuit; six bandits, including one woman, were reported by the police as having died in combat during 1938s first quarter.[5] Lampião himself made his only major public appearances during a trip through Alagoas in the middle part of April. He crossed over into the state from Sergipe not far from Caixeiro's ranch at Canhoba; for many, this was confirmation of the charges that he had been sheltered by Caixeiro and his son all along. On his way across the river, Lampião treated himself to some rare entertainment. Encountering the Pão de Açúcar jazz band in midstream, the bandit gave each of the musicians a bill of substantial denomination and then told them to play.[6] Once in Alagoas, Lampião and his band of seventeen pillaged several villages and ranches in the area stretching from Traipú to Arapiraca. One of the major raids was on the sizable village of Jiraú. There, on April 18, the outlaws looted stores and disrupted homes in search of gold. They also gravely wounded the police sergeant who tried to lead the village's defense. According to one of Jiraú's residents, the band was mounted, well armed, and carrying impressive quantities of ammunition. They were, he also said, extremely ugly, for they were dirty, smelly, and had hair down to their shoulders. In Salomé, another village raided by the band, the people fled from their homes, remaining in the *caatinga* for six days before daring to return.[7]

Following the raids in April, Lampião again went into hiding. Little, apparently, was heard of him outside his circle of friends and protectors until July. A few days before the end of that month, an Alagoas volante had a brief encounter with him in Pão de Açúcar County, just across the river from Sergipe.[8] And the end of the month brought the sensational news that the renowned cangaceiro and ten of his companions had died in their hide-out on the Sergipe side of the São Francisco River. This time, it was no false report. Lampião was dead, the

[5] *Jornal de Alagoas*, February 10 and 13 and March 31, 1938.
[6] *Jornal de Alagoas*, April 1, 1938.
[7] Ibid., April 20 and 28, 1938. See also *O Povo*, April 22.
[8] Antônio Pequeno, interview.

victim of a surprise police attack by an Alagoas volante led by Lieutenant João Bezerra.

In the events at Angicos, João Bezerra was not a willing participant. Known neither for his courage nor his honesty, he was one of those police officers who had long been suspected of trafficking with the bandits.[9] Why it was he, rather than someone of greater devotion to duty, who reaped the fame for killing Lampião was a matter of circumstance. Bezerra was the commander of the volante stationed at Piranhas, one of the counties across from Sergipe that the bandits frequented in those years. By mid-1938, the Alagoas state authorities were prepared to go to considerable lengths to accomplish Lampião's elimination. The reasons for their determination may have been several. There was a new government there, as there was in the other states, as a result of the proclamation late in 1937 by President Getúlio Vargas of his New State—an indigenous version of the fascism current in Europe in that era. Whatever else the New State may have meant for Brazil, it did bring about a heightening of governmental power. It has been asserted, though not proved, that Getúlio himself sent down word that the time had come to get rid of Lampião and that he took the action, at least in part, because of complaints that had reached him from the influential Maurício family of backlands Alagoas. It does seem to be true that Eloy Maurício, one of those whose stores had been plundered by the bandits in the April attack on Jiraú, complained to the authorities and that his complaints reached the presidential palace by way of a member of the family who was well placed in the Church hierarchy. Maurício first complained to Antonio Caixeiro of Sergipe, asking him to intercede with Lampião. Caixeiro told him that he had influence with Lampião only in Sergipe. Maurício then asked Bishop José Maurício to lend a hand.[10]

Whether at the instigation of the Maurício family or not, the Alagoas authorities in mid-1938 resolved to take decisive action. It is known that José Lucena, who commanded the state's campaign against banditry, arrived in the backlands with orders from the police chief to eliminate Lampião quickly. To accomplish the fearsome task, Lucena

[9] Aldemar de Mendonça, Zezito Guedes, João Jurubeba, Dadá, interviews.

[10] Zezito Guedes, interview. Masson, "A aventura sangrenta do cangaço," gives another version of federal government pressure on Alagoas to bring the cangaço to an end.

chose João Bezerra.[11] Almost anyone else might have refused the order or attempted to carry it out only halfheartedly, but Bezerra was in no position to do either. Lucena, it is said, told him to get rid of Lampião within thirty days or suffer the consequences of his unfaithfulness as a police officer. Offered that choice, Bezerra—reluctantly, it is said—chose duty.[12]

Merely locating Lampião, let alone killing him, was not an easy task, as dedicated soldiers who had chased him for years knew. Moreover, that Bezerra and Lampião had engaged in mercenary dealings did not imply that Bezerra had access to knowledge of the bandit's whereabouts, for Lampião normally dealt with officers through intermediaries. If Bezerra was to find the bandit, he would need the assistance of someone who had close knowledge of the band's movements. Fortunately for him, like a piece of a puzzle falling to place by chance, a lead was offered by a coiteiro named Joca Bernardes of Piranhas County.

Bernardes, one of Corisco's coiteiros, was a rustic cowboy on Novo Gosto Ranch. After he met Lampião in 1928, Joca has said, he dreamed that he would be responsible for the famed bandit's death. His chance to play a role in that event now arrived. A cangaceiro who usually rode with Corisco stopped briefly at Novo Gosto Ranch and carelessly told Joca that Lampião had just crossed over from a point nearby into Sergipe. Under cover of darkness, Joca went to Piranhas to inform the police. In Bezerra's absence, the cowboy told Sergeant Aniceto Rodrigues what he had heard. He did not know exactly where Lampião was, he admitted, but he knew who would know. That man was Pedro de Cândido, a coiteiro who lived in Entre Montes, a village a short distance down river from Piranhas.[13] Aniceto, recognizing the potential value of the information, sent a message, by way of the railroad's telegraph facilities, to João Bezerra, who was in nearby Pedra. Couching his information in code to confound any of Lampião's informers who might see it, Aniceto wired: "Bull in the pasture."[14]

[11] Reported in *Jornal de Alagoas*, July 29, 1938. Also see: Goís, *Lampião*, p. 229, and Silva, *Lampião*, pp. 179–180.

[12] Aldemar de Mendonça and Zezito Guedes, interviews; Moacir Vieira Nunes, interview, Piranhas, Alagoas, August 20, 1975.

[13] Joca Bernardes, interview.

[14] Aldemar de Mendonça, untitled MS; Lima, *O mundo estranho*, p. 286; Bezerra, *Como dei cabo de Lampeão*, p. 85.

Lampião, indeed, was nearby. He was at Angicos, a modest ranch on the Sergipe side of the river between Piranhas and Entre Montes. Lying in a remote region of Sergipe, its main contacts were with the towns and villages across the river in Alagoas, especially Entre Montes and Piranhas. While there, Lampião's most trusted coiteiro was Pedro de Cândido, whose family owned Angicos. The outlaw chieftain and his immediate followers had arrived at the ranch a few days previously. They were camped along Tamanduá Creek, a precipitous stream that lies in a slight depression between two steep hills; the river is only a few hundred yards away. Covered with dense and spiny vegetation, the location would seem to have been a good hide-out. Sentries strategically posted on the prominent positions that dominate it would have a commanding view of the surrounding area.

In conformance with Lampião's custom, the bandits had settled in for a stay of only a few days, prudence demanding that they move frequently to avoid detection. But, since their lives were spent in such a fashion, they had made their place of abode as comfortable as possible. The bandits and their women had constructed small brush arbors or lean-tos as protection against the mist and rains that often come along the river in that season. And, as always, their shelters were widely dispersed—scarcely more than a man and his woman or two male companions in each one—as a precaution against an unexpected police attack. A sewing machine had been obtained and brought to the camp for Maria, who, in the peace and quiet of that mountain camp, could attend to some of her domestic duties.[15]

Lampião had come to Angicos to call a meeting of the various bands operating under his command. The purpose of the reunion has been variously described. It may have been simply that the outlaw leader had the need now and then to see his bands, and this was one of those occasions.[16] Ângelo Roque, who operated mostly in Bahia, came and departed, going to the house of a coiteiro to try to recuperate from

[15] I visited Angicos in July, 1975. The description at the time of Lampião's death comes mostly from my interviews with Antônio Correia Rosa and João Leandro dos Santos (Piranhas, Alagoas, August 23, 1975), the latter being one of the soldiers who composed the attacking force.

[16] Corisco's woman, Dadá, told me that the purpose was to plan an ambush of José Rufino's volante (interview). The cangaceiro, Vila Nova, reported that it was for general planning purposes (interview with Vila Nova in *Jornal de Alagoas*, October 25, 1938).

the flu. He told Lampião, he later claimed, that Angicos was a dangerous place to camp, since the only escape was uphill over the top.[17]
When the night of Wednesday, July 27, approached, approximately
fifty to sixty bandits were camped at the site, including a few of the
women. One of those who had not yet arrived was Corisco. He had
learned on Monday from a coiteiro in Pão de Açúcar County that
Lampião wanted to see him, but, he had told the coiteiro, he would be
able to go to Angicos only on Friday.[18] By then, there would no longer
be any reason for the journey.

On Wednesday, in response to Sergeant Aniceto's telegram, João
Bezerra and his troop left Pedra for Piranhas, making a deceptive exit
by announcing that they were bound for Agua Branca, where, they
said, they had just learned Lampião was. Before leaving, Bezerra arranged for the loan of a machine gun from a Bahia force that was in
the area but did not reveal to them the true end to which it was destined.[19] Reluctant to share the glory of vanquishing the bandits and,
crucially, the treasure that they carried, he did not invite the Bahia
force to go along. Sergeant Aniceto, accompanied by his volante, departed from Piranhas at approximately the same time to meet Bezerra.
They traveled in a commercial truck that had been temporarily expro-
priated for the occasion. Aniceto, too, kept his real purpose concealed
by announcing in Piranhas for all to hear that he was going to Pedra to
join Bezerra in a search for the bandits at a still more distant location.
He was certain that news of his announced plans would reach Lampião
shortly, for Wednesday was the market day when the rural folk came
into town to do their trading, and among those within hearing range,
the sergeant knew, were some of the bandit's coiteiros. Aniceto sur-
mised that, upon hearing the news, Lampião and his men would be inclined to pass a carefree night, unworried about an attack from Alagoas. Aniceto and Bezerra, together with their forces, met each other
half way between Piranhas and Pedra. They then planned their strate-
gy, deciding to return to Piranhas only after the coming of night in
order to conceal their movements from the bandit's informers.

Lampião, in the meantime, received the news that virtually all of
the troops had left Piranhas in the opposite direction. Pedro de Cân-

[17] Interview with Roque, reported in *O Povo*, May 10, 1952.
[18] Antônio Pequeno, interview.
[19] José Izidro, interview.

dido, coming to the camp with provisions, gave the information. While the coiteiro was still there, Zé Sereno, one of the bandits, came up and told Lampião that they ought to break camp. They had been there several days, he reminded the chief, and remaining any longer might be dangerous. In reply, Lampião looked over at Pedro and assured Sereno that, with a trusted friend like that to depend on, they need fear only God. Lampião added that the men could sleep in their undershorts that night, there being no danger of an attack. The cangaceiros were prepared to spend an uneventful night. Lampião had decided that they would leave Angicos on the following day.[20]

On Wednesday evening, Bezerra and his troops returned to Piranhas, entering the town in stealth. There, Bezerra's forces, also accompanied by Officer Candidate Francisco Ferreira de Melo, joined Aniceto and his men to form a total of forty-five soldiers. Around eight o'clock, they embarked in three sailboats for the trip down the river. They were unsure of their exact destination, for, as yet, they did not know where the bandits were camped. They expected to obtain this information from Pedro de Cândido in Entre Montes, and, when the party was just short of that village, two soldiers were sent to bring him out. Under interrogation, the coiteiro at first denied any knowledge of the whereabouts of the outlaws, but, when threatened with death within minutes if he did not cooperate, he revealed that their hide-out lay only a short distance away on the other side of the river. Forcing Pedro to accompany them, the troops crossed the river and made their way to the Angicos ranch house, there taking on the coiteiro's younger brother as an additional guide. By then the hour was well past midnight. Low, dark clouds hung over the São Francisco and a light rain was falling as the two coiteiros led the soldiers over the rough terrain toward their meeting with Lampião. Beset by doubts and fears, Bezerra proposed that the attack be delayed until reinforcements could be obtained, but, when Ferreira adamantly insisted that he and his men would go alone if Bezerra dropped out, the commander consented to follow the plans already made.[21]

Arriving in the vicinity of the bandits, the troops divided into four

[20] The preceding account of Pedro de Cândido's visit is based on my interviews with Antônio Correia Rosa and João Ferreira, the former having heard the story from Pedro, the latter from Zé Sereno.

[21] Mendonça, untitled MS.

groups. Protected by the thick vegetation and the night, they stealthily began to encircle the camp. They encountered no sentries, for none, apparently, had been posted. Lampião's dogs raised no ruckus, probably because they had sought shelter for protection from the rain. The police were having uncommonly good luck; the famed caution of the bandits was not in evidence. Actually, Lampião probably had spent many carefree nights in the course of his long career, secure in the darkness and isolation and protected by the fear that his name inspired. Many times as well, no doubt, fortune had favored him. By the coming of dawn on that Thursday morning of July 28, 1938, the bandit's allotment of luck had been expended.

When the first rays of day appeared, some of the soldiers found that they were only a few feet from the outlaws. They could hear them talking and stirring in their widely scattered shelters as they began to arouse from sleep. Then, somewhere in the camp, a cangaceiro realized that something was wrong. Maybe it was a noise, or a movement, or some other telltale sign that a person attuned to nature would recognize as out of character. Whatever it was, the man gave the alarm, and the soldiers, discarding their plan to open fire only on a signal from Bezerra, launched their attack. Numerous rifles and three machine guns brought the surprised and disorganized cangaceiros under withering fire. Lampião, reportedly in a soldier's rifle sight when the alarm was sounded, fell, mortally wounded. All over the hillsides, the desperados sought to beseige their attackers and cut out a path of escape. Among them was Luís Pedro, the man who had walked in the stead of the dead Antônio for more than a decade. As he tried to flee, Maria called to him, reminding him that he had sworn to die by the side of his chief. Luís Pedro then turned back and, according to the police, offered heroic resistance until he too was cut down by a soldier's bullet.[22]

The attack was over scarcely more than twenty minutes after it began. Some forty or more of the outlaws had succeeded in escaping, but eleven bandits had died, including Lampião, Luís Pedro, Maria, and one other woman. One soldier had been killed, and another wounded; Bezerra himself received a light injury.

As the battle ended, the jubilant soldiers looted and mutilated the dead. Their money, gold, and precious stones fell to whoever got to

[22] Ibid.

them first. Scenes of savagery—credible enough to those who know the history of the cangaço but shocking, perhaps, to others—took place. One soldier chopped off the hand of Luís Pedro and stuck it in his packsack so he could strip it of its rings at his leisure.[23] The body of Maria was left in a grotesque position, its legs pulled apart and a large stick rammed up the vagina.[24] As had happened so many times before, the bodies of the outlaws were decapitated. Attempting to justify the acts, Bezerra later argued that carrying the bodies would have been too much of a task, and proof was needed that Lampião and his companions had really died. Otherwise, few would have believed it.[25] Their jobs done, the troops departed for Piranhas with their grisly trophies. The headless bodies were left where they lay, to be ogled by the many who would go there to view the site during the next few days. Eventually the bones, picked clean by vultures, would be carried down to the São Francisco by the rushing waters of a tropical rainstorm.[26]

As in the case of the deaths of so many famous personages, there is an alternative story of how Lampião died. There are several versions of the story, but the central argument alleges that the bandits were dead when the soldiers arrived at Angicos and that Pedro de Cândido, acting in concert with João Bezerra, had poisoned them. He had brought, most versions assert, bottles of wine laced with strychnine on his afternoon visit. When the force arrived on the next morning, their

[23] Mendonça, *Pão de Açúcar*, fact no. 245.

[24] Antônio Campos, a soldier who visited the site on the afternoon of the attack, saw Maria's body (interview, Piranhas, Alagoas, August 21, 1975).

[25] Bezerra, *Como dei cabo de Lampeão*, pp. 89–90. In his book, Bezerra denies that he ordered the beheading of the bodies, but a journalist who interviewed him shortly after the event reported that Bezerra said that he ordered the decapitation (Rocha, *Bandoleiros*, p. 30).

[26] Virtually every work on Lampião contains an account of his death. My account is derived mainly from the following sources: Mendonça, untitled MS, which contains the story of Lampião's death based on interviews with participants; Bezerra, *Como dei cabo de Lampeão*, pp. 83–90; Lima, *O mundo estranho*, pp. 277–91, containing interviews with Francisco Ferreira and João Bezerra; *O Povo*, August 15, 1938, containing interviews with Francisco Ferreira and Aniceto Rodrigues; my interviews with Antônio Correia Rosa (Pedro de Cândido's nephew) and João Leandro dos Santos, one of the soldiers who participated in the event. Other sources are noted in my account. Also see Antonio Amaury Corrêa de Araujo, *Assim morreu Lampião*, which contains interviews with various persons concerning Angicos, the most valuable being with Durval Rodrigues Rosa (pp. 99–100), Pedro de Candido's younger brother. Durval accompanied his brother and the police force to Angicos, and his account adds additional details.

firing was only to convince the area population that a battle had occurred. The death of the one soldier and the wounding of Bezerra and another, it is argued, were arranged to provide more convincing evidence of a battle. Others argue that Bezerra was wounded by mistake when, having ordered the volleys, he miscounted and, in his eagerness to plunder the dead, rushed in before the final volley was fired. All of the bandits at Angicos did not die, it is said, because only those of Lampião's immediate group drank the wine. The soldiers were sworn to secrecy on the matter under penalty of death.

Such stories began to appear within two or three years after Lampião died. However, even the seemingly most reliable ones come secondhand. For example, a Recife priest, Father Frederico Bezerra Maciel, states that he was told such a story many years ago by a person who said that he was a cangaceiro who was present at Angicos. Others say that they were told the story by persons claiming to be soldiers present at Angicos. One version was said to have been told by a man who said he was an ex-tenant on Angicos Ranch.[27]

Such stories are most widely believed by the Pernambucans, especially by those who, like the Flor family and other Nazarenos, feel cheated because, in their view, the bandit was killed by a corrupt and cowardly Alagoas officer who was not worthy of the honor. That honor by rights, they feel, should have belonged to them. The unworthy Bezerra could get Lampião only by trickery, not with honor and bravery in a fair fight, as they would have done. The story also appeals to those who assert Lampião's invincibility and believe that the police would never have overcome him by fighting fairly; only through deceit could they kill the celebrated outlaw.

Many of those who believe the story cite as additional proof the subsequent untimely deaths of some of those who allegedly were parties to the plot. They, it is said, were killed to prevent their telling the truth. It is true that some of the soldiers who were at Angicos eventually met violent deaths, but this is not surprising, for soldiers in the raw society of that era led dangerous lives. The death of Pedro de Cândido three years after Angicos, nonetheless, is an intriguing matter. After Angicos, Pedro Rodrigues Rosa (known as Pedro de Cândido), was taken into the state police for his own protection. He was killed on Au-

---

[27] Not one of the persons telling me the story had any sustained contact with the alleged firsthand witness; the meetings of all of them were casual.

gust 22, 1941, in Piranhas de Baixo, a small group of houses just a few hundred feet downstream from the town of Piranhas. The former coiteiro was killed just after dark by a young man who testified that he thought he was killing the monster (*bicho*) that community residents believed to be in the area. Seeing a dark, formless thing approaching him, he said, he plunged his knife into it. He then shouted for help and rushed to the house of acquaintances, where he excitedly related the story of his encounter with the monster. His friends, returning to the area with him, found Pedro lying dead in the street. Strange as it was to outsiders, his story was accepted by most of Piranhas' residents. Like northeastern Brazilians in general, they believed in the existence of unidentified monsters who would come out of the dark to prey on people. The young man's fear was understood, and in his trial the following year he was acquitted. But, for those who believe the poisoning story, João Bezerra had merely arranged to eliminate the one who could tell the shameful story most convincingly.

While, no doubt, controversy over the cause of Lampião's death will continue, the proponents of the poisoning hypothesis will have to produce more convincing evidence than they have offered thus far— and at the same time disprove weighty evidence to the contrary—if they are to be taken seriously. As of now, their case, resting on such an elaborately contrived conspiratorial argument, does not offer a reasonable alternative to the standard version.[28]

News of the death of the celebrated Lampião soon flashed across Brazil. Special editions of newspapers were published and reporters flocked to Alagoas to give firsthand accounts. Several foreign news-

[28] The most convincing and complete version of the poisoning story was offered me in interviews with João and David Jurubeba of the Flor family. Additional information, both pro and con, was obtained from interviews with Wilson Antônio Pereira (Princeza, Paraíba, August 10, 1975), Manoel Arruda d'Assis, Zezito Guedes, Father Frederico Bezerra Maciel (Recife, Pernambuco, June 14 and 15, 1974), and numerous others, including many persons from the Piranhas–Pão de Açúcar area of Alagoas who contest the belief that Lampião was poisoned. Also see Luna, *Lampião*, pp. 120–122. For a somewhat different story of the poisoning, see Noblat, "Lampião morreu envenenado"; this article is based on an interview with Padre José Kehrle, who also believes the poisoning story. The information on Pedro de Cândido's death is extracted from the criminal proceedings against Sabino Francisco dos Santos, Pedro's slayer, August 22, 1941, Cartório, Piranhas. Freyre gives an imaginative discussion of the common belief in monsters in *The Masters and the Slaves*, pp. 139–141.

papers also reported the event, including the *New York Times,* which announced in its heading to the story that "One-Eyed Lampiao . . . One of Most Ruthless Killers of Western World" had been slain.[29] In Rio de Janeiro, Sergipe's interventor, Eronides de Carvalho, granted an interview to discuss the demise of the bandit. While he asserted that his forces had always fought the bandits with devotion—a statement that was patently false—he apparently could not refrain from acknowledging his acquaintance with the renowned figure. He showed the reporters a photograph of Lampião that, he said, he had snapped in 1929 when the outlaw visited a ranch where he was staying.[30] The official press in Sergipe also asserted that the state's forces, led by Eronides, had always engaged the bandits in constant war.[31] They had killed, the release continued, several of them, including the infamous José Bahiano. This was a blatant lie, since it was common knowledge that Bahiano had been killed by civilian coiteiros who had betrayed him. The Sergipe police's record of having killed not even one of Lampião's men apparently stood until the end.

In the aftermath of Angicos, much interest in the area centered on the heads. While they were being shown in Piranhas, they were requested by the authorities in Maceió. The heads were in an advanced state of putrefaction by the time they reached the capital, for, although they were transported in cans of kerosene, they were taken out for display numerous times along the way, usually lined up on the steps of some public building like birds in a shooting gallery. And they went on display again on August 1 in Maceió.[32] Presumably, the main reason for bringing them to the capital, other than to satisfy curiosity, was to permit the study of them by local police physicians, who claimed to double as physical anthropologists. At any rate, they were examined, measured, and classified. But Alagoas was not a major center for the study of criminal typology, and, when institutions in other areas requested the heads, it was decided to relinquish them. Several places wanted them, including an institution far away in Berlin. With respect to that request, one Brazilian journalist commented that surely German

[29] July 29, 1938.

[30] *Correio de Aracajú,* August 5, 1938.

[31] *Diário Oficial* of July 29, 1938, reported in *Correio de Aracajú,* August 5, 1938.

[32] *Jornal de Alagoas,* August 1, 1938.

scholars could find more fitting subjects closer to home. Compared to "certain demons" of their own, he wrote, Lampião might be called gentle.[33] In the end, it was not Berlin but Salvador that was favored. The heads of Lampião and Maria were sent to the Nina Rodrigues Institute; the others were interred in Maceió. In Salvador, the heads of the famed desperado and his lover joined those of several of their comrades already there, and for many years—disfigured and grotesque—they served as the Nina Rodrigues (later Estácio de Lima) Museum's main attraction.

With the celebration in the backlands of Lampião's death came the realization that, while the chief might be dead, several dozen of his band were still on the loose. Among them was Corisco, long known for the ferocity and deliberate cruelty of his vengeance. On the same day that the events at Angicos happened, Corisco learned of the deaths when he talked to a coiteiro who had just been brought the news. Both the outlaw and Dadá cried, the coiteiro has said, upon learning of the event, and Dadá, turning to her mate and his followers, declared to them that they were not men if they failed to avenge the deaths. Corisco's revenge came against Domingos Ventura and his family on Patos Ranch, a property in Piranhas County owned by João Bezerra's father-in-law. Domingos was a coiteiro, but his links to Bezerra made him vulnerable. It has been charged that Joca Bernardes—who had informed on Lampião—deflected Corisco's suspicions of him with false accusations that it was Domingos who perpetrated the betrayal.[34]

Five days after Angicos, Corisco and his band arrived at Patos, seeming to come in peace as usual, and ate supper with Domingos and his family. Afterwards, the outlaw, having asked for a pencil and paper, wrote a note. His men, meanwhile, invited Domingos and one of his sons to step outside into the night for a word in private. The bandits then came back for two other sons. It was then the turn of Domingos' wife and his adult daughter. When they were brought to the corral, they found the bodies of the four men lying on the ground, their heads cut off; a similar fate was then meted out to them. Their lives, Corisco said, were taken in exchange for the two women killed at Angicos. Only the three small children were spared—for the purpose, the bandit lead-

[33] Rocha, *Bandoleiros*, p. 65. Rocha also reprints the physician's report of the examination of Lampião's head (pp. 58–61).

[34] Antônio Pequeno, interview; Mendonça, untitled MS.

er told them, of telling the story of what happened. The massacre over, Corisco ordered the heads placed in a sack and sent them to Piranhas. Attached to the bloody package was the note he had written, informing Bezerra that three of the heads were for him while the remaining three were destined for the state interventor.[35] For those who lived within the crude world of the cangaceiros, justice had been done. Notice was also served that the cangaço was not yet dead.

If the cangaço was not dead, it was nonetheless on its way toward extinction, for within two years after Lampião's death it had passed from the scene, seemingly forever. There was speculation immediately following Lampião's death that someone else—Corisco, most likely— would assume the role of chief and that the cangaço would continue to constitute a threat of virtually undiminished strength. But that did not happen. Instead, Lampião's bandit empire quickly weakened and fragmented. A cangaceiro who turned himself in—having shown his willingness to reform by killing one of his comrades and beheading him in early September in Alagoas—declared Corisco to be a failure. He was, the twenty-year-old bandit said, spending much of his time drunk. The bandits were quarreling among themselves and many of them were ready to leave the cangaço, he continued.[36] Similar reports came from Bahia where three bandits had surrendered to police. Again, one of the bandits brought in the head of a comrade to prove his change of heart. Officials there, perceiving an opportunity to accomplish their aims without further resort to large-scale violence, passed the word along the Bahia-Sergipe border that cangaceiros who turned themselves in would be accorded kind treatment. The response from the bandits was more than encouraging: in October seventeen delivered themselves in Jeremoabo, fifteen on one day. Meanwhile, six bandits surrendered without a fight when they were surrounded by police in Poço Redondo, and, elsewhere, four were killed.[37] Others turned themselves in or were apprehended during the remaining months of the year. By the end of the year, the number of cangaceiros still free was quite small, since at least thirty-five had been killed or

[35] Mendonça, untitled MS; Rocha, *Bandoleiros*, pp. 67–78; *Jornal de Alagoas*, August 4, 1938.

[36] Interview with Barreiros in *Jornal de Alagoas*, September 9, 1938.

[37] *A Tarde*, October 22 and 24, 1938; *Jornal de Alagoas*, October 18 and 19, 1938.

captured or had turned themselves in after Angicos. Including the eleven killed there, the number no longer on the loose—for whatever reasons—came to no fewer than forty-six.[38] Only Corisco and Ângelo Roque, of the better-known bandits, remained to be dealt with.

Ângelo Roque continued to operate in the Bahia-Sergipe border region until 1940 and was yet the author of vicious crimes. Near Bebedouro in 1939, he beat a woman to death with a mallet while her four small children (the oldest was five) looked on. He apparently bore the woman no personal enmity, for he had come to kill her husband on the request of a coiteiro; he killed her instead when he found that the man was not at home. By April of 1940, Roque too was willing to accept police assurances that his own life would be spared and that he would be given the opportunity to reform himself. He and eight companions, including four women, surrendered at Bebedouro.[39]

The most recalcitrant of the prominent cangaceiros who survived Angicos was Corisco. More than any of the others, he seems to have been afraid to surrender, believing that he would be killed. That he should have felt that way is understandable, in view of his evil reputation. After the Patos massacre, Corisco and Dadá, together with their band, settled down to operating quietly, attracting a minimum of attention. They did not attack villages and ranches but limited themselves to requesting money, using coiteiros as intermediaries. Even though the cangaço was in a dying state, the name of Corisco still was sufficient to induce most persons of wealth and property to make the requested contributions.[40]

The police continued to be Corisco's major problem. There were still volantes in the field, and a combat occasionally occurred, as in August, 1939, when three bandits were killed.[41] Then, late in that year or in early 1940, Corisco himself was seriously wounded in a battle and lost the use of his right arm as a result. In the months following the injury, he began seriously to consider turning himself in, at one time asking a priest in Porto da Folha, Sergipe, to intercede for him and, at another, sending a letter to the commander of the Bahia forces.

[38] My calculation, based on newspaper reports.

[39] Criminal proceedings against Ângelo Roque, June 8, 1939, Cartório, Jeremoabo, Bahia; *A Tarde*, April 1 and 2, 1940.

[40] The band's activities were described by one of its members, Velocidade, who surrendered to police in May, 1940 (*A Tarde*, May 29, 1940).

[41] Ibid., August 17, 1939.

When on the latter occasion everything seemed to be arranged for his surrender, he backed down after a fortune teller told him he would be killed if he went through with the plan. He then set out on a trek westward across Bahia, accompanied by Dadá, an eleven-year-old girl whom Dadá had taken a liking to, and another bandit and his woman. On their departure, Corisco talked of leaving the cangaço and seeking refuge in some far-away place.[42]

The police soon learned of Corisco's leaving and sent José Rufino and his volante after him. They caught up with the bandits, disguised as gypsies, in Brotas de Macaúbas County in the state's remote interior not far from the São Francisco River. In the battle, Corisco— who faced the police with a pistol in his left hand—was injured and soon died. Dadá, who offered fierce resistance, received a serious leg injury.[43] The eleven-year-old girl was uninjured and was returned to her family by the police. Dadá was taken on an agonizing trip in the back of a truck to Jeremoabo—a distance of near 250 miles over rough dirt roads—her foot hanging to her leg only by the fleshy parts, the bone having been shot away. Gangrene had set in by the time the party reached its destination, and the foot and a portion of the leg subsequently were amputated. Corisco's body, which had been buried near Miguel Calmon on the trip back, was not left to rest. Alleging that the cause of death had not been determined and that all the legal formalities of a proper declaration of death had not been executed, authorities in Salvador sent a physician from the Nina Rodrigues Institute to exhume the body. It is apparent, professed reasons notwithstanding, that what the authorities wanted was the bandit's head; the physician, of course, returned with it. It was added to the collection.[44]

With the killing of Corisco, the cangaço was brought to a close.

[42] Felipe Borges de Castro, the commander of the forces in northeastern Bahia at the time, related to me Corisco's difficulties and his desire to leave the cangaço. Also see *A Tarde*, January 22, April 4, and June 13, 1940.

[43] The story of the pursuit and battle was told to me by Severiano Ramos, one of the soldiers in the force (interview). Also see *A Tarde*, May 27 and 28, 1940, and Lima, *O mundo estranho*, pp .71–72.

[44] *A Tarde*, June 3 and 4, 1940. Curiously, Dadá—who, aided by Colonel João Sá, was released by authorities after her recuperation—later went to Miguel Calmon and dug up the remaining parts of her husband's body. As of this writing, she still has the bones in her possession, keeping them in a nicely polished wooden box under hers and her present husband's bed in Salvador. She now has a grandson who attends the police academy in that city.

There were, to be sure, some few individuals of one or another of the bands still on the loose. Some of those were later apprehended; others sank quietly back into the anonymity of the peasantry from which they came and were never called to pay for whatever crimes they may have committed. But the colorful, roving bands of outlaws—of distinctive dress and fearsome renown—who had haunted the northeastern *caatingas* for so many years were no more.

The fact that the cangaço became extinct within two years of Lampião's death strongly suggests that his passing was a major determining factor in its demise. And, beyond reasonable doubt, that was true. It was his ability as a bandit leader and warrior that gave the cangaço a longevity that extended beyond its time. Logically, the cangaço—and Lampião—should have been fatal casualties of the Pernambuco campaign of the late 1920s, when banditry was virtually extinguished in the area in which it had been endemic. But the wily Lampião survived that campaign and, on the other side of the São Francisco, built a new bandit empire that prolonged his career—and the cangaço—for several years. When he died, the cangaço effectively died too, for its force was spent. Those few remnants of his bands that led an increasingly fragile existence for two years were little more than his lengthening shadow.

In 1940 a Rio de Janeiro editorial on the death of Corisco suggested another reason for the end of the cangaço. It had become, the editorial said, an anachronism: there was no place for Corisco and Lampião in the Brazil of schools, airplanes, and the Ford.[45] Their extinction, it seemed to the writer, resulted from the entry of the backlands into the twentieth century. In short, progress had overtaken the cangaço and eliminated it. The view of the editor—who, if he was a typical Rio journalist, knew virtually nothing of significance about the backlands—has come to be the commonly accepted explanation for the end of the cangaço. If not overdrawn, the view has some validity, for there were indications by 1940 that Brazil was changing. Just how much change had come to the backlands by that date is a matter of importance.

The most decisive difference, it is usually suggested, was the im-

[45] Reprinted in *A Tarde*, June 1, 1940.

provement in communications. Roads were constructed in the back-lands during the 1930s, some of them for the specific purpose of facilitating the campaign against Lampião. But such roads were only primitive dirt trails built by human and animal labor, and vast areas continued to lie outside their reach. Trucks for transporting soldiers, moreover, were few, and those that were furnished often could not be used, either because they so frequently broke down or because the roads were impassable from rains and washouts. For that matter, motorized transport remained a novelty in the backlands throughout the 1930s for soldiers and civilians alike. In Bahia, for example, usually no more than two or three trucks and automobiles existed in each of the backlands counties; some counties had none at all.[46] The fact is that the war against the bandits continued to be waged mostly on foot. Governor Magalhães of Bahia stated in 1937 that, while the new roads made greater vigilance against the bandits possible, the bandits' main incursions into the state were being made in places like Bebedouro and Paripiranga, where there still were no roads.[47] Of course, trucks were useful, where and when conditions permitted their use, in transporting soldiers between major towns and in the more rapid formation of a force—as, for instance, the one that attacked Angicos. It would be injudicious to deny that improved communications hastened the end of the cangaço, but it should be kept in mind that improvements were not extensive.

Other signs of material progress in the backlands during the 1930s would be difficult to uncover, the optimistic opinions of the Rio editor notwithstanding. Airplanes were not used against the bandits; schools, even of the lowest elementary grades, were almost unknown outside of sizable towns, and many county seats had none that regularly functioned. If material improvements had reached the backlands, they were not much in evidence in places like Bebedouro and Poço Redondo.

It has been suggested that, after 1930, a new era in the nation's economy opened with a surge toward industrialization that, creating

[46] Based on the *Annuário estatístico da Bahia*, published annually in Salvador, containing vehicle registrations by county. All the soldiers and officers with whom I have talked about the last years of the campaign told me that trucks and automobiles were seldom used in their day-to-day operations.

[47] Bahia, *Mensagem do Governador Juracy Magalhães . . . em 2 de Julho de 1937*, p. 40.

opportunities for employment—especially in the South—ended the can- gaço by drawing off the surplus population. However, before we can affirm with assurance that Lampião and the cangaço were ended by an expanding capitalism, we need to know far more than is presently known about the effects of Brazil's larger economic development before 1940 on remote backlands communities. Probably not until well after 1940 did migration from the backlands to São Paulo and other southern cities reach a level significant enough to produce any changes in the country of the cangaço.[48]

A trend toward the modernization of government, including more effective penetration of governmental authority into the backlands, ap- pears to have been of greater consequence in eliminating the cangaço than either material improvements or outward migration. Although this change affected different places at different times and varied in inten- sity from place to place, it was becoming evident from the late 1920s forward that the old order was being eroded. No longer were the lords of the backlands left untrammeled in their dominions in exchange for professions of loyalty and the delivery of votes to the state and national political machines. The war against the bandits and their coiteiros in Pernambuco in the late 1920s stands as evidence of the onset of the trend. The changes wrought by Getúlio Vargas' regime during the next decade, but especially after 1937, demonstrate—however haltingly, at times—the continuance of it. Parts of the old order and the new existed side by side, of course. For example, authorities in Alagoas in 1938 were moved to take drastic steps to ensure the elimination of the can- gaceiros, while Interventor Eronides in neighboring Sergipe remained able to offer them the traditional protection. But, as uneven as the man- ifestations of the trend were, when we view the history of the back- lands from early in the century to 1940, it is clear that incidences of more effective governmental authority during the last fourteen years or so of that period contributed measurably to the passing of the cangaço.

---

[48] Queiroz in "Notas sociológicas," pp. 506–507, argues that migration from the backlands helped to end the cangaço and in "Os cangaceiros," p. 193, sets the beginning of significant migration at 1935. The more complete discussion of migra- tion in T. Lynn Smith, *Brazil: People and Institutions*, especially pp. 154–156, 171, suggests that the movement of people out of the area did not reach a significant level until after 1940.

None of the foregoing discussion, of course, explains fully the events that culminated in Angicos. As in so much of history, it may have been chance that held the center of the stage in that drama. Nonetheless, changes that were taking place in the larger society made Angicos—or a similar happening on some other day—more likely.

13. A Social Bandit?

By 1940, when Corisco was killed, large numbers of cangaceiros were in the custody of the authorities in Bahia and Alagoas. Many of them hoped for mercy, especially those who had voluntarily turned themselves in. But the crimes of some of them were too well known to be excused, and a few, like Ângelo Roque, were given long prison sentences.[1] In the cases of many others, no criminal proceedings had ever been initiated and none were started after their arrest. If they were guilty of crimes, as many of them were, no one came forth to accuse them. In general, the authorities and the larger Brazilian public exhibited sympathy and leniency for them, a view that sprang logically from the long-standing popularization of the cangaço as a reflection of the ignorance, poverty, and injustice of backlands society: the cangaceiros were not common criminals but victims of circumstances.[2] Their comportment under detention also impressed officials. They were, as one prison official stated it, normal people who, while in prison, worked well and exhibited obedience to authority. Following periods of detention ranging from a few months to as long as three or four years, during which time their disposition was being considered, they were released to society.[3] Of course, some never reached that point. Portu-

[1] Roque's initial sentence was ninety-five years, but it was reduced to thirty and then, in the 1950s, commuted. He died recently in Salvador.

[2] See, for instance, an early call for compassionate treatment in an editorial in *A Tarde*, October 26, 1938.

[3] Castro, *Figuras legendárias*, contains profiles of ten cangaceiros held by Alagoas and also has comments by prison officials on their behavior. It apparently was written to explain why the state released them. The release of cangaceiros who were not charged with crimes was not new. Bahia, for example, freed four in 1935 and sent them outside the area so as to discourage their return to the cangaço (*O Imparcial*, May 22, 1935; *Diário de Notícias*, May 23, 1935). It is a fact that

guês, for example, was killed in Santana do Ipanema in early 1939, shortly after his surrender, by a soldier whose father he had killed five years earlier.[4]

While many of the cangaceiros were being reintegrated into society, the mummified head of their chieftain, along with those of his lover and several companions, sat on display in the museum for curious eyes to see. Indeed, Brazilians were not exceptional in their exposition of bandits' heads, for similar displays in other parts of the world have not been rare. In the United States in the 1850s, a head reputed to be that of bandit Joaquin Murieta was displayed pickled in whiskey in California, and broadsides were posted announcing its arrival.[5] Also in the United States, the exposition in traveling carnivals of mummified bodies alleged to be those of criminals was common from the 1920s until World War II. As a child in Kentucky in the early 1940s, I saw one reputed to be that of Lincoln's assassin, John Wilkes Booth. In 1976, a mummy found in a Long Beach, California, amusement park was identified as the remains of an outlaw named Elmer McCurdy who was ambushed in Oklahoma in 1912. An Oklahoma City sheriff had sold McCurdy's cadaver to a carnival operator who displayed it from 1921 until the early 1940s. After being subsequently stored for several years, it was sold to a wax museum, which in turn sold it to the Long Beach enterprise.[6]

Such barbarous expositions have never set well with many people, and in Brazil, as the years passed, criticism of the Bahia collection became more vocal and widespread. The main obstacle to the interment of the bandits' heads was Estácio de Lima, the museum director and a well-known Bahia scholar. To Estácio, the demands for the removal of the heads were a threat to the state's "cultural patrimony."[7] In time, more sensitive counsel prevailed, and in 1969 the heads were laid to rest quietly in small crypts in picturesque Quintas Cemetery, located atop one of Salvador's many hills.

---

criminal proceedings were never initiated for many of the cangaceiros' crimes, due apparently to the lethargy of backlands officials. I have concluded that Pernambuco authorities generally were the most conscientious in investigating the crimes and initiating proceedings against the authors of them.

[4] *Jornal de Alagoas*, February 14, 1939.
[5] Robert Elman, *Badmen of the West*, p. 73, reproduces the broadside.
[6] *Corpus Christi* (Texas) *Caller*, December 11, 1976.
[7] *Diário de Notícias*, May 21, 1959.

Yet, neither the events at Angicos nor Quintas Cemetery laid Lampião to rest, for he continues in Brazilian popular culture as one of the nation's best-known historical figures. The books and movies on his life and the stories that are told about him ensured his survival for a long time to come.[8] Moreover, in the view of many backlanders, the bandit still lives in the flesh.[9] He is, they believe, now residing on some ranch in one or another of the nation's far western states, enjoying the peace of old age. To them, Angicos was a sham, for Virgulino Ferreira da Silva, commonly known as Lampião, was invincible.

Eric Hobsbawm, the British social historian, has set up a framework for classifying bandits according to their characteristics and the opinions people have of them. He includes Lampião in his study.[10] It might be worthwhile at this point to review some of his ideas about banditry, particularly as they pertain to Lampião. In doing so, perhaps we shall be able to bring the cangaceiro chieftain into clearer focus and also offer, in passing, a critique of the ideas from the perspective of our study of him.

Hobsbawm's interests are directed chiefly to those bandits whom he classifies as social bandits. Social bandits are peasant outlaws whom the people regard as heroes rather than common criminals. They are seen as champions of justice or, at least, as justified in their actions. They kill only for just cause, and they are thought to merit support and protection. Among the social bandits, there are two, and possibly three, types: the noble robber, the primitive guerrilla leader, and, possibly, the avenger. The first of these, the noble robber, fits most securely

---

[8] Movies with cangaceiro themes occupy much the same position in the Brazilian film industry that Westerns do in the United States. The best known of the films on Lampião is *O cangaceiro*, released in 1953. For a history of the cangaceiro films, see Silva, "O filme de cangaço."

[9] The majority of backlanders with whom I have talked in rural areas and small towns hold this opinion.

[10] Hobsbawm's ideas are set forth briefly in *Primitive Rebels*, pp. 13–29, and more extensively in *Bandits*. His comments on Lampião are in *Bandits*, especially pp. 50–53, and in Nirlando Beirão, "No mundo dos bandidos (Entrevista: Eric J. Hobsbawm)," *Veja*, June 11, 1975. As in the instances of the other bandits whom he uses to build his case, Hobsbawm makes no claims that his data about Lampião are true reflections of the historical figure. He chooses freely and often indiscriminately from myths as well as purportedly factual sources, and much of his portrayal comes from the former.

within the definition of the social bandit. He is, of course, the classic Robin Hood. He is admired not only for his daring feats but also for his zeal for justice and his redistribution of wealth.

Leaving the primitive guerrilla leader aside, it is the third group, the avengers, that most concerns us. The avengers are set apart from true social bandits by their extreme use of violence. They are social bandits (if they are that at all) only marginally. If they are regarded with admiration or as heroes, it is not so much for their acts of justice as for their demonstration that the peasant can also be terrible. Their "social justice consists of destruction. To kill, to wound, to burn means, for them, to abolish corruption and evil."[11] Hobsbawm recognizes that Lampião could clearly be terrible and for this reason places him among the avengers. He states that Lampião further fails the test of a true social bandit because of his alliance with landlords. But he adds—in error, I think—that the cangaceiro chieftain defended the poor. Hobsbawm exculpates Lampião for his violence, arguing that in a sense it was involuntary, for, coming at the point of severe social tensions marking the final break between the traditional Northeast and the new capitalist order, it was inevitable.[12]

Hobsbawm's discussions of banditry range widely and overall are neither closely reasoned nor adequately supported by reliable evidence. Confusion results especially from his dealing with bandits as both myth and reality, without, in many instances, distinguishing between the two. Because of this imprecision, his ideas do not readily lend themselves to analysis and, therefore, may best be regarded as tentative suggestions. Perhaps the major problem is that his definition of a social bandit is, it seems, inverted. It rests not so much on the actual deeds of the bandits as on what people thought them to be, or, more precariously, on how they were reported by balladeers and other popular storytellers even generations later. As one of Hobsbawm's critics has said, popular conceptions of bandits are an important field for study, but they are not reliable reflections of reality.[13] Indeed, if the definition

[11] Beirão, "No mundo dos bandidos."

[12] Ibid.

[13] Anton Blok, *The Mafia of a Sicilian Village, 1860–1960*, p. 102. For Blok's criticism of Hobsbawm's ideas of banditry, also see his "The Peasant and the Brigand: Social Banditry Reconsidered," pp. 494–503.

is turned right side up, thus placing the burden of proof on fact instead of myth, there would seem to be so few noble robbers in history as to cast a shadow of doubt on the type as a significant pattern of human behavior.

In addition to Robin Hood—who may or may not have been real —Hobsbawm in the chapter on noble robbers in his major work on banditry identifies only two of that type: Juro Janosik of Slovakia and Diego Corrientes of Andalucía, both shadowy figures from the eighteenth century.[14] To illustrate the type more broadly, he includes several other bandits who, like Ângelo Roque ("Labareda"), are clearly inappropriate. His inclusion of Roque casts doubt on the care with which he chose his examples, for that bloody subchieftain of Lampião's does not belong in any discussion of noble robbers, real or imagined— nor have I ever seen such a designation of him other than Hobsbawm's. If one is interested in portraying bandits as they were rather than as they were popularly imagined to be, neither do Jesse James and Billy the Kid merit inclusion.[15]

While including these bandits who do not fit the type, Hobsbawm, curiously, fails to refer to others—such as the eighteenth-century bandit Angelo Duca of southern Italy—whom he had mentioned in an earlier study as sterling examples of the type.[16] Such use of evidence limits the value of Hobsbawm's work. Much of the problem lies in his intermingling fact and fiction to support his views without indicating (and often not knowing) which was which. A more credible and historically sound approach would have recognized the need for dealing with banditry on two levels: reality and legend. However, such a distinction, requiring the sorting of data according to historical reliability, would have severely restricted Hobsbawm's wide-ranging approach.

In short, the scarcity of noble robbers and the more than adequate supply of the common variety suggests a weakness in Hobsbawm's conceptualization of banditry. There seems to be reason for a strong argument that although his view may make a considerable contribution to

[14] Hobsbawm, *Bandits*, pp. 34–39. On Diego Corrientes, see also Constancio Bernaldo de Queiros and Luis Ardila, *El bandolerismo andaluz*, pp. 37–53.

[15] Hobsbawm, *Bandits*, pp. 36, 38. The scholarly work on Jesse James is William A. Settle, Jr., *Jesse James Was His Name*. A nearly perfect fictional noble robber is portrayed in the Turkish novel by Yashar Kemal, *Memed, My Hawk*.

[16] Hobsbawm, *Primitive Rebels*, p. 14.

the analysis of the myths about bandits, it contributes little, as a tool of analysis, to the study of the bandits themselves.

Of course, by inverting Hobsbawm's definition, we lose sight of his main point. He is, after all, at least as much interested in the myths about bandits as he is in the bandits themselves. He believes that the tendency of peasants to attribute characteristics such as justice to their bandit hero (also their admiration for his success in battling the oppressors) represents a rejection by the peasants of the unjust societies in which they live. Such a bandit need not really possess the traits said to be his; what is important is the kind of stories the peasants tell about him.

An extensive critique of this portion of Hobsbawm's analysis falls outside the purview of this study, for the aim here has been the recreation of the historical Lampião and not the exploration of the folklore about him. Yet, it should be noted that the humble people of the backlands accorded Lampião high marks—however grudgingly, on the part of many—for his success. There also has been the tendency for them to forget some of the horror that accompanied his career but to remember and exaggerate not only his cunning and bravery but also his good traits—and even to invent some. He is known today as a man of his word, and in fact he often was, whether by whim or by design. But, surprisingly, he is also almost invariably said to have been a respecter of women—this, in spite of the evidence to the contrary. Some people also see in him a kind of primitive rebel with a social conscience. When Francisco Julião, the Pernambuco leader of peasant unions, called for the interment of the heads in 1959, he declared that Lampião was the first to fight against latifundia and the injustice of the powerful.[17] And did he not, after all, give alms to the poor and distribute freely the goods of backlands merchants whom he plundered? The myth of the noble robber may someday obscure the real Lampião just as it has so many other ignoble robbers. Indeed, the process of idealization and heroization may be virtually inevitable in his case, for there is just enough truth to feed the legend. Moreover, from his alleged entry into crime to avenge the death of his father to his own ultimate death by betrayal—not to mention so much of what happened in between—

[17] Julião, a member of the Pernambuco state legislature when he made his appeal, was exiled after the 1964 military takeover. His comments are in *Diário de Notícias*, May 23, 1959.

Lampião more than adequately qualifies for inclusion in the pantheon of bandit heroes.[18]

Whether or not the creation of such a legend is fraught with social significance is a matter for speculation. The telling of stories has long been a pastime of rural folk who, living apart from the distractions of town and city life, have to rely mostly on their own resources for pleasant diversion. When people sit in those forgotten corners of the backlands to tell stories under the splendidly adorned sky of a summer's evening, they want to escape the humdrum of their lives and talk of romantic things—of valiantry, of cunning, and of how, as the turtle outwitted the hare, the weak make fools of the powerful. This may be suggestive of what people think of those who are wealthier than they, but, primarily, it is entertaining. It may be that cangaceiros continue to be remembered mostly because they make good stories, not because they are symbols of genuine social disaffection. Moreover, an interest in violence and crime seems to afflict most of us, and interest is heightened when the perpetrators possess the flair of a Lampião. To attempt to translate that interest into the rejection of the society in which the violence takes place is, it may be, to claim an understanding of human nature that man has not yet achieved.

Hobsbawm also thinks that myths are not unimportant in shaping bandits' behavior, and possibly stories and legends of the cangaceiros as defenders of justice and benefactors of the poor—such as those told of Antônio Silvino—affected Lampião's behavior to the degree that he did a good deed now and then in order to improve his image. Lampião, after all, was concerned about his public relations. But it should be remembered that he came from a respectable family of yeoman status, and he yearned for a return to lawful society and respectability. This tended to place some curbs on his conduct, or, at the least, to lead him to deny his participation in indiscriminate violence or ungentlemanly actions. He was never totally brutalized by the nature of his work; until the end he tried to retain an image of himself as a man of honor.

In this connection, Hobsbawm's view that the terrible violence of the avengers is a blind striking out at injustice is poetic and, like much poetry, may contain some truth. It is easy to conceive of any bandit,

---

[18] Kent L. Steckmesser in "Robin Hood and the American Outlaw," *Journal of American Folklore*, 79 (1966), pp. 348–355, discusses the traits that ideal bandit heroes should have. Also see Hobsbawm, *Bandits*, pp. 35–36.

bereft of the chance to live a normal life and chased by the law as hounds pursue a fox, committing acts of unjustifiable violence in frustration and anger. Yet, the overall pattern of Lampião's behavior does not conform to this view. There were times when his violence was indiscriminate, as, for example, his rampages after the deaths of his brothers. There were also times under entirely different circumstances when the cruelty of his vengeance overflowed the boundaries of reason. But, in the main, his violence was deliberate, directed expressly to maintain his personal survival. This is an inevitable development in the lives of many bandits, no matter how they fall outside the law— whether by clear injustice against them or their families or, as with Lampião, by a complex set of circumstances in which blame is cumulative on both sides and not easily assignable. No matter how strong their original desire to avenge the alleged wrongs, bandits who remain in the field very long soon become overwhelmed by the demands of survival. It is to this fact that the violence may most reasonably be attributed, especially in the instance of a successful and calculating man of Lampião's caliber. If there was an influence of equal consequence, it was most likely fear itself, for fear, as has often been noted, is one of the most corrupting of influences.

The political, or ideologically motivated, bandit may stand as an exception to the rule, in that he struggles not to preserve himself but to kindle a flame of revolt and nurture it. However, such considerations are not relevant in the evolution of Lampião, for he had no discernible wish to alter the basic structure of his society.[19] His ties with it were intimate and far reaching, as Hobsbawm has recognized. Indeed, the famed desperado took advantage of an unjust society and profitably and brutally exploited it.

As to the larger question of whether or not banditry is (as Hobsbawm suggests) a form of primitive and prepolitical protest against an unjust society, it is difficult to say whether the Brazilian cangaço during the time of Lampião was that or not. The cangaço had various and diverse origins, some of which were based in human perversity and some of which lay in unjust social conditions. But, even so, it is questionable whether such criminality—almost totally, and usually alto-

[19] An exemplary although naïve, bandit of the political type was Salvatore Giuliano, who operated in Sicily from 1943 to his death in 1950. Gavin Maxwell, *God Protect Me from My Friends*, tells his story.

gether, divorced from any conscious desire for meaningful change in society—was a form of social protest. It may be more meaningful to suggest that it was a symptom of a maladjusted society.[20]

Of course, bandits may contribute to protest under unusual conditions, such as in Mexico during its revolution.[21] Such cases may arise chiefly because the bandits are relatively independent and armed and thus are in a position to occupy a vacuum when established power begins to crumble. What the bandits then become—popular leaders, an army at the behest of one wielder of power or another, power and property usurpers in their own right—depends on many conditions, including mere chance. There would seem to be little in banditry itself that steers them toward the types of revolutionary change that benefit the oppressed classes. This is, it should be noted, a point that Hobsbawm has emphasized on occasion. Social bandits, he wrote in *Primitive Rebels*, protest only excessive deprivation or oppression and then only within the existing social structure; they do not seek revolutionary change.[22]

It is questionable whether even this limited characterization of social banditry is applicable to Lampião. Concern over the oppression of the poor and weak by the wealthy and powerful simply was not one of his preoccupations. He was mainly concerned with his own survival, and in that fight for survival he demanded and received the cooperation and favors not only of peasants but also of wealthy landowners and political bosses. Whether, in return, the recipients of his favors or his terror, as the case might be, were the oppressed or the oppressors made little if any difference. Hobsbawm's uneasiness about including Lampião in his class of social bandits, evinced by his placing him on the margins of the group, is justified.

To determine whether Lampião was, in any sense, a social bandit, we must examine further Hobsbawm's definition. The problem may be that his definition is not only inverted but also unnecessarily narrow. All banditry, broadly construed, may be called social banditry, involv-

[20] On Hobsbawm's views of social banditry as a primitive, prepolitical protest, see his *Primitive Rebels*, especially pp. 13–28.

[21] Hobsbawm notes this in *Bandits*, pp. 84–93, especially p. 90.

[22] P. 24. Somewhat in contrast to this view, the same author in *Bandits* (pp. 19–23, 84–93) makes a major effort to establish an affinity between banditry and revolutionary movements, although in the end his conclusions do not radically change.

ing, as it does, relations between people.[23] So comprehensive a definition, of course, may be unacceptable to some students of banditry. However, a narrower definition should surely include at least those bandits whose criminal origins appear to lie in uncommonly unjust social conditions. If this be allowed—it may be one of the better definitions of social banditry—it can be said that Lampião was a social bandit, even if he was not a noble robber. Although there is little reason to deny that some of his actions may have arisen from a perversity that was his own, it is true that his society was one in which a valiant young man such as he could fall into banditry all too easily. Or as a folk poet has recorded it:

> He was savage, he was evil,
> Virgulino, the Lampião,
> But he was, who would deny it,
> In the fiber of his heart,
> The most perfect picture
> Of the *caatingas* of the backlands.[24]

[23] Blok, in *The Mafia of a Sicilian Village*, p. 99, so defines banditry.

[24] A well-known verse that appears, among other places, in Luciano Carneiro, "Lampeão é nosso sangue," *O Cruzeiro*, September 26, 1953.

Bibliography

Archives

Arquivo Nacional. Rio de Janeiro.
Arquivo, Polícia Militar. Salvador, Bahia.
Arquivo Público. Aracajú, Sergipe.
Arquivo Público. Fortaleza, Ceará.
Arquivo Público. Maceió, Alagoas.
Arquivo Público. Recife, Pernambuco.
Arquivo Público. Salvador, Bahia.
Cartório. Agua Branca, Alagoas.
Cartório. Floresta, Pernambuco.
Cartório. Jeremoabo, Bahia.
Cartório. Piranhas, Alagoas.
Cartório. Princeza, Paraíba.
Cartório. Serra Talhada, Pernambuco.
Instituto Histórico e Geográfico de Alagoas, Maceió, Alagoas.
Museo Histórico, Fortaleza, Ceará.

Published Documents

Bahia. Directoria Geral de Estatística. *Annuário estatístico da Bahia.* Vols. 1930–1940. Published annually in Salvador, Bahia.
Bahia. *Mensagem do Governador Juracy Magalhães em 2 de julho de 1937.* Salvador, Bahia, 1937.
Bahia. Secretaria da Polícia e Segurança Pública. *Relatório de 1929.* Salvador, Bahia, 1930.
Magalhães, Juracy M. *Exposição feita ao Exmo. Snr. Dr. Getúlio Vargas pelo Capitão Juracy Montenegro Magalhães, Interventor Federal no Estado da Bahia, relativo ao exercício de 1932.* Salvador, Bahia, 1932.

Interviews

Alves, José. Piranhas, Alagoas, August 20, 1975.
Barbosa, Hermenigildo. Queimadas, Bahia, July 12, 1974.

Barros, Ana Maria. Floresta, Pernambuco, August 5, 1975.
Bernardes, Joca. Piranhas, Alagoas, August 20, 1975.
Bulhões, Pedro Melo. Santana do Ipanema, Alagoas, June 21, 1974.
Calazans, José. Salvador, Bahia, November 25, 1973.
Campos, Antônio. Piranhas, Alagoas, August 21, 1975.
Campos, Olympo. São José de Belmonte, Pernambuco, July 30, 31, 1975.
Carvalho, João Primo de. São José de Belmonte, July 30, 1975.
Castro, Felipe Borges de. Salvador, Bahia, November 25, 26, 27, 1973.
Correia, Maria. Agua Branca, Alagoas, June 27, 1974.
d'Assis, Manoel Arruda de. Pombal, Paraíba, August 12, 13, 1975.
Diniz, Marcolino Pereira. Princeza, Paraíba, August 10, 1975.
Diniz, Severiano. Princeza, Paraíba, August 12, 1975.
Dourado, Francisco Motinho. Salvador, Bahia, November 29, 1973.
Feitosa, Miguel. Araripina, Pernambuco, July 15, 16, 1975.
Ferreira, Genésio. Serra Talhada, Pernambuco, July 21, 28, 1975.
Ferreira, João. Propriá, Sergipe, December 14, 15, 1973, July 1, 2, 3, 1974.
Guedes, Zezito. Arapiraca, Alagoas, June 29, 1974.
Izidro, José. Salvador, Bahia, November 24, 1973.
Jesus, Sérgia Maria de ("Dadá"). Salvador, Bahia, September 1, 1975.
Jurubeba, David. Serra Talhada, Pernambuco, July 29, 1975.
Jurubeba, João. Serra Talhada, Pernambuco, July 29, 1975.
Leitão, Manuel. Mata Grande, Alagoas, June 24, 1974.
Lopez, Augustin. São José de Belmonte, Pernambuco, July 30, 31, 1975.
Maciel, Frederico Bezerra. Recife, Pernambuco, June 14, 15, 1974.
Marinheiro, Rosal. Piranhas, Alagoas, August 20, 1975.
Melo, Pedro Barbosa de. Mata Grande, Alagoas, June 22, 1974.
Mendonça, Aldemar de. Pão de Açúcar, Alagoas, August 25, 1975.
Nascimento, Diniz Casemiro do. Paulo Afonso, Bahia, August 29, 1975.
Neco, Antônio. Serra Talhada, Pernambuco, July 25, 26, 1975.
Nogueira, Luiz Andrelino. Serra Talhada, Pernambuco, July 30, 1975.
Nogueira, Venáncio. Floresta, Pernambuco, August 5, 1975.
Nunes, Moacir Vieira. Piranhas, Alagoas, August 20, 1975.
Oliveira, José Melquiades de. Pinhão, Sergipe, June 30, 1974.
Pequeno, Antônio. Pão de Açúcar, Alagoas, August 25, 1975.
Pereira, Wilson Antônio. Princeza, Paraíba, August 10, 1975.
Queiroz, Euclides Lunes de. Mata Grande, Alagoas, June 23, 1974.
Ramos, Severiano. Jeremoabo, Bahia, August 17, 1975.
Rodrigues, Francisco. Piranhas, Alagoas, August 19, 1975.
Rosa, Antônio Correia. Piranhas, Alagoas, August 19, 1975.
Santanna, Umbelino. Queimadas, Bahia, July 12, 1974.
Santos, João Leandro dos. Piranhas, Alagoas, August 23, 1975.
Santos, José Gomes dos. Jeremoabo, Bahia, August 15, 1975.
Saturnino, José. Serra Talhada, Pernambuco, July 26, 28, 1975.
Silva, Miguel Vicente da. Mata Grande, Alagoas, June 22, 1974.
Souza, João Ignácio de. Floresta, Pernambuco, August 2, 1975.

Torres, América. Agua Branca, Alagoas, June 27, 1974.
Torres, Delilah. Agua Branca, Alagoas, June 24, 1974.
Valente, Waldemar. Recife, Pernambuco, June 14, 1974.
Vieira, José Fernandes de. Salvador, Bahia, November 30, 1973.

Newspapers

Brazil

O Ceará, Fortaleza, Ceará.
Correio da Pedra. Pedra, Alagoas.
Correio de Aracajú. Aracajú, Sergipe.
Correio do Ceará. Fortaleza, Ceará.
Correio do Sertão. Jatobá, Pernambuco.
Diário da Bahia. Salvador, Bahia.
Diário da Noite. Rio de Janeiro.
Diário de Notícias. Salvador, Bahia.
Diário de Pernambuco. Recife, Pernambuco.
Estado das Alagoas. Maceió, Alagoas.
O Estado de Sergipe. Aracajú, Sergipe.
Gazeta de Alagoas. Maceió, Alagoas.
O Globo. Rio de Janeiro.
O Imparcial. Salvador, Bahia.
Jornal de Alagoas. Maceió, Alagoas.
Jornal do Brasil. Rio de Janeiro.
Jornal do Commércio. Fortaleza, Ceará.
A Luta. Annápolis, Sergipe.
A Noite. Rio de Janeiro.
O Nordeste. Fortaleza, Ceará.
O Norte. João Pessoa, Paraíba.
O Paulistano. São Paulo, Sergipe.
O Povo. Fortaleza, Ceará.
A Província. Recife, Pernambuco.
A República. Natal, Rio Grande do Norte.
Sergipe-Jornal. Aracajú, Sergipe.
A Tarde. Salvador, Bahia.
A Tribuna. Aracajú, Sergipe.
A Tribuna. Petrolina, Pernambuco.
A União. Paraíba, Paraíba.
Verdade. Nova Friburgo, Rio de Janeiro.

United States

Corpus Christi Caller. Corpus Christi, Texas.
New York Times.

Published Works

Books

Abreu, Pedro Vergne de. *Os dramas dolorosos do nordeste.* Rio de Janeiro, 1930.

————, ed. *O flagello de "Lampeão."* Rio de Janeiro, 1931.

Albuquerque, Ulisses Lins de. *Um sertanejo e o sertão.* Rio de Janeiro, 1957.

Andrade, Manoel Correia de. *A terra e o homem no nordeste.* São Paulo, 1963.

Andrade, Mário de. *O baile das quatro artes.* N.p., n.d.

Anselmo, Octacílio. *Padre Cícero: Mito e realidade.* Rio de Janeiro, 1968.

Araujo, Antonio Amaury Corrêa de. *Assim morreu Lampião.* Rio de Janeiro, 1976.

Baptista, Pedro. *Cangaceiros do nordeste.* Paraíba, Paraíba, 1929.

Barbosa, Eduardo. *Lampião: Rei do cangaço.* Rio de Janeiro, 1968.

Barroso, Gustavo. *Almas de lama e de aço (Lampeão e outros cangaceiros).* São Paulo, 1930.

————. *Heróes e bandidos (Os cangaceiros do nordeste).* Rio de Janeiro, 1917.

Bezerra, João. *Como dei cabo de Lampeão.* Rio de Janeiro, 1940.

Blok, Anton. *The Mafia of a Sicilian Village, 1860–1960.* New York, 1975.

Bruno, Ernani Silva. *História do Brasil: Geral e regional.* 7 vols. São Paulo, 1967.

Campos, Eduardo. *Folclore do nordeste.* Rio de Janeiro, 1960.

Carvalho, Cícero Rodrigues de. *Serrote Preto (Lampião e seus sequazes).* 2d ed. Rio de Janeiro, 1974.

Castro, Felipe de. *Derrocada do cangaço no nordeste.* Salvador, Bahia, 1976.

Castro, José Romão de. *Figuras legendárias.* Maceió, Alagoas, 1945.

Chagas, Américo. *O chefe Horácio de Matos.* São Paulo, 1961.

Chandler, Billy Jaynes. *The Feitosas and the Sertão dos Inhamuns: The History of a Family and a Community in Northeast Brazil, 1700–1930.* Gainesville, Florida, 1972.

Crosland, Jessie. *Outlaws in Fact and Fiction.* London, 1959.

Cross, James Eliot. *Conflict in the Shadows: The Nature and Politics of Guerrilla War.* Garden City, N.Y., 1963.

Cunha, Euclides da. *Rebellion in the Backlands (Os sertões).* Translated by Samuel Putnam. Chicago, 1944.

Curran, Mark J. *Selected Bibliography of History and Politics in Brazilian Popular Poetry.* Tempe, Arizona, 1971.

Davies, James Chowning, ed. *When Men Revolt and Why.* New York, 1971.

della Cava, Ralph. *Miracle at Joaseiro.* New York, 1970.

Elman, Robert. *Badmen of the West.* New York, 1974.

Facó, Rui. *Cangaceiros e fanáticos.* 2d ed. Rio de Janeiro, 1965.

Ferreira, S. Dias. *A marcha da Coluna Prestes.* Pelotas, Rio Grande do Sul, 1928.

Figueiredo, Moysés de. *Lampeão no Ceará: A verdade em torno dos factos* (*Campanha de 1927*). N.p., n.d. Epilogue dated December, 1927.

Freyre, Gilberto. *The Masters and the Slaves*. 2d ed. New York, 1956.

Goís, Joaquim. *Lampião: O último cangaceiro*. Aracajú, Sergipe, 1966.

Gueiros, Optato. *"Lampeão": Memórias de um oficial excommandante de forças volantes*. Recife, Pernambuco, 1952.

Gurr, Ted Robert. *Why Men Rebel*. Princeton, New Jersey, 1970.

Hobsbawm, Eric. *Bandits*. New York, 1971.

——. *Primitive Rebels: Studies in Archaic Forms of Social Movement in the 19th and 20th Centuries*. New York, 1965.

Instituto Brasileiro de Geografia e Estatística. *Grande região nordeste* (Vol. 5 of *Enciclopédia dos municípios brasileiros*). Rio de Janeiro, 1960.

Kemal, Yashar. *Memed, My Hawk*. Translated by Edouard Roditi. London, 1961.

Laurindo, Augusto [Trovador Cotinguiba]. *Lampeão: O maior dos bandoleiros*. Propriá, Sergipe, n.d.

Leal, Victor Nunes. *Coronelismo, enxada e voto*. Rio de Janeiro, 1948.

Levine, Robert M. *The Vargas Regime*. New York, 1970.

Lima, Estácio de. *O mundo estranho dos cangaceiros*. Salvador, Bahia, 1965.

Lima, Lourenço Moreira. *A Coluna Prestes*. 2d ed. São Paulo, 1945.

Lins, Wilson. *O médio São Francisco: Uma sociedade de pastôres e guerreiros*. 2d ed. Salvador, Bahia, n.d.

Luna, Luiz. *Lampião e seus cabras*. Rio de Janeiro, 1963.

Macaulay, Neill. *The Prestes Column*. New York, 1974.

Macedo, Nertan. *Capitão Virgulino Ferreira: Lampião*. 3d ed. Rio de Janeiro, 1970.

——. *Sinhô Pereira: O comandante de Lampião*. Rio de Janeiro, 1975.

Machado, Christina Matta. *As táticas de guerra dos cangaceiros*. Rio de Janeiro, 1969.

Maxwell, Gavin. *God Protect Me from My Friends*. London, 1956.

Mendonça, Aldemar de. *Pão de Açúcar: História e efemérides*. N.p., n.d. Introduction dated February 6, 1974.

Montenegro, Abelardo F. *História do cangaceirismo no Ceará*. Fortaleza, Ceará, 1955.

——. *História do fanatismo religioso no Ceará*. Fortaleza, Ceará, 1959.

Moraes, Walfrido. *Jagunços e heróis*. Rio de Janeiro, 1963.

Motta, Leonardo. *No tempo de Lampeão*. Rio de Janeiro, 1930.

Nóbrega, Francisco Pereira da. *Vingança, não: Depoimento sobre Chico Pereira e cangaceiros do nordeste*. Rio de Janeiro, 1960.

Nogueira, Ataliba. *Antônio Conselheiro e Canudos: Revisão histórica*. São Paulo, 1974.

Nonato, Raimundo. *Jesuíno Brilhante: O cangaceiro romântico (1844–1879)*. Rio de Janeiro, 1970.

——. *Lampião em Mossoró*. 2d ed. Rio de Janeiro, 1970.

Oliveira, Aglae Lima de. *Lampião, cangaço e nordeste*. 3rd ed. Rio de Janeiro, 1970.

Parreira, Abelardo. *Sertanejos e cangaceiros*. São Paulo, 1934.

Pinto, L. A. Costa. *Lutas de famílias no Brasil*. São Paulo, 1949.

Prata, Ranulfo. *Lampeão*. Rio de Janeiro, 1934.

Queiroz, Maria Isaura Pereira de. *Os cangaceiros: Les bandits d'honneur brésiliens*. Paris, 1968.

Quirós, Constancio Bernaldo de and Ardila, Luis. *El bandolerismo andaluz*. Madrid, 1973.

Rocha, Melchiades da. *Bandoleiros das caatingas*. Rio de Janeiro, n.d. Preface dated 1940.

Settle, William A., Jr. *Jesse James Was His Name*. Columbia, Missouri, 1966.

Silva, Manoel Bezerra e. *Lampião e suas façanhas*. Maceió, Alagoas, 1966.

Skidmore, Thomas E. *Politics in Brazil, 1930–1964*. New York, 1967.

Smith, T. Lynn. *Brazil: People and Institutions*. Rev. ed. Baton Rouge, Louisiana, 1963.

Souto Maior, Mário. *Antônio Silvino: Capitão de trabuco*. Rio de Janeiro, 1971.

Valente, Waldemar. *O trovador nordestino: Poesias de João Martins de Ataide*. Recife, Pernambuco, 1937.

Vidal, Ademar. *Terra de homens*. Rio de Janeiro, 1944.

Wilson, Luís. *Vila Bela, os Pereiras e outras histórias*. Recife, Pernambuco, 1974.

Zehr, Howard. *Crime and the Development of Modern Society*. London, 1976.

Articles

Amorim, Oswaldo. "O homem que chefiou Lampião." *Jornal do Brasil* (Rio de Janeiro), February 25–27, 1969.

Aston, T. H. "Robin Hood: Communication." *Past and Present* 20 (November, 1961): 7–9.

Audi, Jorge. "Eu sou o Labareda de Lampião." *O Cruzeiro*, October 19, 1968, p. 13.

Beirão, Nirlando. "No mundo dos bandidos (Entrevista: Eric J. Hobsbawm)." *Veja*, June 11, 1975, pp. 3–5.

Blok, Anton. "The Peasant and the Brigand: Social Banditry Reconsidered." *Comparative Studies in Society and History* 14 (September, 1972): 494–503.

Carneiro, Luciano. "O filho de Corisco." *O Cruzeiro*, October 10, 1953, p. 46.

———. "Lampeão é nosso sangue." *O Cruzeiro*, September 26, 1953, p. 6.

———. "Porque Lampeão entrou no cangaço." *O Cruzeiro*, October 3, 1953, p. 7.

Chandler, Billy Jaynes. "The Role of Negroes in the Ethnic Formation of

Ceará: The Need for a Reappraisal." *Revista de Ciências Sociais* 4, no. 1 (1973): 31–43.

Gomes, Bruno. "Volta-Sêca" (exact title varies). *Diário de Notícias* (Salvador), April 25–May 22, 1959.

Lewin, Linda. "The Oligarchical Limitations of Social Banditry in Brazil: The Case of the 'Good' Thief Antônio Silvino." *Past and Present*, forthcoming.

Machado, Maria Christina de Matta. "Aspectos do fenômeno do cangaço no nordeste brasileiro." *Revista de História* 46, no. 93 (1973): 139–175; 47, no. 95 (1973): 177–212; 47, no. 96 (1973): 473–489; 47, no. 97 (1974): 161–200; 49, no. 99 (1974): 145–180.

Masson, Nonnato. "A aventura sangrenta do cangaço." *Fatos e Fotos*, October 20, 27; November 3, 10, 17, 24; December 1, 8, 1962, unpaged.

"Memórias de Balão, um velho cangaceiro." *Realidade*, November, 1973, pp. 45–47.

Noblat, Ricardo. "Lampião morreu envenenado." *Manchete*, April 29, 1972, pp. 154–157.

Queiroz, Maria Isaura Pereira de. "Notas sociológicas sobre o cangaço." *Ciência e Cultura* 77 (May, 1975): 495–516.

Silva, Alberto. "O filme de cangaço." *Filme e Cultura*, November/December, 1970, pp. 42–49.

Souza, Amaury de. "The *Cangaço* and the Politics of Violence in Northeast Brazil," in *Protest and Resistance in Angola and Brazil*, pp. 109–131. Edited by Ronald L. Chilcote. Berkeley, California, 1972.

Steckmesser, Kent L. "Robin Hood and the American Outlaw." *Journal of American Folklore* 79, no. 312 (1966): 348–355.

Unpublished Works

Cunniff, Roger Lee. "The Great Drought: Northeast Brazil, 1877–1880." Ph.D. dissertation, University of Texas, 1971.

Mello, Frederico Pernambucano de. "Aspectos do banditismo rural nordestino." Recife, Pernambuco, 1974. Copy furnished by author.

Mendonça, Aldemar de. Untitled typewritten manuscript on Lampião. Pão de Açúcar, Alagoas, 1975. Copy furnished by author.

Pang, Eul Soo. "The Politics of Coronelismo in Brazil: The Case of Bahia, 1889–1930." Ph.D. dissertation, University of California, Berkeley, 1970.

Index

Aba Filme, 199
Abílio, José, 66, 201
Abóboras Ranch, 48, 60
Abóboras, Bahia: battle of, 117–118
Abrahão, Benjamin, 199–200
agriculture, 8, 11–13
Agua Branca, Alagoas: Ferreiras' trouble in, 29–31; raid on, 38–39
Agua Branca, baroness of, 38–39
Aguas Belas, Pernambuco, 137
Alagoa do Serrote, Paraíba, 60
Alagoas: Ferreiras move to, 29–30; invaded by bandits, 78, 190, 220; fails to oppose bandits, 179; Lampião frequents, 187–188
Algodões, Pernambuco, 74
Almeida, Erico de, 198
Alves, Felix, 190
Alves, José, 170
Ambrósio Ranch, 137
ammunition: sources of, 45, 82, 88–89, 183, 184–187
Angicos Ranch, 222–223
Antônio Pequeno, 169–170
Aranha, Oswaldo, 144
arms: backlanders' attitudes toward, 18, 28; sources of, 71, 95–96, 186–187; types of, 71, 183
Arruda, Isaías, 60, 63; and attack on Mossoró, 95–96, 101, 105–107
Ataide, João Martins de, 197
atrocities: Lampião's early reputation and, 40–43; after Levino's death, 59–60; at Queimadas, 127; at Mandacarú, 133–134; at Ambrósio Ranch, 137; after Ezekiel's death, 147; and Salinas family, 168; at São Paulo Ranch,

169; and Manuel Silvestre, 203; at Patos Ranch, 230–231; of Ângelo Roque, 232. *See also* beheadings; castration; rape
Augusto, Pedro, 61
Aurora, Ceará, 93, 96, 101
Azulão (bandit), 178, 216

backlands: physical conditions of, 6–7; population of, 8–10, 12; social conditions of, 9–19; of Bahia, as area favorable to bandits, 112; disarmament of, 142–143, 184; migration from, 216, 235–236
backlands society: structure of, 8–11; economic conditions of, 11–13, 76; political conditions of, 13–15; illiteracy in, 22; overly protective of women, 25; paternalism of, 86; lack of schools in, 235
Bahia: Lampião's entry into, 111; reacts to Lampião's coming, 114–115; antibanditry campaign of, 138–142, 145–146, 148–149, 157, 160, 161, 179–180; moves against coiteiros, 163–165; campaign declines in, 172–175
Bahiano, José: and branding of women, 155–156; in Bahia and Sergipe, 181, 191; brands man, 202; killed, 192–193
Bananeira (bandit), 158
bandits: dress of, 5; attitudes of, toward police, 34, 75–76, 115, 119, 124, 127; methods of travel of, 45, 99, 116, 118, 123, 125; described, 68–69, 84, 109, 219; camp life of, 84, 149, 175–176,